NEW WINE AND THE BABYLONIAN VINE

BY ROGER OAKLAND

New Wine and the Babylonian Vine

By Roger Oakland

Published by **Understand The Times**
P. O. Box 27239
Santa Ana, CA 92799

TABLE OF CONTENTS

INTRODUCTION: A SIGN OF OUR TIMES

"What will be the sign of Your coming, and of the end of the age?" the disciples asked Jesus.[1] He responded to this question by giving them a number of answers. While the signs that He gave are now in the process of being fulfilled indicating we are indeed living in the last days, there is one sign above all others that is at the top of the list. It was the very first sign that Jesus mentioned. He said the terminal generation could expect widespread deception in His name. This book deals specifically with this last day spiritual deception and the documented reasons why I believe His return will be soon.

Over the past few years I have written two books, which have dealt with deception in the church. The first, *New Wine or Old Deception?*,[2] documented the roots of experience-based Christianity and explained how the Toronto Blessing phenomenon has swept the entire world. The second, *When New Wine Makes a Man Divine,*[3] was written to warn Christians to be on the alert for the apostasy the Bible states will happen before the revelation of the Antichrist.

This book, the third in the "New Wine" series, is called *New Wine and the Babylonian Vine.* My objective in writing this book is to further document the direction experience-based Christianity is heading and how it is joining together with experience-based Catholicism, other religions and a spiritualized environmentalism to form a global spirituality or ecumenical delusion that the

---

[1] Matthew 24:3

[2] Roger Oakland, New Wine or Old Deception: A Biblical View of Experience Based Christianity, (The Word For Today, Costa Mesa, CA, 1995).

[3] Roger Oakland, *When New Wine Makes a Man Divine: True Revival or Last Days Deception,* (Understand The Times, Santa Ana, CA, 1997).

Bible predicts will unfold in the last days. I have attempted to write as a journalist who is accurately examining the spiritual trends of our times from a biblical perspective. As in my two previous books, I have presented my own personal concerns regarding the deception that is masquerading in the church in the name of Christ.

While many have contacted me expressing appreciation for the biblical position I have taken on the New Wine Movement, others have indicated they are disappointed in what I am doing and have stated that I am dividing the body of Christ and blaspheming the Holy Spirit. One person told me I had no right to say the New Wine Movement is connected with the apostasy the Bible teaches will happen before the Antichrist is revealed. By boldly proclaiming, "this is that," I was told, someday I will stand before God and answer for having prevented people from becoming part of the great end-times revival that is supposedly underway in the world today.

Revival or Falling Away?

I am not convinced the Bible teaches there will be a great revival in the last days before Jesus returns. Jesus said that the gospel would be proclaimed worldwide, and then the end would come.[4]

I recognize that there are many around the world today who are responding to the gospel and becoming genuine believers and followers of Jesus Christ. As I have traveled the world over the past two decades, it has become obvious to me that God is touching lives. Many who were once in darkness have been delivered and are now in the Kingdom of God. However, to say that a massive revival is underway and that nearly the whole world will embrace Jesus as their true Savior is not found in the Scriptures. Instead there seems to be strong evidence indicating that Satan will be the inspiration behind a great final delusion that will send many people to hell.

---

[4] Matthew 24:14

The Bible teaches that ever since the Fall, Satan has been active with his scheme to deceive mankind. One of his techniques has been to fool people into believing there is more they need to know than what God has revealed to man through His Word. One of the devil's favorite tactics is to combine God's Word with extrabiblical revelation or experience. Ever since Eve was duped into eating from the forbidden tree, mankind has been vulnerable to Satan's deceptive plan.

The Bible also makes it clear that God has always been faithful to warn the world about the dangers of seeking experiences that can lead people astray. In the Old Testament era, the prophets were used by God to warn His people. As God has warned mankind in the past, so too, His warnings are still relevant today. This is a time for people who love God to check out all they are being taught and do it according to God's Word.

There's a Battle Raging

In the Book of Ephesians, Paul, writing by the inspiration of the Holy Spirit, clarified that our battle as humans is not against fellow humans. There are forces at work in an unseen realm or spiritual dimension whose plan is to separate us from the God of the Universe for eternity. Paul also stated that Satan is a master schemer and a clever manipulator.[5]

Knowing that Satan has a scheme to deceive the world, should we not be alert to his devices? If the most important truth found in the Bible is God's plan of eternal salvation through Jesus Christ, would it not be reasonable to assume Satan would try to convince people they were going to heaven in Christ's name, when in reality they were not?

The Battle Plan

Today many people are redefining the term "salvation." The way to heaven that Jesus said was narrow is becoming wider every day according to them. There are many who believe salvation is based upon tradition or what some man or organization

[5] Ephesians 6:10-12

has claimed to be true. Others are convinced they are believers because they have experienced the miraculous in Jesus' name.

We also know that Christianity based on teachings that are extrabiblical can be misleading. Certainly Christians can have experiences, but these experiences must be Bible-based. Satan is a master at counterfeiting the spiritual gifts that God has given. When people seek after extrabiblical experiences or use these practices as a focus to draw people together in unity for unity's sake, the resulting unity may be spiritually catastrophic.

The Bible teaches true faith is based upon hearing God's Word.[6] Therefore, apostasy, a falling away from the faith, produces a faith that is not biblically based. If someone is an apostate, he has fallen away from a faith in God and His Word for a faith in something else.

Thy Word is Truth

I have written this book as a love letter and a wake-up call to all people who profess the name of Jesus Christ. Therefore, this book has been written to all Protestants and Roman Catholics. It is also my desire that others who do not profess to be Christians would read this book.

I want to make it clear that I am not saying that all who are in the New Wine Movement and are embracing extrabiblical experiences are apostates. I know many people who are part of this group and I know they are sincere God-loving people. They desire to live effective lives for Jesus Christ. However, many of these same people are being misled. They say they have discovered new manifestations of the power of God, when there is no basis for these manifestations in the Word of God.

As this book was being written, I prayed daily for the wisdom and the ability to present what God had placed upon my heart in a way that would not offend readers. Because of the controversial nature of this book, I recognize that some who read it will no doubt still be offended. My challenge to the reader is

[6] Romans 10:17

that every page be examined according to the Word of God. Anything that I have written that is not biblically based should be rejected.

The Counterfeit Bride

The inspiration for the title of this book came from the words written by the apostle John, found in the Book of Revelation. In the seventeenth chapter we read:

> Then one of the seven angels who had the seven bowls came and talked with me, saying to me, "Come, I will show you the judgment of the great harlot who sits on many waters, with whom the kings of the earth committed fornication, and the inhabitants of the earth were made drunk with the wine of her fornication." So he carried me away in the Spirit into the wilderness. And I saw a woman sitting on a scarlet beast which was full of names of blasphemy, having seven heads and ten horns. The woman was arrayed in purple and scarlet, and adorned with gold and precious stones and pearls, having in her hand a golden cup full of abominations and the filthiness of her fornication. And on her forehead a name was written: MYSTERY, BABYLON THE GREAT, THE MOTHER OF HARLOTS AND OF THE ABOMINATIONS OF THE EARTH.[7]

Throughout the New Testament, the true church is represented as the bride of Christ. We know that the only way to become a part of this true church is by the narrow path that is through the gospel of Jesus Christ. In the Book of Revelation, the harlot represents a counterfeit bride that prepares the way for a counterfeit christ. This ecumenical religion that is in the name of Christ will be based upon a religious worldview that embraces many of the pagan practices that originated at Babylon as recorded in the Book of Genesis.

In the eighteenth chapter of the Book of Revelation we learn more about the incredible impact this false religious movement is going to have upon the whole world. John stated:

---

[7] Revelation 17:1-5

> For all the nations have drunk of the wine of the wrath of her fornication, the kings of the earth have committed fornication with her, and the merchants of the earth have become rich through the abundance of her luxury. [8]

Then in the nineteenth chapter of Revelation, John explains what will happen to the counterfeit bride. In his own words:

> After these things I heard a loud voice of a great multitude in heaven, saying, Alleluia! Salvation and glory and honor and power belong to the Lord our God! For true and righteous are His judgments, because He has judged the great harlot who corrupted the earth with her fornication; and He has avenged on her the blood of His servants shed by her. [9]

Judgment is Coming

The Bible states that a terrible time of judgment is coming upon this earth for those who have willingly rejected the true gospel of Jesus Christ. While many have said they have joined a new movement, tasted of the "new wine" and know that it is real, because they have "become drunk in the Spirit," I am concerned these same people may have become spiritually deluded. This is a time for sober contemplation. As Paul wrote:

> Therefore let us not sleep, as others do, but let us watch and be sober. For those who sleep, sleep at night, and those who get drunk are drunk at night. But let us who are of the day be sober, putting on the breastplate of faith and love, and as a helmet the hope of salvation. [10]

Searching for the Truth

Finally, I have written this book because God has given me a passion for the truth and a compassion for the deceived. My plea is that you will read what I have written, compare it with Scripture, and keep an open mind. Although some have stated that

---

[8] Revelation 18:3
[9] Revelation 19:1-2
[10] I Thessalonians 5:6-8

my style of writing is too analytical because of my science background, the whole objective for writing this book is not to be a good scientist, but to point people toward the truth. One of my favorite verses found in the Bible is Matthew chapter twenty-two and verse twenty-nine. Jesus said to the Sadducees: "You are mistaken, not knowing the Scriptures nor the power of God." It is not a matter of just the "Word" or just the "Spirit." Our spiritual lifeline should be based upon a balance between the Word and the Spirit, and this balance only the Word can reveal.

What a great privilege it is to know we have been given His Word and His Spirit to reveal His truth! The Word of God has been given to us by God and will help us to understand Satan's deceptive plan for the last days. My prayer is that everyone who reads this book will reverence and trust the Bible more than before and see the danger of tasting the *new wine from the Babylonian vine* before it is tragically too late.

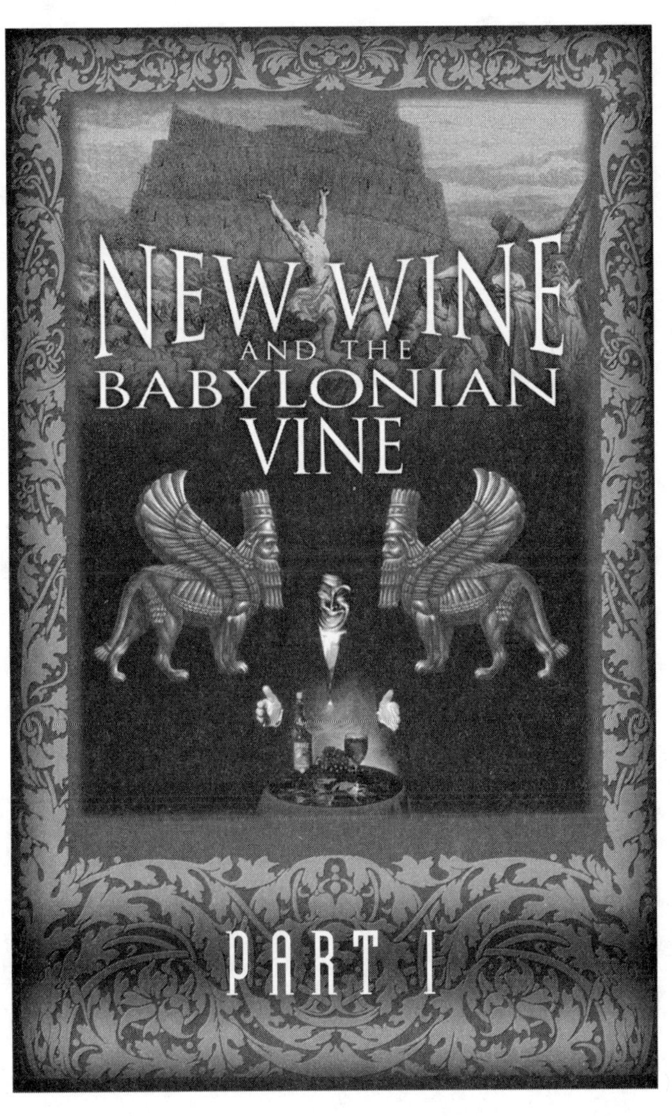

UNDERSTANDING DECEPTION

1

BEWARE OF DECEPTION

Each one of us as we look back over our past, can recall certain events or experiences that have been life changing. Sometimes at the moment the incident happens, we do not realize how significant the event actually was. Then there are other times when we immediately become aware that the experience we have just encountered will affect us for as long as we live.

Not long ago, I was thrust into a situation that changed the way I will think for the rest of my life. This experience started when I dropped off my car at a service station for some maintenance work. As the mechanic told me he would have the work completed in about an hour, I decided to walk down the street to a restaurant and make use of this time by having a cup of coffee and reading a book. As it was another beautiful Southern California morning, I decided to sit outside where there were a number of tables.

While I was sitting there I looked up a few times and noticed several other people seated nearby. Everyone, like me, seemed to be enjoying the beautiful day. But the quietness was shattered by the sound of people scuffling. When I looked up to see what was happening, I was startled to see that a man and a woman who had been sitting in front of me were on top of a man who had been seated at a table beside me. Before I even had time to think, there were three more men piled on top of them. Looking behind me, I could see there were police cars everywhere.

A few moments later, this man was dragged to his feet. His arms were handcuffed behind his back. Then several officers escorted the man over to a police car and he was driven away. Still somewhat startled, I asked one of the officers that remained on the scene if he could tell me what had just happened. He said the man they had taken in custody was a very dangerous criminal who had been on the most wanted list. Because of the seriousness of the crimes this man had committed, he would now spend the rest of his life in jail.

I will never forget the thoughts that went through my mind that day as I drove back to my office. At one moment, this man who had been seated next to me was free. Just a split second later he was held captive against his will and now would be destined to spend the rest of his life locked up in a jail. Although I had never seen the man before in my life, I felt like I knew him. Like a father who is concerned about the welfare of his son, I tried to imagine the thoughts that would be going through this man's mind as he was being driven to jail.

Then another thought popped into my mind: Although this man will spend the rest of his life in jail, a life incarcerated in prison is minor compared to what will happen to many of the people I personally know. As they are headed down the road of life believing everything is fine, some day death will rudely intervene. From that moment on they will spend eternity in hell.

As the result of this life-changing experience I am now far more aware of the consequences of being spiritually deceived. I know many moral people who are in bondage to spiritual deception. Some are caught up in a system of religiosity, believing their church has saved them from their sins. There are others who believe that God looks upon their good works as the basis of their salvation. Then there are those who are going about their daily lives completely oblivious to what will happen to them after they die.

One of the main purposes for writing this book is to challenge the reader to consider what the Bible has to say about the consequences of spiritual deception. The Bible makes the claim that its words are inspired by God and therefore the truth. Should we not be more concerned about the consequences of being spiritually deceived?

Deception in His Name

Although the New Testament was written almost two thousand years ago by men inspired by God, every Bible-believing person knows the words are still relevant and applicable to spiritual matters today. On one occasion, when Paul was writing the church at Corinth, he warned them about leaving the simple truth of the gospel and getting caught up in deception that would attack them three different ways. In Paul's words:

> But I fear, lest somehow, as the serpent deceived Eve by his craftiness, so your minds may be corrupted from the simplicity that is in Christ. For if he who comes preaches another Jesus whom we have not preached, or if you receive a different spirit which you have not received, or a different gospel which you have not accepted; you may well put up with it! [11]

If we were able to translate what Paul wrote to the Corinthian church into modern-day language, it would sound something like this:

> Don't complicate the gospel. Keep it simple. Watch out that the same devil that tricked Eve doesn't trick you. Just because you are a Christian doesn't mean you are immune to deception. Satan likes to trick people in the name of Christ, and in order to do so, he makes people think they believe in Jesus, when in reality they don't know Jesus at all. Rather than being led by the Holy Spirit, an unholy deceptive spirit can delude you into believing in a counterfeit gospel instead of the true gospel.

Correction or Compromise

The trend preparing the world for an experience-based Christianity continues to escalate. More people are traveling to

---

[11] 2 Corinthians 11:3-4

an increasing number of places where they say God is manifesting Himself through signs and wonders. Those who caution others to beware of deception in the name of Christ are now becoming a minority.

Christianity that is biblically based must always be focused on a personal relationship with Jesus Christ. However, history reveals there has always been a tendency for Christians to stray away from this essential tenet of the faith. There are many ways to have our worship and devotion diverted. Seeking after extrabiblical revelation from angels, or placing too much emphasis on a biblical personality like Mary, are two examples that head the list.

Although the gospel is not complicated, it is easy to complicate. Satan, God's adversary, is a master at deceiving mankind. Because the gospel is a narrow way that is predicated upon faith in Jesus Christ alone, Satan has numerous schemes for inspiring people to believe in a counterfeit form of Christianity. The imitation may look and feel like the real thing, but in reality it is an abomination to the One who shed His blood on the cross.

A study of the apostle Paul's writings reveals that the early church was constantly falling into Satan's plan to complicate the gospel or pervert the basic message in some way. After warning the Corinthians about leaving the simple gospel for another gospel, he told them why the church was being led astray. He wrote:

> For such are false apostles, deceitful workers, transforming themselves into apostles of Christ. And no wonder! For Satan himself transforms himself into an angel of light. Therefore it is no great thing if his ministers also transform themselves into ministers of righteousness, whose end will be according to their works.[12]

It is obvious Paul was concerned about false doctrines that were being propagated by false teachers who were Satan's agents masquerading as followers of Jesus Christ. In his letter to

---

[12] 2 Corinthians 11:13-15

Timothy, Paul warned that these "doctrines of demons" would intensify in the last days as part of the apostasy that would impact the body of Christ.[13]

Nowhere in any of Paul's writings do we find a precedent that permits believers to compromise and embrace teachings that are not biblically based. Although Paul wrote about the importance of unity and brotherly love, neither he nor any other writer whose words were inspired to appear in the Bible, gave us authority to seek after unity for the sake of unity and forsake the truth.

The Scriptures teach that Paul corrected the church when it embraced error. He never made a practice of building a bridge to the false doctrines that were propagated by false teachers. He always corrected false teaching with a passion for the truth and a compassion for the deceived. Are we willing to follow Paul's example? Although confronting heresy may not be popular, it is biblically correct!

[13] I Timothy 4:1

2

THE SERPENT'S LIE

A foundational principle of Christianity is that the Bible is true. So if the Bible is true and the Bible states that God has an adversary, would it not be reasonable to believe that Satan, God's adversary, would do everything possible to deceive people and keep them from coming to the knowledge of the truth? What methods does Satan use to accomplish his plan? Are these methods still in effect today?

The Bible, consisting of the Old and the New Testament, contains the good news of the gospel of Jesus Christ. The gospel of Jesus Christ proclaims that individuals can be reconciled to God and spend eternity with Him if they will acknowledge their sin and accept the sacrifice Jesus made on the cross. The Bible also makes it clear that Satan has an agenda to blind mankind from understanding this plan. Since the fall of man in the Garden of Eden, hundreds of millions of people throughout the generations have fallen into Satan's plan.

Although the Bible states that hell was prepared for the devil and his angels, man who willfully rejects God's plan of salvation has the same destiny.[14] The apostle Peter warned us about Satan's tactics. He said: "Be sober, be vigilant; because your adversary the devil walks about like a roaring lion, seeking whom he

---

[14] Matthew 25:41

may devour."[15] John described Satan's agenda in the Book of Revelation by saying Satan was the one "who deceives the whole world."[16] Satan is alive and well and his plan to deceive is still very effective.

Figure 1: The fall of Adam and Eve brought the curse upon the original creation. Every generation since that time has been influenced by Satan's agenda to deceive mankind.

[15] 1 Peter 5:8

[16] Revelation 12:9

He's a Schemer

So how does Satan go about deceiving, and how can we identify when someone has been deceived unknowingly? Does the Bible indicate what we should look for that will help prevent us from falling into the same trap?

The best way to understand man's vulnerability to deception is to briefly review what happened when man was first deceived. Satan, whom the Bible calls the father of lies,[17] came to the first woman, Eve, and initiated a conversation that triggered the Fall. The Bible states:

> Now the serpent was more cunning than any beast of the field which the LORD God had made. And he said to the woman, Has God indeed said, 'You shall not eat of every tree of the garden'? And the woman said to the serpent, We may eat the fruit of the trees of the garden; but of the fruit of the tree which is in the midst of the garden, God has said, 'You shall not eat it, nor shall you touch it, lest you die.' Then the serpent said to the woman, 'You will not surely die. For God knows that in the day you eat of it your eyes will be opened, and you will be like God, knowing good and evil.'[18]

It is obvious that Satan caused Eve to doubt what God had stated. As well, he suggested to her that additional revelation was the key for her successful future. It was this lie that brought about the fall of mankind. Certainly Satan's deceptive methods have not changed to this day.

Nothing New under the Sun

According to the inspired words of Solomon, there is nothing new under the sun. Whatever has happened in the past will reoccur. History merely repeats itself in cycles.[19] So if Satan has a master plan to dupe mankind, and if his plan has been successful in the past, should we not expect that he is still at work today?

---

[17] John 8:44

[18] Genesis 3:1-5

[19] Ecclesiastes 1: 9-10

Secondly, the Bible reveals that an understanding of the physical realm is not complete unless we consider the spiritual dimension that God also created. All of us have grown accustomed to analyzing the world around us through the use of our senses. We can touch, feel, smell, taste and hear what is going on around us. Although the spiritual dimension is just as real, we are not able to perceive its presence under normal everyday experiences.

In order to fully comprehend the history of mankind, it is necessary to understand the part the fallen spiritual dimension has played since the fall of man in the Garden of Eden. The Bible makes it clear we are not the only intelligent beings that exist in the universe. God also created the angelic realm. These spirit beings are able to manifest themselves to humans and then dematerialize.

We know that Satan, the leader of the fallen angelic realm, was the first spirit being to interfere in the affairs of man. He appeared to Eve in the form of a serpent and enticed her to disobey God and His Word.[20] He suggested that there was another dimension that was available to her if she took of the forbidden tree. Instead of being confined here on earth with limited knowledge, man could know both good and evil and have the capability of being "like the gods."[21]

What Satan claimed was partially true. If he could get man to disobey God and follow him, he would be able to take humans captive with him as hostages on his way to hell. Certainly biblical history reveals that Satan's plan has been fruitful. There is a clear pattern that has been repeated many times. Although God has revealed His grace to mankind throughout the ages, fallen human beings still have a tendency to resist God's plan of salvation and instead follow after the fallen angelic realm that has an objective to deceive mankind.

---

[20] Genesis 3:1-5

[21] Ibid. K.J.V.

It's Not Flesh and Blood

In the sixth chapter of Ephesians, Paul wrote: "For we wrestle not against flesh and blood, but against principalities, against powers, against the rulers of the darkness of this world, against spiritual wickedness in high places."[22] These words are absolutely true in spite of what many Bible skeptics would like us to believe. Yes, according to the Bible, intelligent spirit beings do exist. Some are holy and some are not. The unholy ones are commonly called demons or fallen angels. When mankind attempts to communicate with this spiritual dimension he will be deceived.

The Bible states we are not to be involved in an attempt to contact the fallen spirit world. Paul wrote: "For there is one God and one Mediator between God and men, the Man Christ Jesus."[23] Are we rejecting these words and being set up for a final delusion? The Scriptures say yes! And we will see that such a delusion is presently underway.

---

[22] Ephesians 6:12
[23] 1 Timothy 2:5

3

THE BABYLONIAN VINE

The Old Testament is a historical record given by God to man. It was intended to tell us about the significant events leading up to the appearance of His Son, Jesus Christ here on earth. Since Jesus came, we have lived in a period of history known as "the day of grace." The New Testament was given in order to help us understand God's plan of salvation -- the gospel-- also called the good news. However, it is still important that we refer to the Old Testament for insight and understanding into God's overall plan for mankind. Without the entire Bible as our foundation, we are unable to see the whole picture that God intends for us to see.

It is clear from reading the Old Testament that there are serious consequences when man willingly rejects God's inspired Word and goes his own way. Although the Bible makes it clear that our real blessing is the result of being obedient to what God has said in His Word, the tendency has always been for humans to break God's ordinances and look for other answers that are beyond biblical parameters.

We have already seen how Satan's plan brought about the fall of man. The curse, which came upon mankind as the result of the Fall, has affected mankind throughout subsequent generations. By the sixth chapter of Genesis we read that the world was so corrupt that God was grieved that He had ever created man:

Then the LORD saw that the wickedness of man was great in the earth, and that every intent of the thoughts of his heart was only evil continually. And the LORD was sorry that He had made man on the earth, and He was grieved in His heart.[24]

Figure 2: The Genesis record gives us an account of the worldwide flood that God brought upon the world to destroy the original creation. Noah and his family were the only human survivors.

[24] Genesis 6:5-6

Chapters seven and eight of Genesis describe the terrible destruction God brought upon this planet. The great Flood of Noah was the physical calamity God used to destroy the original earth. There were only eight human survivors who were supernaturally preserved. After the Flood, Noah and his family were instructed to disperse and repopulate the planet. However rather than obeying God, they were disobedient and built a city in rebellion against God. Just as before the Flood, man rejected God's instructions and chose to do his own thing. Based upon man's previous record, the consequences were predictable.

A City and a Tower

The eleventh chapter of Genesis describes a pivotal event that took place during Old Testament times. Although it is essential to understand Satan's lie recorded in the third chapter of Genesis, in order to comprehend man's fallen nature, it is also important to grasp the meaning of what happened at Babylon. Our sinful nature separates us from God; our Babylonian nature reveals man's innate desire to unite in rebellion against God.

The rebellion that occurred at Babel by the descendants of Noah happened in two stages: first, man chose to unify in order to build a city, defying God's instructions that they were to disperse and fill the earth. Following the construction of the city of Babylon, a tower was constructed in order to "reach the heavens." This second stage of the rebellious process helped fill the spiritual vacuum that was created because man had turned away from God. As the Genesis account states:

> Now the whole earth had one language and one speech. And it came to pass, as they journeyed from the east, that they found a plain in the land of Shinar, and they dwelt there. Then they said to one another, "Come, let us make bricks and bake them thoroughly." They had brick for stone, and they had asphalt for mortar. And they said, "Come, let us build ourselves a city, and a tower whose top is in the heavens; let us make a

name for ourselves, lest we be scattered abroad over the face of the whole earth."[25]

It is obvious from this portion of the Bible that the survivors of the Flood had very short memories. They fell into the same trap as their pre-Flood ancestors. Their own desires became foremost. Once more God was angered by mankind's refusal to be obedient to Him. The Bible declares that God put an end to the construction of the Babylonian tower by supernaturally confounding their communication. The Bible states:

> But the LORD came down to see the city and the tower which the sons of men had built. And the LORD said, "Indeed the people are one and they all have one language, and this is what they begin to do; now nothing that they propose to do will be withheld from them. Come, let Us go down and there confuse their language, that they may not understand one another's speech." So the LORD scattered them abroad from there over the face of all the earth, and they ceased building the city. Therefore its name is called Babel, because there the LORD confused the language of all the earth; and from there the LORD scattered them abroad over the face of all the earth.[26]

Archeology bears out the fact that the remains of ziggurats exist in the region between the Tigris and the Euphrates, the very location where the Bible claims civilization sprang up after the Flood of Noah. These structures substantiate the biblical claim that the ancient Sumerians were focused on involvement with the spirit world. As an article titled "The Men Who Built the Tower of Babel" from a book called *The World's Last Mysteries* states:

> Soaring in platforms towards the sky, bold in their design, capped with temples, the towering structures known as ziggurats were the crowning glory of the city-states that emerged in Mesopotamia 5,000 years ago. Eclipsing them all was Baby-

[25] Genesis 11: 1-4
[26] Genesis 11:5-9

lon's ziggurat [the ziggurat of Etemenanki] - renowned as the Tower of Babel. But their function remains a mystery. Were they royal tombs, astronomers' observatories or gigantic stepping stones for the gods to come down to earth? [27]

Figure 3: The Tower of Babel was built by the rebellious survivors of the Noahic Flood. These were people who willfully chose to be disobedient to the God who made everything. The ancient Sumerians built structures like the Tower of Babel in order to worship the fallen satanic realm.

[27] "The Men Who Built the Tower of Babel," *The World's Last Mysteries*, (Reader's Digest Association, Pleasantville, NY), 169.

Although the Tower of Babel is not available for us to examine today, there are other archeological sites in the area that provide insight into the purpose of the Tower of Babel and why God was angered by what the ancient Babylonians were doing. For example the ziggurat at Ur, the Sumerian capital for several centuries, is the best preserved. Ur, which is located in the south of Iraq, is the Ur of the Chaldees mentioned in Genesis and was the location from which Abraham originated.

Nimrod: Legend or Reality?

While it is possible to verify that there were physical structures like the biblical Tower of Babel existing in ancient Sumeria, there is another important factor that confirms that Babylonian worship was concentrated on contacting spiritual powers in heavenly places. Once more archeology, the study of the facts left to us by the ancient people from the past, supports the fact that Babylon was the mother of all spiritual harlotry.

One of the individuals who played a significant role in leading the Babylonians into their mutiny against God was a man by the name of Nimrod. He is briefly mentioned in the tenth chapter of Genesis. The Bible states: "Cush begot Nimrod; he began to be a mighty one on the earth. He was a mighty hunter before the LORD."[28]

Although these two verses do not seem to indicate that Nimrod had an agenda to lead people into rebellion against God, other sources show that this is what happened. The name Nimrod comes from the Hebrew word *marad* and means, "he rebelled." The expression that he was a mighty one "before the Lord" can express a hostile meaning --the word *before* can carry the meaning "against" the Lord. The *Jewish Encyclopedia* says that Nimrod was "he who made all the people rebellious against God."[29]

---

[28] Genesis 10:8

[29] Gross, "The Heathen Religion," *Jewish Encyclopedia*, 60.

The Microsoft Encarta 98 Encyclopedia's account of Nimrod adds additional insight to the importance of this biblical character. It states:

> Nimrod, a character in the biblical Book of Genesis described as "the first potentate on earth" and "mighty hunter in the eyes of Yahweh (God)" (Gen. 10:8-9). In Genesis he is identified as the son of Ham and grandson of Noah, and an empire-builder whose lands included large areas of Southern Mesopotamia. The epithet "mighty hunter" applied to Nimrod in Genesis has traditionally been interpreted as indicating that "his prey was man." In the 17th-century epic poem *Paradise Lost* (Book XII, 11. 24-63), by English writer John Milton, Nimrod appears as the lawless and impious tyrant whose ambition led to the disastrous episode of the building of the Tower of Babel. Nimrod instructed his people to construct a tower to reach heaven. God punished Nimrod's arrogance and halted construction by condemning the human race to speak separate and mutually unintelligible languages and by scattering it all over the world. Legend locates the tomb of Nimrod in Damascus, Syria. In English literary tradition, the name "Nimrod" is often applied to a skillful or daring hunter.[30]

The noted Jewish historian Josephus also added another dimension to the character of Nimrod. He wrote:

> Now it was Nimrod who excited them to such an affront and contempt of God. He also gradually changed the government into tyranny, seeing no other way of turning men from the fear of God. The multitudes were very ready to follow the determination of Nimrod and they built a tower, neither sparing any pains, nor being in any degree negligent about the work: and by reason of the multitude of hands employed in it, it grew very high... the place wherein they built the tower is now called Babylon.[31]

---

[30] "Nimrod," Microsoft Encarta Encyclopedia, 1998, CD-ROM.

[31] Flavius Josephus, Wm. Whiston, translator, *The Complete Works of Josephus,* (Kregel Publications, Grand Rapids, MI, 1981), 30.

Jewish Babylonianism

The Jews, God's chosen people, were influenced by the Babylonian practice of worshipping male and female deities known as the gods and goddesses. In the thirtieth chapter of Deuteronomy, God, speaking through the prophet Moses, laid out the consequences of worshipping the fallen spiritual realm. He stated:

> See, I have set before you today life and good, death and evil, in that I command you today to love the LORD your God, to walk in His ways, and to keep His commandments, His statutes, and His judgments, that you may live and multiply; and the LORD your God will bless you in the land which you go to possess. But if your heart turns away so that you do not hear, and are drawn away, and worship other gods and serve them, I announce to you today that you shall surely perish; you shall not prolong your days in the land which you cross over the Jordan to go in and possess.[32]

In the Book of Judges, the Bible explains what happened because the people refused to take God seriously. The very thing that God told them not to do, the children of Israel did. The Bible states:

> Then the children of Israel did evil in the sight of the LORD, and served the Baals; and they forsook the LORD God of their fathers, who had brought them out of the land of Egypt; and they followed other gods from among the gods of the people who were all around them, and they bowed down to them; and they provoked the LORD to anger. They forsook the LORD and served Baal and the Ashtoreths.[33]

Ashtaroth was the name by which the goddess or queen of heaven was known to the children of Israel. Certainly God's chosen people, the Jews, were not immune to Satan's devices. In fact, it is apparent from the Old Testament that the Jews fell into this trap of the devil over and over again. The Book of Jeremiah

---

[32] Deuteronomy 30:15-18

[33] Judges 2:11-13

records the actual words of defiance by God's people as they openly rebelled against Him. As the Bible states:

> As for the word that you have spoken to us in the name of the LORD, we will not listen to you! But we will certainly do whatever has gone out of our own mouth, to burn incense to the queen of heaven and pour out drink offerings to her, as we have done, we and our fathers, our kings and our princes, in the cities of Judah and in the streets of Jerusalem. For then we had plenty of food, were well-off, and saw no trouble. But since we stopped burning incense to the queen of heaven and pouring out drink offerings to her, we have lacked everything and have been consumed by the sword and by famine.[34]

Roman Babylonianism

Centuries later, Jesus Christ was born of a virgin, was crucified and rose from the dead to atone for the sins of the world. Those who turned from their sin and placed their faith in Jesus comprised and began what we now call the Christian Church. However, history reveals that by the third and fourth centuries, the church based in Rome had made a great departure from a scriptural basis for the Christian faith. This "falling away" was characterized by the acceptance of various pagan customs and beliefs. Unconverted pagans were allowed to be a part of the Christian church by slightly altering certain occult rites and customs in order to give them Christian respectability.

Several books have been written attempting to document a connection between Roman Catholicism and Babylonianism. In some cases, these books have been based on faulty or incomplete statements, the authors quoting other writers who had not properly documented their claims.[35] However well–respected historian, Will Durant has come to the same conclusion. Regarding Augustine's observation of the pagan beliefs infiltrating Catholicism, Durant has written:

---

[34] Jeremiah 44:16-19

[35] Ralph Woodrow, "The Two Babylons: A Case Study in Poor Research Methodology," *Christian Research Journal,* vol. 22, no. 2, 1999, 54-56.

> Augustine's argument against paganism was the last rebuttal in the greatest of historic debates. Paganism survived in the moral sense, as a joyous indulgence of natural appetites; as a religion it remained only in the form of ancient rights and customs condoned, or accepted and transformed, by an often indulgent Church. An intimate and trustful worship of saints replaced the cult of the pagan gods, and satisfied the congenial polytheism of simple or poetic minds. Statues of Isis and Horus were renamed Mary and Jesus; the Roman Lupercalia and the feast of the purification of Isis became the Feast of the Nativity; the Saturnalia were replaced by Christmas celebrations, the Floralia by Pentecost, an ancient festival of the dead by All Souls' Day, the resurrection of Attis by the resurrection of Christ. Pagan altars were rededicated to Christian heroes; incense, lights, flowers, processions, vestments, hymns which had pleased the people in older cults were domesticated and cleansed in their ritual of the church; and the harsh slaughter of a living victim was sublimated in the spiritual sacrifice of the Mass. Augustine had protested against the adoration of saints, and in terms that Voltaire might have used in dedicating his chapel at Ferney: "Let us not treat the saints as gods; we do not wish to imitate those pagans who adorn the dead. Let us not build them temples nor raise altars to them."[36]

Durant also documented how the Catholic adoration of Mary is rooted in the ancient pagan religions that are clearly associated with Babylonianism. He wrote:

> The finest triumph of this tolerant spirit of adaptation was the sublimation of the pagan mother-goddess cults in the worship of Mary. Here too the people took the initiative. In 431 Cyril, Archbishop of Alexandria, in a famous sermon at Ephesus, applied to Mary many of the terms fondly ascribed by the pagans of Ephesus to their "great goddess" Artemis-Diana; and the council of Ephesus that year, over the protests of Nestorius, sanctioned for Mary the title of "Mother of God."

[36] Will Durant, *The Story of Civilization: A History of Medieval Civilization – Christian, Islamic and Judaic – from Constantine to Dante: AD 325-1300*, (Simon and Schuster, New York, 1950), 75.

> Gradually the tenderest features of Astarte, Cybele, Artemis, Diana and Isis were gathered together in the worship of Mary. In the sixth century the Church established the Feast of the Assumption of the Virgin into heaven, and assigned it to August 13, the date of the ancient festivals of Isis and Artemis.[37]

The Bible makes it clear that Mary worship was never intended to be a part of the original Christian faith. God said, "Thou shalt have no other gods before me."[38] The Bible does record that Mary, was a special woman that God chose to be the mother of Jesus, and that she was a dedicated and godly woman. However, to make Mary into more than what the Bible teaches, is to embrace ideas or dogmas without scriptural basis. This point is even admitted by *The Catholic Encyclopedia,* which states:

> Devotion to Our Blessed Lady in its ultimate analysis must be regarded as a practical application of the doctrine of the Communion of Saints. Seeing that this doctrine is not contained, at least explicitly, in earlier forms of the Apostles' Creed, there is perhaps no ground for surprise if we do not meet with any clear traces of the cultus of the Blessed Virgin in the first Christian centuries, the worship of Mary being a later development.[39]

Learning from the Past

Solomon, writing in the Book of Ecclesiastes, said there is really nothing new under the sun. Whatever has happened before, can and will happen again. History merely repeats itself.[40]

---

[37] Ibid., 745-746.

[38] Exodus 20: 3

[39] "Virgin Mary," *The Catholic Encyclopedia,* vol.15, 459.

[40] Ecclesiastes 1:9

Figure 4: Depictions of the Catholic belief that Mary is the "Queen of Heaven" are found worldwide. Numerous paintings and statues depict "Mary" wearing a crown, or she is in the process of being crowned.

Figure 5: Statues of the crowned Madonna holding a baby Jesus are common throughout the Catholic Church. This represents the importance of the Catholic view of "The Queen of Heaven."

The scenario that developed at Babylon as documented in the Book of Genesis, provides important insight for anyone who takes the Bible seriously. When one chooses to rebel against God by ignoring His Word, there will be consequences. Spiritually we can see what happens when mankind willingly joins forces to defy God. Man, operating without God and inspired by fallen spiritual forces, will attempt to set up his own rebellious and ultimately doomed kingdom.

There are numerous other examples we could point to from the Bible, showing that the Babylonian incident was not unique to the period of time shortly after the Flood. In reality, what Babylon represents has been repeated many times. In fact, the same pattern of human behavior is alive and well throughout the world today. Should we not be more concerned about what could happen in our society today if we continue to ignore the warnings that God has revealed through His Holy Word?

4

APOSTASY AND BIBLE PROPHECY

The Bible is a unique book. No other book has ever been written that places its entire credence upon the claim that the statements it contains about the future must occur with one hundred percent accuracy.

While this statement may seem too incredible for skeptics who refuse to believe the Bible is the Word of God, there are many who study Bible prophecy that stand firmly behind this claim. History reveals that countless Bible prophecies have already been fulfilled. Current events that are unfolding show numerous prophecies are in the process of being fulfilled. This chapter will present the biblical foundation showing the Bible predicts that great deception will take place in the name of Christ in the last days.

Deception in His Name

In Matthew chapter twenty-four, the Bible relates that one day Jesus' disciples approached Him privately and asked what signs would indicate His Second Coming was near. "Tell us," they said, "when will these things be, and what will be the sign of Your coming, and the end of the age?"[41]

Jesus responded to them by presenting a list of events that could be expected before His Second Coming. He mentioned there would be wars and rumors of wars and that nations would rise up against other nations.[42] He said famines and earthquakes would be common all around the world.[43] He claimed that human behavior would be characterized by lawlessness, and that society would be just like it was in the days of Noah.[44] As well, Jesus said another sign that His return would be soon would be that "the gospel would be proclaimed to all the nations as a witness and then the end would come."[45]

While Jesus talked about all of these signs that would indicate His Second Coming was near, it seems He emphasized one sign above all others. The first sign that He mentioned is that there would be many who would mislead many.[46] More specifically, the last days would be a time when deception would take place in His name. He clarified this by saying:

> Then if anyone says to you, 'Look, here is the Christ!' or 'There!' do not believe it. For false christs and false prophets will rise and show great signs and wonders to deceive, if possible, even the elect. See, I have told you beforehand.[47]

This statement Jesus made was not just for the disciples that were gathered together with Him on the Mount of Olives. The statement is relevant and true for anyone who is willing to take His Word seriously today. If Bible prophecy is about knowing the future in advance with absolute accuracy, then it would be good to pay attention. It is obvious that Jesus said what He said for the purpose of warning those who would live in the days

---

[41] Matthew 24:3
[42] Matthew 24:6-7
[43] Matthew 24:7
[44] Matthew 24:12
[45] Matthew 24:14
[46] Matthew 24:3-4
[47] Matthew 24:23-25

before His return so that they would be aware of being deceived. Notice that He made it very clear that the deception that was going to sweep the world would be in His name – the name of Christ.

Great Apostasy or Great Revival?

There is a lot of talk today in Christian circles about "the great revival that must take place before Jesus can return." While every genuine Bible-believing Christian should have a desire to see unbelievers saved so that they will not face judgment, it is also important for them to be aware of the deception that Jesus said would impact believers in the last days.

Jesus warned that lying signs and wonders would be instrumental in leading people astray before He returned.[48] We also know that lying signs and wonders have the potential of sending people to a lost eternity. When Jesus was speaking at the Sermon on the Mount, He stated that people would stand before Him on Judgment Day and actually be convinced that they are believers when in reality they will end up going to hell. In Jesus' own words:

> Not everyone who says to Me, 'Lord, Lord,' shall enter the kingdom of heaven, but he who does the will of My Father in heaven. Many will say to Me in that day, 'Lord, Lord, have we not prophesied in Your name, cast out demons in Your name, and done many wonders in Your name.' And then I will declare to them, 'I never knew you; depart from Me, you who practice lawlessness!'[49]

It seems apparent that these words of Jesus should be taken seriously. The cost of being deceived into believing you are a Christian, when in reality you are not, is eternal separation from God. Believing in Jesus requires a true understanding of the gospel, not just an experiential encounter in the name of Christ.

---

[48] Ibid.

[49] Matthew 7:21-23

The Miracle Man

The apostle Paul also warned that lying signs and wonders in the last days would deceive people. This would occur as part of the delusion that would be the prerequisite for the Antichrist. The deluding influence would be part of Satan's strategy to seduce the world into the preparation for the counterfeit bride for the counterfeit Christ. As Paul stated:

> The coming of the lawless one is according to the working of Satan, with all power, signs, and lying wonders, and with all unrighteous deception among those who perish, because they did not receive the love of the truth, that they might be saved. And for this reason God will send them strong delusion, that they should believe the lie. [50]

Paul also stated that the church would play a key role in the prelude to the revelation of a man who will claim to be God. This whole scenario could not happen, Paul wrote to the Thessalonians, until after apostasy happened. He stated:

> Let no one deceive you by any means; for that Day will not come unless the falling away comes first [apostasy], and the man of sin is revealed, the son of perdition, who opposes and exalts himself above all that is called God or that is worshiped, so that he sits as God in the temple of God, showing himself that he is God. [51]

The word *apostasy* means a falling away from the faith. [52] The Bible states that "faith cometh by hearing, and hearing by the Word of God." [53] Therefore, an apostate faith is a faith that is based on extrabiblical ideas or experiences that convince people they are genuine believers when they are not.

---

[50] 2 Thessalonians 2:9-11

[51] 2 Thessalonians 2:3-4

[52] 646. apostasia, ap-os-tas-ee'-ah; fem. of the same as G647; defection from truth (prop. the state) ["apostasy"]:--falling away, forsake. *Strong's Exhaustive Concordance of the Bible*, (Abingdon, Nashville, TN, 1980).

[53] Romans 10:17

Doctrines of Demons

Although the Bible teaches the day is coming when "every knee shall bow" to Jesus Christ, that day is still in the future. Satan and his followers still have a powerful influence upon the world in which we live. The "god of this world"[54] that Paul wrote about, is still alive and active.

As well, the Bible teaches that end-times deception is not an exception. Instead, it is the rule. Although God's power is greater than what the devil has to offer, this does not mean we can ignore Satan's devices. The Bible warns that the great deceiver is "like a roaring lion seeking whom he may devour"[55] and at any hour.

In other words, it is wise to be alert to what the Bible has to say about deception. Some have said, "We have to have more faith in God's ability to bless us than in Satan's ability to deceive us."[56] Although there is an element of truth in this statement, there is much more that needs to be said. When people willingly ignore what God has warned about in His Word, they become sure candidates for the doctrines devised by demons.

In light of Bible prophecy, we need not speculate about Satan's ability to be involved in sowing the seeds for apostasy. This is a biblical fact. As Paul wrote to Timothy: "Now the Spirit expressly says that in latter times some will depart from the faith, giving heed to deceiving spirits and doctrines of demons."[57]

If this were the only verse in the entire New Testament that indicated there would be spiritual deception in the last days, would that not be enough? But there are numerous others that add to the deception complexion. Satan is the deceiver and deception is his game. In the last days his agenda intensifies.

---

[54] 2 Corinthians 4:3-4

[55] 1 Peter 5:8

[56] John Arnott. *The Father's Blessing*, (Creation House, Orlando, FL, 1995), 110.

[57] I Timothy 4:1

Jannes and Jambres

Finally, a word of warning about the danger of using signs and wonders as an end-times tool for evangelism. We know from the Old Testament that Satan is a master at conjuring up signs and wonders as a means of showing that he can operate in the supernatural realm.

One example can be found in the Book of Exodus where we see a situation in which Moses, Aaron and Pharaoh were involved in a supernatural signs and wonders demonstration. When Aaron's staff was turned into a serpent, the Pharaoh called for his sorcerers and magicians to do the same.[58] In the New Testament Paul identifies these Egyptian signs and wonders experts by name. As part of his end-times dissertation to Timothy, he warned about the appearance of similar last day charlatans:

> Now as Jannes and Jambres resisted Moses, so do these also resist the truth: men of corrupt minds, disapproved concerning the faith; but they will progress no further, for their folly will be manifest to all, as theirs also was.[59]

Once more we see how the Bible teaches there will be a concentrated demonic effort in the last days to deceive people from the authentic faith that is based upon the Bible. With this in mind, it is interesting to note that we are living in a period of history when many people are talking about faith. But what is this faith they are talking about? If the whole world is going to come to a biblical faith, then why would Jesus have said: "Nevertheless, when the Son of Man comes, will He really find faith on the earth?"[60]

This is a time to be serious about faith. A faith that is based upon tradition, dogma, or a belief system that has been introduced by some extrabiblical experience may not be biblical faith at all. If we do not heed the warning from Scripture, then we could be fooling ourselves.

---

[58] Exodus 7:8-11

[59] 2 Timothy 3:8-9

[60] Luke 18:8

Figure 6: While the Bible teaches that God is a God of miracles, Satan is also capable of working miracles. The Bible teaches that lying signs and wonders will be repeated in the last days.

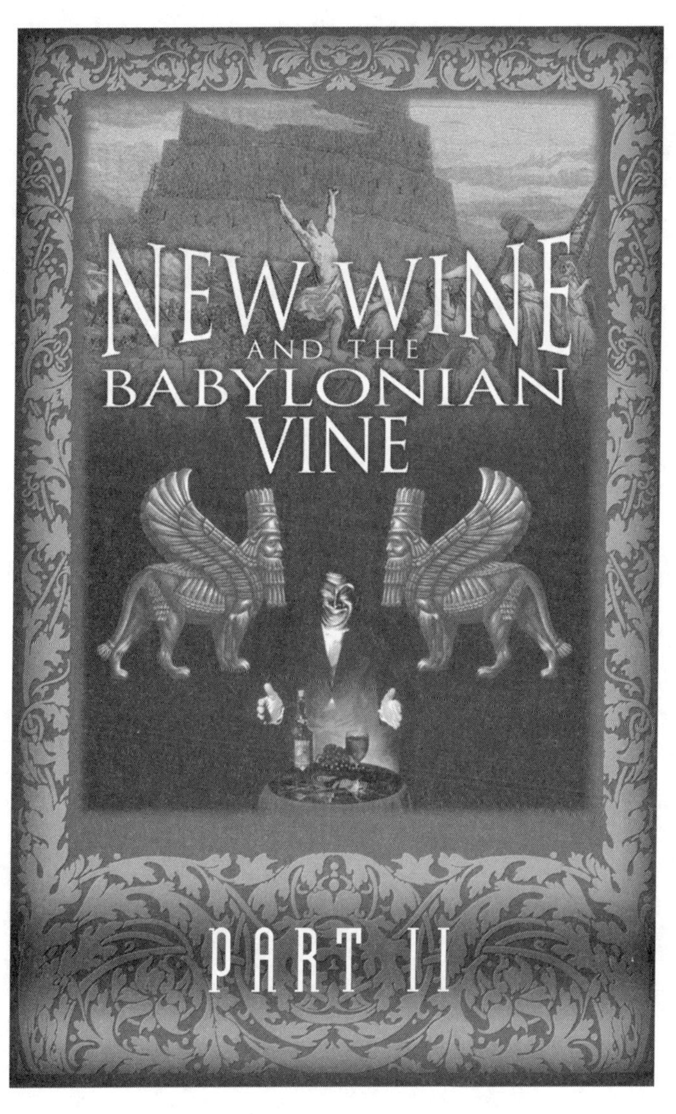

THE GOSPEL REDEFINED

5

THE WIDE WAY, THE NARROW WAY

We have already established that a faith that is not biblically based is not biblical faith. Given the fact that the Scriptures state we are saved by faith in Jesus,[61] should we not earnestly contend for the faith that was once delivered unto the saints?[62]

For the unbeliever, the idea of being saved by grace through faith alone is nonsense. As Paul wrote to the Corinthians: "For the message of the cross is foolishness to those who are perishing, but to us who are being saved it is the power of God."[63]

Many say they are unable to understand the gospel or that it is just too difficult to comprehend. However, the gospel was never intended to be difficult. Even a child can comprehend what this message is all about. Jesus defined the gospel in a single verse: "For God so loved the world that He gave His only begotten Son, that whoever believes in Him should not perish but have everlasting life."[64]

---

[61] Ephesians 2: 8

[62] Jude 1:3

[63] I Corinthians 1:18

[64] John 3:16

Another Gospel

We know the Bible teaches there is another gospel.[65] We also know the true gospel is based upon believing who Jesus is and what He has done. Without His blood having been shed on the cross, there would be no gospel. The Creator, who made us, became a man and sacrificed His life for us. Our part is to recognize we are doomed to hell because of our sinful nature and practices. When we are sincere and ask Jesus to forgive us, He will. Our human spirit is then born again, and we can spend eternity with Him.

Throughout the history of the church we have seen this simple message perverted over and over again. While many Protestants are quick to point out they are the only true defenders of the faith, it is important to keep one thing in mind. Error is error, whether propagated by Catholics or Protestants. Teachings that are not Bible based and are not corrected will always have the potential to lead people into spiritual deception. In other words, it is imperative to always examine what men are saying and compare it with what God has already said.

History reveals that major shifts in thought occur very slowly. At first, new ideas have little perceived impact. Then very rapidly, an old worldview becomes obsolete and is then replaced by a new worldview that is heralded as the way, the truth and the light. There are some, including myself, who are saying that this is happening now to the church. Christianity is undergoing a paradigm shift.

But does the gospel change from generation to generation? If not, then why is there such an organized effort to redefine the gospel in order to permit a wide variety of extrabiblical beliefs? Why are there so many people from so many different backgrounds lifting up the banner of unity? While we know that unity and brotherly love are important if we are going to be followers of Jesus Christ, how far can we go to seek unity, if truth is not the common ground?

---

[65] Galatians 1:6

The Reformation

The Bible contains a number of references that make it clear it is very helpful to examine the past if we want to understand the present and the future. As Solomon stated: "Is there anything of which it may be said, "See, this is new"? It has already been in ancient times before us."[66] Or in the Book of Job, the Bible challenges us to check out what happened to our ancestors:

> For inquire, please, of the former age, and consider the things discovered by their fathers; for we were born yesterday, and know nothing, because our days on earth are a shadow. Will they not teach you and tell you, and utter words from their heart?[67]

It is with these words in mind that we want to go back and reconsider another paradigm shift that happened in the church about five hundred years ago. When the word *reformation* is mentioned today, many Christians are not informed. They have never taken the time to study how this famous revolution of the past changed the course of Christianity.

I have found it interesting to read a variety of history books in order to get a broader view of the different perspectives there are on the Reformation. While secular historians see this crucial period of time as merely a revolutionary movement, books that are written from a Roman Catholic viewpoint look upon the Reformation as a revolt by Protestants against the Universal Church. They see Protestantism as a heretical schism that destroyed the theological and ecclesiastical unity of the medieval Roman Church. From this point of view Martin Luther was a heretic. On the other hand, Protestant historians consider the Reformation as a sovereign movement of God that brought Christianity back to the pattern laid out in the New Testament.

The reformers, many of whom shed their blood for the cause, were totally committed to developing a theology that would be in complete accord with the teachings of Paul and the

---

[66] Ecclesiastes 1:10

[67] Job 8:8-10

other New Testament writers. They realized this would never become a reality as long as the church was the authority, rather than the Word of God.[68]

Reasons for Reformation

According to the book, *Foxe's Christian Martyrs of the World*, the early reformers stood against the Church of Rome in four important areas:[69] 1) they denied the value of pilgrimages; 2) they refused to worship the saints; 3) they insisted on reading Scriptures for themselves; 4) they did not believe the physical body of Christ was present in the sacramental bread.

This last area of disagreement was particularly important to Rome and led many reformers to the stake. Author R. C. Ryle makes this historical fact clear:

> The point I refer to is the special reason why our reformers were burned. Great indeed would be our mistake if we supposed that they suffered in the vague charge of refusing submission to the Pope, or desiring to maintain the independence of the Church of England. Nothing of the kind! The principal reason why they were burned was because they refused one of the peculiar doctrines of the Romish church. On that doctrine, in almost every case, hinged their life or death. If they admitted it, they might live, if they refused it, they must die. The doctrine in question was the real presence of the body and blood of Christ in the consecrated elements of bread and wine in the Lord's Supper...[70]

While the early reformers disagreed on many other issues, such as indulgences and papal supremacy, the doctrine known as transubstantiation was paramount.

---

[68] Earle E. Cairns, *Christianity Through the Centuries*, (Zondervan, Grand Rapids, MI, 16th printing), 300-301.

[69] John Foxe, *Foxe's Christian Martyrs of the World*, (Barbour & Company, Uhlrichville, OH), 50-51.

[70] J. C. Ryle, *Light from Old Times - Volume 1*, (Charles Nolan Publishers, Moscow, ID, 1890), 54-55.

Transubstantiation

Transubstantiation is the Catholic belief that the actual "presence of Christ" appears in the Eucharist. For Catholics who believe and accept the Catholic Church's teachings, the most important tenant of faith, without dispute, is the Holy Eucharist. It is in this Holy Eucharist, under the appearance of bread and wine, that Jesus Christ is believed to unite with His people. While this dogma is rejected by the secular world and almost all other Christian churches, it is the source, unity and summit of the Catholic faith. By receiving Holy Communion, the Catholic Church teaches that a person is in obedience to the Lord's command to "eat His body and drink His blood."[71]

According to Dr. Thomas W. Petrisko and the Catholic view of church history, "throughout the fourteenth century, Eucharistic miracles, saintly visions and apparitions abounded, as Heaven continued to pour out its signs and wonders in order to strengthen the faithful."[72] While these "eucharistic miracles" were claimed to be from God, there is no biblical precedent found in the Word of God. Following are two examples of fourteenth century eucharistic miracles that Petrisko reported in his book *Mother of the Secret: From Eucharistic Miracles to Marian Apparitions Heaven has sought to illuminate and defend what was once the Church's greatest secret*:

> On March 15, 1345, a very sick man named Ysbrant Dommer received Holy Communion at his home in Amsterdam, Holland. After the priest departed, Ysbrant expelled the contents of his stomach into a basin. A woman who was there then threw it into a large open fire in the hearth. The following day the same woman discovered the Host, shining and whole in the coals. She placed it in a cloth and then into a chest. A priest came and took it to the parish church of Saint Nicholas, where he placed it into a pyx. The next morning the priest found the pyx empty. Somehow, the Host reappeared in the woman's

[71] Thomas W. Petrisko, *Mother of the Secret: From Eucharistic Miracles to Marian Apparitions Heaven has sought to illuminate and defend what was once the Church's greatest secret,* Queenship Publishing Company, 1997, p xix
[72] Ibid., 51

> chest. After a third incident, the priest became convinced of the entire miracle. An inquiry was held, and the bishop's verdict was favorable for the events. Over the centuries, celebration of this miracle has continued.[73]
>
> At the church of Santa Maria Assunta in Bagno Di Romagna, Italy in the year 1412, a priest was struggling with his faith. As he was offering Mass one day, he continued to have his doubts about the True Presence of Jesus in the Eucharist. Suddenly after the consecration, the priest looked into the chalice and saw the wine had turned into blood. The red blood began to boil! This caused some of it to spurt out of the chalice and onto the corporal. The blood seemed to be alive. The priest alerted the congregation who experienced a powerful conversion. Almost 400 years later, after Pope Pius VI convened a commission to investigate, the relics were put on display to venerate. In 1912, a large celebration was held to commemorate the miracle. In 1958, a scientific study confirmed that the stain on the corporal cloth was blood.[74]

These Eucharistic "signs and wonders" were not always accepted as miracles from God. Several critics risked their lives in their attempt to warn "experience-based" Christians of the importance of basing their faith upon Scripture alone. As previously mentioned, numerous reformers lost their lives for the stance they made against the Catholic Church's position on transubstantiation. To this fact of history, Thomas Petrisko makes the following comment:

> An Oxford scholar named John Wycliffe (1330-1384), who had little serious study of Scripture, published his translation of the Bible. Wycliffe taught that the Bible, not tradition, was the sole rule of faith, It quickly became one of the most well-circulated works of the times. Most significantly, Wycliffe's ideas about transubstantiation then affected others, such as John Huss (1369-1415). These critics then led an increasing number of people to rebel against Church teachings. Accord-

[73] Ibid., p 53

[74] Ibid., p 56

> ing to scholars, all these circumstances were the early sparks of Protestant uprising. But again, it must be emphasized that during this period, a plethora of miracles, accompanied by reports of numerous mystical interventions occurred.[75]

I find it very intriguing to investigate the Protestant and Catholic views of church history and then ask some legitimate questions. Is it possible to determine from Scripture, whether the Catholic view of transubstantiation is God's truth or man's tradition? If one argues that it is the truth, then how would it be possible to justify that people were burned at the stake for taking a position against the literal appearance of Christ in the Eucharist? And then one final question that may stimulate some thought: If people died for standing up against the Catholic view of transubstantiation, is it possible, if history repeats itself, that it could happen again, some time in the future?

Martin Luther

Martin Luther is the name most people recognize when it comes to the topic of the Reformation. He was born November 10, 1483 in the small town of Eisleben, Germany. His father encouraged him to study law, but Luther, frightened by a severe lightning storm in July of 1505, promised Saint Anne that he would become a monk if his life was spared. About three weeks later he entered a monastery of the Augustinian order at Erfurt. It was there in 1507 that he was ordained and celebrated his first mass.[76]

During the winter of 1510 and 1511 Luther was sent to Rome on business for his order. There he had a "Roman revelation." He saw the corruption and luxury of the Roman Church and realized there was a great need for reform.

In 1511 Luther was transferred to Wittenburg, Germany. During the next year he became a professor of Bible and received his doctor of theology degree. At this time he was given an office

[75] Ibid., p 51-52

[76] Cairns, 313-314.

in the tower where he came to his realization of justification by faith, a teaching that was to spread all over Germany. A reading of Romans 1:17 convinced him that only faith in Christ could make a human being just before God. From that time on, justification by faith and *sola scriptura,* (the view that the Scriptures are the only authority for sinful man in seeking salvation), became the main points of his theological position.[77]

In 1517 the sale of indulgences, a means of raising funds for the Catholic Church, began. Church officials claimed that repentance was not necessary for the buyer of an indulgence and that the indulgence gave complete forgiveness of all sin. Luther was upset about the exploitation of the people by this scheme and decided to make a public protest. On October 31, 1517 he posted his Ninety-five Theses on the door of the Castle Church in Wittenburg.

He condemned the abuses of the indulgence system and challenged anyone to debate him on this issue. Although his original objective was to be a reformer, between 1518 and 1521 he was forced to accept the idea that separation from the Roman Church was necessary. The only way for reform to occur, he finally decided, was to completely abandon the heretical teachings that had been embraced by his church and return to the truth as revealed in the Scriptures.

[77] Ibid., 314.

Figure 7: Martin Luther was one of the founding fathers of the Reformation. He and others risked their lives to speak out against the extrabiblical teachings of the Catholic Church

Did the Counter Reformation Succeed?

As has been documented, the Reformation was an attempt to turn away from a man-made religious system masquerading as Christianity, to a biblically based Christianity centered upon the

Word of God. While the Reformation resulted in a separation that ended in what has been called the Protestant faith, there was also a profound effect on the Catholic Church. The Counter Reformation is a term that has been coined to describe the changes that happened in the Roman Catholic Church between 1545 and 1645. This was an attempt to stabilize and strengthen the church after its heavy losses to Protestantism as the result of the Reformation.

While the Counter Reformation may have appeared to some to have been an admission that all was not well within the Catholic Church, the violent nature of the Counter Reformation, indicated that true repentance had not been achieved. Many lives ended prematurely, as blood was shed for the cause of the Roman Catholic Empire.

But today, as part of the "convergence movement," touted as the prerequisite for a last-days worldwide revival, Protestants are being asked to forgive and forget the past and join with Catholics to evangelize the world. Protestants and Catholics really do believe in the same foundational tenants of the faith, the promoters of the ecumenical movement are saying. We need to agree on what is agreeable and lay aside anything that would separate us for the cause of Christ, the claim is made.

However, there are some Protestants, perhaps a remnant who have the same concerns that Martin Luther had, who believe that reconciliation that is not centered on the cross, is not reconciliation at all. Joining together with a group of Christians who embrace another gospel could be dangerous, these concerned Christians say. As we stated in the first chapter of this book, Paul told the Corinthian church that it was spiritually dangerous to embrace another gospel and that this would mean the church had fallen for Satan's lie.[78] As well, he told Timothy[79] and the church at Thessalonica[80] there would be an intensification of this deceptive process in the last days.

---

[78] 2 Corinthians 11:3-4

[79] I Timothy 4:1

[80] 2 Thessalonians 2:3

A Personal Testimony

T. A. McMahon is a friend of mine. He has co-authored several books including *The New Spirituality* and *The Seduction of Christianity*. As a former Catholic, he is distressed about the trend he sees happening in the church today. Although he still has fond memories of a number of individuals in the Catholic Church who taught him when he was younger, he is very concerned about the teachings the church itself still embraces. In his own words:

> The priests and nuns of the various grade schools and of the high school and military school I attended were precious people in my life. I still have loving memories of each of those individuals who, for a quarter of a century, so profoundly impacted my life. I grew up respecting those who took part in personally rearing me, and those feelings haven't changed. What has changed drastically, however, is what I believe about the Church to which they dedicated their lives.[81]

T.A. McMahon's present knowledge of Catholicism comes from two perspectives. One is as a born-again, Bible-believing Christian who has studied the official teachings of the Roman Catholic Church; the other is as one who lived under twenty-five years of teaching by nuns and priests. Because of his background, he is uniquely qualified to discuss what he calls "the significant seduction taking place in these last days before His return."[82]

McMahon, like myself, recognizes that being a Protestant does not necessarily make one a genuine born-again believer. Certainly there are Catholics who are genuine believers, just as there are Protestants who believe they are Christians but are on their way to hell. It is not our "Protestantism" or our "Catholicism" that saves us. What saves a person is a genuine understanding of the gospel and a personal relationship with Jesus Christ.

---

[81] T. A. McMahon, "The Evangelical Seduction," *The Berean Call*, April 1996, 1.

[82] Ibid.

The following statement by McMahon explains the concern he has about a trend he sees developing as the gospel is being confused:

> As we have listened intently to Catholics who dialogue with evangelicals, or to those evangelical leaders who to a large degree defend Roman Catholicism, I've noticed a couple of very disturbing points. First, the language used by Catholic apologists is largely "evangelical speak," i.e. terms and phrases very familiar to Bible-believing Christians, but not common to Catholics. They talk about being saved, being born-again, taught by the Holy Spirit, having a personal relationship with Jesus Christ, engaging in group Bible studies etc. I never heard such terms when I was growing up, so why are we hearing them now?[83]

While many hopeful evangelicals are convinced there is a genuine renewal movement happening, McMahon believes there is reason not to get too excited. Although, it is worth repeating - there are Catholics who are sincerely coming to faith in Christ, just as there are Muslims, Hindus and New Agers coming to faith - it is still important the gospel be proclaimed according to biblical parameters, not by man-made descriptors. As McMahon states:

> I'm concerned that, for tactical purposes, Catholics use words to identify with practices which are meaningful to evangelicals, but without disclosing that they have completely different meaning for the Catholic. Whatever their motives are for introducing them, the practice can be very deceptive. "Salvation by grace," for example, means "without works" to evangelicals. To Catholics, however, grace is the means by which they believe meritorious works are performed in order to "earn salvation." So in that rare instance when a Catholic might claim that he also believes in salvation by grace, he does

[83] Ibid.

> not mean what an evangelical means. The difference is not a matter of semantics but of eternal destiny.[84]

And finally, McMahon also has something to say about the numerous lay-Catholic apologists (meaning they may be used by the church, but don't speak officially for the church) and evangelical ecumenists who tell Protestants what Catholics believe. Although their words may be impressive to evangelicals, it is foreign to the official doctrine and practice of the Catholic Church. McMahon suggests there is a delusion underway that is seducing the body of Christ. He states:

> For instance, the Catholic apologist claims and the evangelical scholar concurs – after checking with Catholic scholars, of course that "Catholics don't worship Mary nor do they pray to her as one would to God." I grew up worshipping Mary and praying to her more passionately than to God, and so did all my Catholic friends and relatives. We did not merely slip into idolatry against the teachings of the Church; we were taught it. The rosary with its 156 prayers to Mary, was not our invention. And to the thousands of other prayers to Mary you could add litanies to a legion of saints, many whom regularly displaced my time with God the Father, and with Jesus. My experience is not unique; it's the common, everyday Catholic experience.[85]

What's Wrong with this Picture?

So what is going on? Is there really a "seduction of Christianity" happening or is this the idea of a few paranoid soothsayer-extremists who are misleading the church and actually hindering the great revival so many are saying is underway? If the Catholic Church really has "turned over a new leaf" then why has there not been a public program designed to expose all practices and beliefs that have so clearly reflected a connection to the Babylonian vine? Since the time of Constantine when Christian doctrines were perverted to bring pagan beliefs under the canopy of the church, there has never been a clear-cut papal an-

---

[84] Ibid.
[85] Ibid.

nouncement that has declared that a combination of Christianity and Babylonianism is wrong.

In fact it can be documented the very opposite has occurred. For example, in 1986, at Assisi, Italy, the Vatican hosted many of the world's religious leaders in a special day of prayer for peace. Buddhists, Hindus, animists and "Christians" of various denominations gathered together by invitation of the pontiff from Rome. All prayed to the gods or goddesses of their choice. The pope who had called for this gathering never presented the gospel of Jesus Christ. Maybe that would have been a hindrance to the unity for peace that he was endeavoring to attain.[86]

There are hundreds of millions of Catholics who believe they are saved by allegiance to the rules and regulations of their church. Shouldn't the Catholic apologists be devoting their time to the warning of their own flock about the dangers of embracing paganism? As T. A. McMahon states: "Instead, their efforts are focused on deluding the Vatican's greatest threat to its worldwide empire – the Bible-believing, gospel-preaching church of Jesus Christ."[87]

How Wide Can Narrow Be?

One of the ways that Satan deceives people is to convince fallen man that the gospel has no validity. However, another effective way is to confuse the message so that people think they understand the gospel, when in reality they do not.

Sometimes as a teaching method, I have found it is useful to express what the Bible does not say, so that people will pay more attention to what the Bible does say. In order to demonstrate this point, I am going to purposely misquote the words of Jesus as recorded in the Book of Matthew chapter seven. Jesus said: "Enter by the [wide] gate; for [narrow] is the gate and [narrow] is the way that leads to destruction, and there are [few] who go in by

---

[86] Richard Ostling, "A Summit for Peace in Assisi," *Time*, November 10, 1986, 78.

[87] McMahon, 1.

it. Because [wide] is the gate and [easy] is the way which leads to life, and there are [many] who find it."[88]

Anyone who has read these verses and understands the gospel will immediately recognize what I have just stated is wrong. Not only is it wrong, it is heretical. The way to eternal life is very narrow. The wide way is the path of deception and there are many who travel this road. Jesus clearly said that He alone was "the way," the "narrow way."[89]

Now, recognizing this foundational biblical truth, I believe it is important to consider the current trend that is underway in the name of Christ. Many who once believed the way was narrow, seem to have fallen for the idea that the road to eternity needs to be widened. It seems that Christianity is becoming an "all embracing" kind of faith. "The preaching of the cross, is just too offensive because it's just too narrow," some say.

I believe that the gospel is the narrow way, and the only way to an eternal relationship with God in heaven. If the narrow way is expanded or compromised, then it merely becomes the wide way. Remember Jesus taught that in the last days, there would be many deceived by many, in His name.[90] Don't fall in the trap.

---

[88] Matthew 7:13-14 Words in brackets are misquotes

[89] John 14:6

[90] Matthew 24:4-5, 23-24

6

A ROMAN REVELATION

When I was a child I remember hearing about how traveling to another country could play an important role in the education process. Now that I have had the opportunity to travel around the world, I can certainly affirm that this is true. While visiting the city of Rome, my mind was expanded tremendously. This chapter will explain why.

Normally when I travel to a country on a missionary trip, my objective is to get there as quickly as possible without any stops on the way. In November of 1997, the itinerary that was arranged for me to travel to Albania was an exception. As the result of Air Italia's flight rescheduling, an overnight stop in Rome actually turned into two full days.

Although I was familiar with some of the important historical sites in Rome, this was my first opportunity to go there and see some of these places in person. I booked a full day tour of Rome that was designed to take tourists to some of the key historical locations. What I learned in Rome during this brief tour has been life changing.

Figure 8: The Trevi Fountain was constructed in Rome in 1751 by order of Pope Clemens XII. The fountain was dedicated to the sea god Neptune.

The Trevi Fountain

The first place our tour guide took us was to the Trevi Fountain. Although this was just another sculpture built during the Renaissance period of history, I discovered something about this site that bothered me. Pope Clemens XII had commissioned the building of this fountain in 1751. Although the fountain was spectacular, it was not the fountain itself that attracted my attention. A figure of the god Neptune is the most prominent feature of the fountain. Pope Clemens XII, like all other popes, was supposed to be the spiritual head of the Catholic Church. As everyone knows, a pagan god such as Neptune is an abomination to the God of the Bible.

No one else on the tour seemed to be troubled by this important piece of information provided by the guide. You don't have to be a biblical scholar to realize that a form of Christianity that embraces paganism is not Christian at all. I purchased a book at the location to make sure the guide knew what she was talking about. Everything that she had told us was confirmed.

As I stood gazing at the fountain, a thought came to my mind. My ancestors on my maternal grandfather's side had come to America from France via the Netherlands as immigrants at about this same period of history. As Huguenots, they had fled their homeland because of persecution from the Catholic Church. Many of their relatives were not able to make the trip. They had been brutally killed because they had stood up against the heresies of the Catholic Church.

For a brief moment my emotions welled up inside me: Now I have a little glimpse of what my ancestors must have experienced, I thought.

Although some may say the Catholic Church has reformed its theology since the sixteenth century, I did not see any signs at the Trevi Fountain stating this was the case. If I were part of the present day Catholic hierarchy, I would not want tourists to be confused. It would be very beneficial if the present pope would clear up any confusion by declaring the Trevi Fountain a pagan site. I will be the first to applaud him for this noble effort.

The Pantheon

The second stop on my brief tour of the city of Rome was the Pantheon. Constructed in 27 BC by Marcus Agrippa, this building was designed as a sacred place dedicated to many gods. It was located where mankind could renew, establish and maintain its mutual pact with the divine.[91]

Figure 9: The Roman emperors constructed the Pantheon as a temple for the worship of all the gods of nature. Today the same building is used as a Roman Catholic Church.

Although the Pantheon is over 2000 years old and still remains in magnificent shape, there is another factor that is far more interesting and impressive. This pagan temple was constructed as an ancient astronomical observatory. Like other pagan cultures around the world, the Romans were obsessed with contacting their gods on the high holy days – the summer and winter solstices that are the longest and shortest days of the year and the spring and fall equinoxes when the day and night are equal. The building was architecturally designed with a circular opening in the dome so that the entire building acted as a sacred sundial. As the *Guide to the Pantheon* explained:

> Sunlight defined in the classical sense as the "great regulator" had been commonly used with sundials and obelisks to

[91] Gianfranco Ruggieri, *Guide to the Pantheon,* (ATS Italia, Rome, 1995), 3.

fix during equinoxes the orientation of given sites, and generally as a time teller; in the case of the Pantheon a revolution occurs: sunlight falling on the interior structure, indicates precisely not only the dates of the equinoxes and solstices, but also the passing of the hours. For this reason an area corresponding with the present position of the great altar remains in the shade while, while from the entrance it is possible to see the sun at noon.[92]

Figure 10: A hole is constructed within the domed-roof of the Pantheon. The building was constructed as a sundial to determine the solstice and equinox days.

Notice the reference to "the great altar" and the description of how and where the light now shines in the Pantheon. This "great altar" is presently the altar for a Catholic church. Around the interior of the building are fourteen other tabernacles that have been dedicated to various Catholic saints.

For example, the third tabernacle called the *Madonna of Stone* contains a sculpture done in 1523-24 by Lorenzo Lotto. The fa-

[92] Ibid., 8.

mous artist Raffaello, who had chosen the Pantheon as his burial place, commissioned this statue. The tomb was opened in 1833 to verify whether or not it actually contained the remains of Raffaello. At this point, Pope Gregory XVI donated a Roman sarcophagus to preserve what was left of the body. An epigraph inscribed on this sarcophagus states: "Here lies Raphael, by whom Nature, the mother of all things feared to be overcome whilst he was living, and, whilst he was dying, herself to die."[93]

It is interesting to note that the Catholic Church has used the Pantheon for special holy days. As the *Guide to the Pantheon* states:

> The feasts of the Ascension and Assumption were celebrated in the church with particular solemnity. On these occasions a sacred representation took place in which the statues of Christ and the Virgin were drawn up until they disappeared in the cupola, and at Pentecost rose-petals were dropped down from above. On the fourth Sunday of Pentecost the Pope blessed the golden roses which were to be sent to those Christian kings who had merited them.[94]

As I observed these things, a portion of Scripture from the Book of Joshua seemed appropriate:

> Now therefore, fear the LORD, serve Him in sincerity and in truth, and put away the gods which your fathers served on the other side of the River and in Egypt. Serve the LORD! And if it seems evil to you to serve the LORD, choose for yourselves this day whom you will serve, whether the gods which your fathers served that were on the other side of the River, or the gods of the Amorites, in whose land you dwell. But as for me and my house, we will serve the LORD.[95]

Throughout the Old Testament, we see that God always instructed His people to tear down the pagan sites, never use them

---

[93] Ibid., 22.
[94] Ibid., 17.
[95] Joshua 24:14-15

for locations of worship. Christianity and Babylonianism should never be combined. It makes God angry!

Figure 11: The Pantheon, once the house of the gods, is now a Roman Catholic Church. The pagan gods that were once located around the inside of the building have now been replaced by the Catholic "saints"

The Basilica

The third and final stop of my Roman tour took us to the Vatican. Our bus driver parked several blocks away. As we filed off the bus one by one, our tour guide called us into a huddle and gave our tour group an orientation of the site.

We were standing along the curb of a wide, straight boulevard adorned by a procession of obelisk-shaped streetlamps. From our position on Via del Conciliazione, we could see a great dome looming in front of us. In front of the dome, a huge Egyptian obelisk could be seen coming up out of the ground perfectly aligned with the spire at the top of the dome. As we walked down the avenue, the boulevard opened into a circular area. The large obelisk that I had seen was in the center of a circle that was surrounded by two semi-circular colonnades. These colonnades were attached to the large building that supported the dome I had seen from the location where the bus was parked. I stood there gazing all around me while our guide explained some of the details about the city of the pope.

Our guide gave everyone a few minutes to take pictures. I walked over to her and asked if she could tell me why the pagan obelisk from Egypt had been placed in this specific spot. Although she wasn't able to give me an answer, later that same day I purchased a book describing the Vatican and the Sistine Chapel. This is what I read about the obelisk:

> The 25-meter high monolith dates back to 1935 BC and is mentioned by Pliny in his *Natural History.* It was imported by the Emperor Caligula for his Circus Vaticanus, later called the Circus of Nero, where Peter was martyred, to be buried in the vicinity afterwards by his small persecuted flock of Christians.[96]

This same book not only explained where the obelisk came from, it also gave some very important insight into why it was placed in the location where it is now found. The book stated:

> The obelisk thus represents more than just the prestigious embellishment of the square that grew up around it a century after its relocation there. It is one of the antecedents of the cult of St. Peter and the very first milestone in its history, a colossal "relic of contact" in no way different from the more modest relics that are worshipped by Christians for having touched the bodies of the saints.[97]

---

[96] Franceso Papafava, *The Vatican*, (KINA Italia, Milan, 1996), 6.
[97] Ibid.

Figure 12: An obelisk is located at the center of St. Peter's Square in the city of Rome. Obelisks, also known as phallic symbols, were sexual images associated with the worship of the Queen of Heaven in Jeremiah's day.

I find no place in Scripture for Christians to be contacting the spirit world other than Jesus Christ. The Bible states: "For there is one God and one Mediator between God and men, the Man Christ Jesus."[98] The Egyptians and other pagan cultures used pillars of stone for contact points with the demonic realm. In the Bible, these phallic symbols were called the Asherah.

---

[98] I Timothy 2:5

In the fifteenth chapter of the First Book of Kings, we read about an interesting scenario that involved one of these pagan objects:

> In the twentieth year of Jeroboam king of Israel, Asa became king over Judah. And he reigned forty-one years in Jerusalem. His grandmother's name was Maachah the granddaughter of Abishalom. Asa did what was right in the eyes of the LORD, as did his father David. And he banished the perverted persons from the land, and removed all the idols that his fathers had made. Also he removed Maachah his grandmother from being queen mother, because she had made an obscene image of Asherah. And Asa cut down her obscene image and burned it by the Brook Kidron.[99]

Once more we see that the God of the Bible strongly commands that satanic idols be destroyed. Although there may be some who say these physical objects that Roman Catholics have incorporated into their worship locations are spiritually benign, I am convinced that this is not the case. It seems that there are some foundational principles of the Catholic faith that also need to be examined critically and biblically. When the gospel of Jesus is confused with extrabiblical beliefs it can open the door to another gospel. And this can lead people into dangerous spiritual territory.

Tradition

Have you ever attempted to talk to someone about a particular unbiblical practice or belief they have accepted or endorsed and been met with stiff opposition? "We believe that what we are doing is right according to our tradition," they say. So what about this argument? Is it all right to accept tradition as an authority that can guide and direct our lives?

Tradition, as defined by the dictionary is the transmittal of the elements of a culture, a mode of thought or the practice of a particular behavior from one generation to another.[100] For many

---

[99] 1 Kings 15:9-13

[100] "Tradition," *Webster's Ninth New Collegiate Dictionary*, (Merriam-

cultures and religious views, tradition becomes a very powerful motivating force for continuing to do things as they have been done in the past. Some find it impossible to change or discontinue a practice even though they may come to realize the practice is no longer valid or even that it is wrong.

Christianity, a belief system that follows the teachings of Jesus Christ, is not without its own traditions. However, the traditions held by many people who call themselves Christians are often not found in the Bible. These traditions are the ideas and the speculations of human thought that have been added to the Bible as extrabiblical revelation.

In the Book of Colossians, Paul warned about this particular danger. He said: "Beware lest anyone cheat you through philosophy and empty deceit, according to the tradition of men, according to the basic principles of the world, and not according to Christ. For in Him dwells all the fullness of the Godhead bodily."[101]

It would be good of course if all Bible-believing Christians followed these words that Paul wrote with diligence and great care. The words of the Bible are sufficient for all our spiritual needs. However, as we are all aware, the Bible teaches that Satan has always encouraged mankind to seek after additional revelation. And for such an error there is always a price to pay.

Jesus Himself was very outspoken when it came to setting people right about their reliance on the traditions of men. Quoting the Old Testament prophet Isaiah who proclaimed God's warning, Jesus said to the Pharisees:

> Well did Isaiah prophesy of you hypocrites, as it is written: 'This people honors Me with their lips, but their heart is far from Me. And in vain they worship Me, teaching as doctrines the commandments of men.' For laying aside the command-

---

Webster, Springfield, MA, 1988).

[101] Colossians 2:8-9

> ment of God, you hold the tradition of men; the washing of pitchers and cups, and many other such things you do.[102]

Could the words of Isaiah and Jesus be any clearer regarding the subject of the authority of tradition? Certainly it would be in our best interest to separate truth from tradition and live our lives solely for Him.

When is a Saint a Saint?

The word *saint* is a biblical term. However, there are some Christians who seem to have their own definition of what the word means. Some believe you become a saint because of good works. Others say that a saint is a person who realizes they can never be good enough. So what is the right definition of a saint?

There are some who teach that church officials can grant people who live exemplary lives the status of a saint. They can be elevated to this title because of the good deeds they have done or for the things they have accomplished. Those who take the Bible more literally and seriously, see that their ticket to eternity must come by realizing that Jesus is the only perfect One. In fact, they see their own works "as filthy rags" before God. "No matter how good you are, you just can't be good enough", they say.

In order to resolve which group is right and which group is wrong, it is important to spend time searching the Scriptures. There is not one verse in the Bible that justifies a person becoming a saint based upon human effort. So if this is the case, why are so many people being taught that good works can earn sainthood?

---

[102] Mark 7:6-8

Figure 13: A brass statue of St. Peter is located inside St. Peter's Basilica. The foot has been worn by the millions of pilgrims who have touched or kissed the statue hoping to receive a blessing from God.

In order to understand the true meaning of Christianity it is necessary to know the reason why Jesus died on the cross. Sin, the Bible states, is the transgression of the law, and condemns mankind to death. There are none who can say they are righteous - not one. Jesus Christ is the only perfect One. And believing on Him is the only way to be saved.

It seems to me that when a Christian leader professes someone can become a "saint" because of human goodness, this is wrong. It is a serious offense to lead people astray. According to the Bible, the only way to become a saint is to be saved. Salvation is a gift from God, not a title that is bestowed on a human by another human.

While I was at St. Peter's Basilica, I saw people praying at the shrines of the dead people. The dead people they were praying to have been given sainthood by the Catholic Church. Apparently the people who were praying believed this would get them closer to God. The Bible states that praying to a dead person is an abomination to God.[103] Such a practice will not bring one closer to God; it can only separate him further.

The Holy Door

There were so many things I learned while on the one-day tour of Rome. It would take a lifetime to be able to absorb all there is to see in this city. However, in the few hours that I was able to be there, a few basic principles came to light, which for me, will last a lifetime.

Although St. Peter's Basilica certainly stands in a category of its own structurally and artistically, there was something else I noticed that was far more impressive than these physical characteristics. Before entering the sanctuary, our guide took us over to a location in front of the "Holy Door."

---

[103] Deuteronomy 18:9

Figure 14: The Holy Door located at St. Peter's Basilica, is one of four doors that is opened by the pope on the Catholic Jubilee. According to Catholic dogma, pilgrims who go to Rome and pass through all four doors receive a pardon for sins during the Jubilee year.

The inner sanctuary of St. Peter's can be entered into through five large doors. Four of these doors are open. The fifth door called the Holy Door is only opened on the Catholic Jubilee year, which now occurs every twenty-five years. The significance of the Holy Door is outlined in a book sold at the Vatican called *The Vatican:*

> The last to the right, the work of Vico Conforti (1950), depicts in sixteen classical panels the theme of Salvation, of which the Jubilee is part. The door is the Holy Door. It stands open only in Holy Years. At all other times it is bricked up in a wall, which at the beginning of each Jubilee the pope symbolically breaks down with the silver hammer. [104]

An article found in *The Vatican* helps us to understand the importance of the Catholic Jubilee and the Holy Door. Author Laura Draghi states:

> Yobhel – Jubilee – was the name that the ancient Hebrews gave to the ram's horn whose blast every fifty years proclaimed a year of freedom from old bonds: debts were forgiven, slaves emancipated, and property restored to its former owners. It was only logical then, that the name be adopted for the great year of plenary indulgence first granted by Boniface VIII at 1300 to the members of the faith who drew upon the Treasury of Merit won by Christ and the saints and demonstrated their penitence in a pilgrimage to the four apostolic basilicas of Rome – St. John Lateran, St. Peter's, Santa Maria Maggiore, and San Paolo Fuori le Mura. [105]

Of course penitence has always been an important aspect of the Catholic view of salvation. Although the Bible teaches we are saved by faith in Christ alone, the dogmas of "penitence" and "purgatory" have proven to be very profitable fund-raisers for the Catholic Church throughout the years. Although originally the Catholic Jubilee year took place every one hundred years, it was shortened to fifty years and then later to twenty-five years. Laura Draghi further documented the history of how this happened in her article:

> But the idea of the Jubilee was not a creation of Boniface. He merely sanctioned the vox popoli expressed in the rumor of

---

[104] Papafava, 20.
[105] Ibid., 18.

> a great pardon that swept through the exceptionally large crowd of pilgrims thronging St. Peter's basilica for the thirteenth centennial of the Nativity at Rome. The papal bull was transcribed on a tablet in the basilica. It announced in catchy Latin verse that "each hundredth year there will be a Jubilee in Rome." When the Curia moved to Avignon the Romans held fast to their celebration and even insisted on shortening the interval to fifty years, after the manner of the Hebrews. But the pilgrims, who came to Rome in 1350 found the throne of St. Peter empty, the city devastated by an earthquake and the population decimated by the plague of 1348. For a century the anniversary alternated between the fifty years of the Hebrews and the thirty-three years of Christ. Sixtus IV finally settled the matter by establishing a Holy Year celebration every twenty-five years to give each generation the chance to benefit from the pardon.[106]

The idea that people can be pardoned from their sin because they have made a pilgrimage to a certain place is not found in the Bible. This was one of the many errors that the Catholic Church had embraced that upset Martin Luther. Historically it is possible to trace how this "pilgrimage-indulgence" heresy came about.

> In 1475 the term first made its appearance in official acts and in the 'printed' papers that circulated news and prayers among the faithful. In 1500 Pope Alexander VI Borgia, that far from unblemished character, acquired some merit by his attention to the liturgy and its introduction of the beautiful rite of opening the Holy Door.[107]

While you may be wondering why I have taken so much space to write about the Catholic Jubilee and its connection to the Holy Door, there is a reason. While I was on my own personal Roman pilgrimage, our guide told us that the Holy Door would be opened by the pope on the Jubilee year of 2000. On

---

[106] Ibid.
[107] Ibid.

Christmas Eve, December 24, 1999, Pope John Paul II officially opened the Holy Door for Catholic Jubilee.

Millions of Catholics travel to Rome during the Catholic Jubilee year. Of course passing through the Holy Door is an added incentive. I asked our guide if she was planning to take advantage of this unique offer to obtain salvation. "Oh yes," she said enthusiastically. "I have the advantage of living in Rome," she said. "I plan to walk through the door every day because I have a lot of sins."

Although Catholic officials may argue that the Holy Door is merely symbolic and was never intended to be a means of salvation, once more there needs to be a clearer representation of what the church actually believes. It was obvious to me that my guide, who was a Catholic, did not understand the true meaning of salvation. For her, salvation was some sort of ritual or dogma that was sanctioned by the Holy Father.

Again it is very important the real gospel not be confused with another gospel. Walking through a door on a Jubilee year never has, and never will save anyone. There is only one door to enter that provides salvation. Jesus said, "I am the door. If anyone enters by Me, he will be saved, and will go in and out and find pasture."[108]

Salvation by Mary

"The Meaning of Mary: A Struggle Over Her Role Grows Within the Church," was the title of the feature article that appeared in the August 25th 1997 issue of *Newsweek*. While the Catholic Church has always placed a strong emphasis on a sacred devotion to the mother of Jesus, this article documents that "Mariology" is in the process of being elevated to higher ground. According to this article there are many Catholics from all over the world who are petitioning the pope to declare a new dogma. They would like Mary to be promoted from mother to "Core-

---

[108] John 10:9

demptrix, Mediatrix of All Graces and Advocate for the People of God."[109]

Mark Miravalle, a professor at the Franciscan University in Steubenville, Ohio, is one of the petitioners. In order to promote his belief, he has written three books and met with the pope on several occasions.[110]

"Personally, I'm confident that there will be this recognition of Marian truth before the year 2000," he stated. An infallible papal recognition of this idea would put this revised doctrine "at the highest level of revealed truth," he concluded.[111]

While Miravalle's mission to have Mary declared Co-Redeemer might seem blasphemous to some, there are plenty of supporters who are willing to back him up. More and more people are visiting the shrines where it is claimed Mary is manifesting herself. Fatima, Guadalupe, Medjugorje along with numerous other locations, have become spiritual hot-spots for the masses.

Such a move would elevate Mary's status well beyond what the Bible teaches. The New Testament reveals that she was a virgin but not ever virgin, and the mother of the Son of God. However, history reveals that the Catholic Church has embraced other dogmas around Mary such as "the immaculate conception" and "the assumption" in order to give Mary her preeminent status.

The *Newsweek* article reported that the pope has received over four million signatures from 157 countries – an average of over 100,000 per month supporting the new dogma. Among the notable supporters are the late Mother Teresa of Calcutta, nearly 500 bishops and 42 cardinals, including the late John O'Conner of New York.[112] According to *Newsweek,* "nothing like this organized petition drive has ever been seen in Rome." As writer

---

109 Kenneth Woodward, "Hail, Mary," *Newsweek*, August 25, 1997, 49.

110 Ibid.

111 Ibid.

112 Ibid.

Kenneth Woodward stated: "It isn't often that Catholics beg a pope to make an infallible pronouncement."[113]

Although Pope John Paul II has not yet made a formal announcement regarding a decision to make a decree for a new infallible doctrine, Kenneth Woodward, the author of the *Newsweek* article believes the possibility for him to do so is very real. In his article he documented the following:

> As the patron saint of Poland, Mary has always been especially important to this pope from Wadowice. He also credits her with saving his life during the 1981 assassination attempt. He has referred to her as "Coredemptrix" at least five times, though never as a formal declaration of dogma. He has reflected on her role in more than 50 weekly addresses, often emphasizing her "co-operation" in redemption.[114]

If the petition succeeds, historical Christianity will again have been completely altered by the Roman Catholic Church and new doctrines embraced. Mary will participate in redemption provided by the shed blood of Jesus. As well, prayers and petitions from the faithful will have to flow through Mary, who then supposedly will bring them to the attention of Jesus.

It will be interesting to follow what happens in the Catholic Church in the years to come. The Bible teaches clearly there is only one mediator between God and man – and that person is Jesus Christ.[115] Wouldn't it be wise for those who are petitioning that Mary be elevated to the status of Co-Redeemer to consider the Bible? When we blatantly ignore what God has said and enthusiastically embrace what fallible humans conjure up in their minds, we can be deceived.

---

[113] Ibid.
[114] Ibid., 51.
[115] I Timothy 2:5

Figure 15: The famous statue sculpted by Michelangelo, located on the inner side of the Holy Door at St. Peter's Basilica, typifies the Catholic view of Mary.

We have already seen that the Bible warns about a great deception that will occur in the name of Christianity before Jesus returns. Is it possible the deception is already underway? Although I am sure the pope has read the New Testament, it would be beneficial for him at this time to review what Paul stated in the Book of Colossians, chapter one. Under the inspiration of the Holy Spirit, Paul wrote:

> He has delivered us from the power of darkness and conveyed us into the kingdom of the Son of His love, in whom we have redemption through His blood, the forgiveness of sins. He is the image of the invisible God, the firstborn over all creation. [116]

Who is Panchamama?

Dr. Carol Damian is professor of the visual arts department of Florida International University in Miami. A noted scholar and authority on the art of Latin America, she is author of a book called the *Virgin of the Andes.* The inspiration for this book came when the author visited a Catholic convent in Cuzco, Peru, the mile-high city that was once the capital of the Inca Empire.

In an article published in the November 1996 issue of LanChile's monthly airline magazine, Dr. Damian tells how her research started:

> The paintings were particularly fascinating, especially as the young woman of the Convent museum described them. Gazing up at a larger-than-life image of the Virgin Mary (or what I thought was the Virgin Mary), the guide reverently described the painting as that of Panchamama, the Earth Mother and patroness of the Andes. [117]

Dr. Damian went on to describe in her article how shocked she was when she first heard the guide's description of Panchamama. Wanting more information she asked:

> Please explain why you called the Virgin Mary Panchamama? Who is Panchamama? She looks like the Virgin Mary of my Catholic experience, even if she is painted differently than the images I am more familiar with. How could someone in a Roman Catholic convent say such things? [118]

---

[116] Colossians 1:13-15

[117] Dr. Carol Damian, "Who is Panchamama?," *LanChile*, November 1996, 32.

[118] Ibid.

According to the article Dr. Damian returned to the convent every year for fifteen years. As well she visited many rural churches in Peru. She examined more paintings of the Virgin Mary and listened to the stories of the parishioners translated from the Kechwa language by her guides. She stated:

> The story was always the same. The Virgin Mary took on different titles, wore different costumes and headdresses and was surrounded by different objects and attributes but she was an Andean virgin. She was Panchamama the Earth Mother and she also was the Moon Goddess and the royal vision of the Inca Queen who they called Coya, and they loved her. [119]

Someone critical of Dr. Damian's research might say this is just her distorted interpretation of Mary. But there are many other examples of pagan practices masquerading in Catholic churches in other parts of the world. For example, a few years ago outside a Catholic church near San Christobal in southern Mexico, I saw chickens nailed on crosses. Inside the church there were numerous shrines to dead people. The worshippers were offering sacrifices that included some of their most prized possessions. Shouldn't someone tell the Catholic Church leaders in Rome what is going on? Shouldn't Catholic churches that mix Christianity with paganism be removed from the Catholic fellowship of believers?

Until this happens I will continue to be very concerned. In 1994 a document called "Catholics and Evangelicals Together: The Christian Mission for the Third Millennium" was signed by evangelical leaders like Chuck Colson, Pat Robertson and Bill Bright. Its seems to me until Catholics clear up the confusion about what the gospel is and what it is not, then a pledge to unite together for the purpose of evangelism is an unholy alliance.

---

[119] Ibid., 34.

Pat Robertson and the Pope

For years the Catholic hierarchy had purposely set up a system to convince the masses that only a select group with proper credentials could interpret God's Word for the masses. Thus the people were kept in ignorance from the full council of God. A few verses here or there mixed together with tradition and dogma does not provide a well-balanced spiritual diet. The Bible states that "All Scripture is given by inspiration of God, and is profitable for doctrine, for reproof, for correction, for instruction in righteousness, that the man of God may be complete, thoroughly equipped for every good work."[120]

It is also important to point out, that although Protestant evangelicals have always had the freedom to read and study the Bible, they are not always diligent to do so. In fact there are many who seem quite comfortable to do exactly what the Catholics were once forced to accept in the past. Rather than reading and studying the Word, they allow others to tell them what the Word states. Bible study is something we all should do. As Paul told Timothy: "Be diligent to present yourself approved to God, a worker who does not need to be ashamed, rightly dividing the word of truth."[121] If we rely upon leaders who do not "divide the word of truth" correctly, we could be misled.

Today there are a number of very prominent evangelical leaders who are convinced that reconciliation with Roman Catholicism is the key to a worldwide revival. For example, Pat Robertson, one of the signers of "Evangelicals and Catholics Together: The Christian Mission in the Third Millennium" strongly believes that this is the case. In one of his newsletters, the following report appeared:

> After CBN founder Pat Robertson met with His Holiness, Pope John Paul II… [he] described their meeting as warm. "I think this meeting was historic," said Robertson, who joined with other religious leaders in greeting the Pope at the New York residence of His Eminence Cardinal John O'Connor. The

---

[120] II Timothy 3:16-17
[121] 2 Timothy 2:15

> meeting came just hours after Robertson [led] an Ecumenical Procession at the Papal Liturgy in New York's Central Park. Robertson called the Pope, "a humble and caring servant of the Lord"... Robertson presented a letter to the Pontiff underscoring CBN's commitment to work for Christian unity and world evangelization. Robertson also wrote that he was "encouraged" by the Pope's recent encyclical on Christian unity, *That All May Be One,* and praised the Pontiff for his recent call to Catholics to be more committed for Christian unity...[122]

The Pope and Pat Robertson

While Pat Robertson and others seem quite enthusiastic about this new alliance with the pope and the Catholic Church, it seems the pope does not see it quite the same way. As T. A. McMahon pointed out in an article called "The Evangelical Seduction," either the press has made a serious error in what they are reporting, or Pat Robertson is being deceived into believing that ecumenical unity is a two-way street. *The Oregonian* ran two headlines which seem to frustrate Robertson's goals: "POPE WILL FACE PROTESTANT TREND IN LATIN AMERICA"[123] and "POPE ISSUES CALL TO DEFEND CHURCH'S PLACE IN CENTRAL AMERICA."[124]

The first article carried this Associated Press summary: "The Pontiff's visit this week will include efforts to win back Roman Catholics who have converted to other churches."[125] The second article was clearer yet regarding the pope's view of "evangelical-Catholicism." It stated: "Directly confronting the challenge to his church's traditional dominance in central America, Pope John Paul II accused Protestant missionaries Tuesday of sowing 'confusion and uncertainty' among Roman Catholics."[126]

It seems very apparent that the kind of unity that Pat Robertson and the other evangelical ecumenists are striving for, is not

---

122 *Frontline*, CBN newsletter, Nov., 1995.
123 *The Oregonian*, Feb. 7, 1996, A3.
124 *The Oregonian*, Feb. 4, 1996, A3.
125 *The Oregonian*, Feb. 7, 1996, A3.
126 *The Oregonian*, Feb. 4, 1996, A3.

the same kind of unity that Rome is planning to embrace. For example, consider the following statement by Cardinal Augustin Bea, president of the Vatican Secretariat for Promoting Christian Unity:

> The Roman Catholic Church would be gravely misunderstood if it should be concluded that her present ecumenical adventuresomeness and openness meant that she was prepared to reexamine any of her fixed dogmatic positions. What the church is prepared to do is to take a more imaginative position and contemporary presentation of these fixed positions.[127]

Finally, to set the record straight, months before Pat Robertson met with the pope in New York, John Paul II had announced to his weekly audience at the Vatican:

> Christian unity will not become a reality unless all churches accept the authority Christ entrusted to St. Peter and his successors. This unity will not be fully manifested until all Christians accept Christ's will for the Church and acknowledge the apostolic authority of the bishops, in communion with the successor of Peter.[128]

How would it ever be possible for Christian unity to materialize if the Catholic Church is unwilling to compromise on the very doctrines that have so long separated them from their Protestant counterparts? Are there any trends that are currently underway in the Protestant evangelical church that could provide some insight?

---

[127] "Quotable," *The Berean Call,* April 1997.

[128] Cindy Wooden, "Pope: for Unity Churches must accept Papal Authority," *Catholic Moments*, Aug. 10, 1995.

7

THAT ALL MAY BE ONE

A review of the history of the Christian Church will reveal a wide spectrum of ideas and beliefs that have come and gone. Although there have been many changes through time, never in such a short period, have so many changes taken place so quickly.

As the outline for this chapter was prepared, an illustration I once heard came to my remembrance. Every lily pond begins with a single lily pad. The first leaf that appears on the pond is inconspicuous. This single original mother pad divides and becomes two. The two pads divide to become four, the four become eight, the eight divide to become sixteen, and the process continues until eventually the entire pond is covered. Before the very last division takes place, the pond is only half-covered. The single pad that was once inconspicuous has now become much more significant. As we can see, the process of covering the pond did not happen at a linear rate. The pond was covered by a process we call a geometric progression.

The paradigm shift that has taken place within Christianity over the past several decades has occurred in a similar fashion as our lily pond illustration. Not only have the changes occurred in this way, the numbers of people that are concerned about these changes have diminished by the same process. Today, the word *discernment* in many churches is an evil word. Those who express their concerns about the direction the evangelical church is going are often labeled as "divisive," "critical," "dangerous," or "judgmental." Why is it that in the last days when the Bible teaches we should be careful about a strong delusion taking place in the name of Jesus Christ,[129] more and more people are convinced that God is doing "something new"?

Unity for the Sake of Unity?

In spite of all kinds of weird behavior that is happening in the name of Christ, the vast majority of the church is calling for reconciliation rather than repentance. "This is a time to forgive one another," these people say, especially when it comes to holding grudges about what other Christians believe. Many are laying down their differences and joining together, saying, "Let's just agree to disagree. The important thing is that we just accept everyone who calls himself a Christian."

While Christian unity is a very important biblical principle, we must ask ourselves "How diverse can Christian unity become before it becomes too diverse? How far should a Bible-believing Christian go in the process of accepting the beliefs of others? Is it possible to go too far?"

An article in the "Focus on Religion" section of the November 1, 1997 edition of the *Orange County Register* may provide the answer to this question. The headline stated: "Church to Ask Indians to Forgive." Author Dave Schleck, writing for the *Newport Virginia News* reported:

> In 1606, King James I granted a charter allowing English businessmen to colonize Virginia and spread "Christianity" among the "savages" who "live in darkness and miserable ignorance." More than three centuries later, the Episcopal Church -- an American outgrowth of the Church of England -- will ask American Indians for forgiveness and reconciliation at a noontime ceremony today on Jamestown Island.[130]

---

[129] II Thessalonians 2:9-10

[130] Dave Schleck, "Church to Ask Indians to Forgive", *Orange County Register*, November 1, 1997, 14.

Although the Bible teaches reconciliation, the New Jamestown Covenant took reconciliation beyond biblical parameters. Statements included in the five-page document announced that Episcopalians and Indians would "work together to find new resolutions in social and political challenges" and "start together to protect and nurture our home, the Earth."[131]

American Indian music, prayers and dance punctuated the ceremony, while Indian drums pounded in the background. According to the article, the New Jamestown Covenant, approved by the 70th General Conference of the Episcopalian Church in July of 1997, initiated "a decade of recognition, remembrance and reconciliation leading up to the 400th anniversary of the Anglican faith in America."[132]

We know the Bible emphatically teaches that unity centered on a common bond in Jesus Christ is very important. "Bind us together Lord," should be a prayer that is always on the hearts of believers. God's love should shine through us. As John wrote: "Beloved, let us love one another, for love is of God; and everyone who loves is born of God and knows God. He who does not love does not know God, for God is love."[133] But if we compromise the gospel and promote a new gospel where people end up being deceived and going to hell-- is that really love?

The Bible also teaches that Christians are to always love and forgive each other. This love for our brothers and sisters in Christ should be very obvious to the world. Others should know we are Christians because we have a love for each other, based on a oneness in Jesus Christ. In fact John stated:

> If someone says, "I love God," and hates his brother, he is a liar; for he who does not love his brother whom he has seen, how can he love God whom he has not seen? And this com-

---

[131] Ibid.
[132] Ibid.
[133] I John: 4:7-8

> mandment we have from Him: that he who loves God must love his brother also.[134]

However, Christian unity must always remain centered on the truth. If those that we are uniting with have not unified with Jesus, they will not spend eternity with Jesus Christ. Christian unity must always be centered at the cross; unity must not be accomplished at any cost.

Brotherly Love

On October 4, 1997, I was watching a television broadcast of a Promise Keepers gathering of Christian men at the Capitol Mall in Washington D.C. It was exciting to see so many men gathered in one place, committing themselves to be better husbands, fathers, church members and citizens of America because they wanted to be better men of God.

Promise Keepers, founded by Bill McCartney is a non-denominational Christian organization for men. In just a few years, the organization grew from obscurity to having a following of millions. Meetings have been held in major baseball and football stadiums throughout the United States. Men from every background and denomination were represented at these rallies. Well-known Christian leaders have presented motivational messages and the men in attendance have responded.

According to the goals and objectives presented by founder Bill McCartney at the Washington D.C. rally on October 4, 1997, Promise Keepers had much more to promise in the future. Towards the latter part of the seven hour Promise Keepers Rally, McCartney took the platform and made the following statement:

> Hallelujah! We're in that part of the program now, where we talk about extraordinary hope. It's my privilege to cast a vision! We need a precise plan! Can't be a guy leave here without knowing exactly what we're going to be doing, so that the

[134] I John 4:20-21

> right hand will know what the left hand's doing. We have a plan![135]

Mr. McCartney, a former college football coach, is a gifted strategist, motivator and speaker. He certainly is well versed in knowing how to come up with a game plan designed to bring success. However, the plan that he presented at the Washington rally had nothing to do with football. The plan he was talking about was designed to mobilize and unify the forces that comprise the Promise Keepers gatherings. Reiterating that the greatest achievement accomplished that day at the Washington rally was the establishment of a unity among the brethren, McCartney stated:

> And where are we going? The reason there's momentum -- and there's great optimism -- is because we've been divided, and a house divided cannot stand! But now we're being reunited, we understand that this is a unity with diversity! This is diversity without dissension![136]

Promise What?

It seems almost ludicrous to express even the least bit of concern about this platform of unity Promise Keepers was so strongly promoting. Who would ever dare say that men coming together in unity in the name of Jesus could be wrong?

However, there are reasons why many today are concerned about the kind of unity that the Promise Keepers leaders were promoting. For example, at the Washington rally, several statements were made which cause concern. About half way through the seven-hour program, Jack Hayford, pastor of Church on the Way, took the platform. As acting moderator, Pastor Hayford indicated there was a strategy that was about to be presented for the men to consider. He stated:

---

[135] Promise Keepers Rally, Washington, D.C., October 4, 1997, Trinity Broadcasting Network, transcript of live broadcast.
[136] Ibid.

> What we're talking about right now are two small steps, but they're not easy ones. And the impact would be a giant leap for mankind. And it's if we, who name the name of the living Christ and walk in the love of God, will come to terms with two issues that are coming to the table as we seek to construct a covenant that would please God and sign our name to it, and say "As men who seek to be godly men, we will covenant these things."[137]

Pastor Hayford then went on to describe why he believed a covenant needed to be established. He said:

> There is a horrible sectarianism that rips the Body of Christ. I'm not talking about a quest for one Church. We're talking about the people of God acknowledging each other, that we are all one people though we are different families, and persuasions and practices. We love Jesus Christ and have been born of the Spirit of God. But loved ones, listen to me, please. We have been taught to suspect those who are not the same as us. We have been taught to look down on those who are different in their practice and doctrine.[138]

At this point in the meeting, author and speaker Max Lucado took the podium. His message clearly re-emphasized what Pastor Hayford had already stated about the need for reconciliation. Lucado said:

> And our prayer this afternoon is that God can, once and for all, do a miracle on the millennium -- that he can inaugurate a new day -- that He can bring about a new era – something that our eyes have never seen. Why? Because Jesus says that when we are one in Christ, then the world will be won for Christ![139]

Although part of Lucado's statement quoted the words Jesus used regarding the importance of Christian unity, to carry this one step further and say the Bible indicates there is a basic formula that can be used to "win the world" for Christ is not right.

---

[137] Ibid.
[138] Ibid.
[139] Ibid.

Especially in light of the kind of unity that Promise Keepers was promoting at the Washington rally. Max Lucado further clarified the Promise Keepers definition of unity by asking the men in attendance the following question:

> Have there been any occasions in which you have categorized or pigeonholed religious groups unfairly, in which you have made blanket summaries about entire denominations or groups? If so, at this hour confess to God that you apologize for defaming the body of Christ.[140]

Then Lucado took the act of repentance one step further. He said that if anyone had ever said anything against Promise Keepers, they needed to repent for that as well.[141]

According to the Promise Keepers' definition of repentance, Christians must forgive each other, if they have ever disagreed with *anything* that another Christian has believed. But what if there are groups or individuals that call themselves Christians, who have embraced serious error? What if someone has accepted a false gospel rather than the real gospel? The Bible never teaches that we compromise with false teaching. The Bible exhorts us to correct false teaching and point these people to the truth of God's Word in love.[142]

The Silent Agenda

True repentance is based upon asking God to forgive us for our sins. If we have wronged a brother or a sister, we do need to repent. However, to make a statement that repentance is required for having spoken out against false teachings, dogmas, or extrabiblical doctrines is absurd. Once more, it bears repeating: The Bible teaches that error leading to a counterfeit gospel needs to be addressed. If we ignore this error, we ourselves are guilty of becoming part of the problem and we are actually nurturing deception rather than warning people about its consequences.

---

140 Ibid.
141 Ibid.
142 2 Timothy 4:1-5

Following Max Lucado's remarks, Michael Timmis, a very important addition to the Promise Keepers board of directors took the platform. Michael Timmis, a leader in the Roman Catholic charismatic renewal movement, continued on the theme of the evils of sectarianism by saying: "Sectarianism is disunity; it is division; it is the seed of the devil! Unity is of God; disunity is of man."[143]

Then Michael Timmis offered a solution to this problem of disunity that the Promise Keepers were focusing in on at the Washington conference, as he made the following claim:

> God created us equals before Him, but we have divided ourselves! We must rid ourselves of the disunity that is in our spirits, and go back to the way God created us! God created the Church to be His bride -- to be married to Him -- to be pure! Therefore to be in a state of disunity is a sin before God![144]

These statements made by Timmis and Lucado on the surface seem to be right. But the Bible states that what seems to be right to man may not necessarily be right to God.[145] What many people do not realize is the fact that there is a silent agenda underway. There is an agenda to bring all people who call themselves Christian under one church. This canopy has its headquarters in Rome. The plan is to build the Universal Church that will usher in the Kingdom of God.

Papal Power

While Jack Hayford, Max Lucado and Michael Timmis were doing their best to convince the men at the Washington rally that sectarianism could be defeated and that repentance is the prerequisite for bringing about the unity required for revival, there was a very important point that had not been communicated. In order to get a full understanding of the brand of Christian unity that the Promise Keepers were promoting, it is important to re-

---

[143] Promise Keepers Rally, Washington, D.C., October 4, 1997, Trinity Broadcasting Network, transcript of live broadcast.

[144] Ibid.

[145] Proverbs 14:12

view an article from the July 20, 1997 edition of *Our Sunday Visitor,* a Roman Catholic newspaper. This article helps to provide insight into the events that went on at the Washington rally as well as to provide another perspective of the kind of unity that Promise Keepers promotes.

The following portion of this article will make my point clear:

> At its March meeting, Promise Keepers board of directors welcomed Mike Timmis as a new member. A Detroit-area lawyer and a businessman, Timmis is a longtime leader in the Catholic charismatic renewal. At several rallies this year, Promise Keepers has spotlighted Catholic evangelist Jim Berlucchi as a speaker. In June, Promise Keepers hosted a "Catholic summit" at its headquarters in Denver, sounding out Catholic volunteers and leaders from around the country. And earlier this year, Promise Keepers amended its statement of faith, revising the lines that Catholics found offensive.[146]

As we have already pointed out, Promise Keepers is made up of a fellowship of men that represent various backgrounds from a broad spectrum of the Christian faith. Although Catholic men were already participating, there had been something that some called offensive that was holding some Catholics back. The article continued:

> Promise Keepers founder Bill McCartney told *Our Sunday Visitor* recently that full Catholic participation was his intention from the start. "Back in 1992, at our first stadium event, we very clearly stated from the podium that we eagerly welcomed participation of Roman Catholics, and we've had scores of Roman Catholics attend and go back to their churches excited."[147]

---

146 "Making New Catholic Men? Promise Keepers' 'gospel for guys': Is it just the thing Catholic men need? Or is it bound to loosen bonds to the Church?," *Our Sunday Visitor,* July 20, 1997, 10.

147 Ibid.

However *Our Sunday Visitor* carefully pointed out that there were other Catholics who were less enthusiastic. The article stated:

> Yet because Promise Keepers is an overwhelmingly evangelical Protestant phenomenon, many Catholics have hesitated to get involved. Some feel uncomfortable with the revivalist style of worship. Others worry about any renewal effort that excludes elements central to the Catholic faith, such as the sacraments, the authority of the pope and the bishops, and Catholic doctrine on marriage and sex. [148]

The article then explained how John Sengenberger, director of Christian outreach at Franciscan University of Steubenville, Ohio, and a Catholic who is very supportive of the Promise Keepers, has had an influence in educating members of the Promise Keepers board to be more sensitive to these Catholic concerns. In an interview with *Our Sunday Visitor*, he explained why he had sponsored his own Catholic men's conferences since 1995. According to Sengenberger:

> At that time Promise Keepers was having an incredible impact on men across this country. It was spreading like wildfire. But it didn't have all the things we'd want in it as Catholics. [149]

It was because of these differences that Sengenberger invited representatives from Promise Keepers to visit the university [Franciscan University]. "We've had some frank discussions and told them we needed to see some Catholic involvement on the leadership level," Sengenberger stated. [150]

In 1995, two Promise Keepers officials responded to the invitation: Dale Schlafler, who at that time was the chairman of the board, and Glen Wagner, a vice president of Promise Keepers. According to Sengenberger:

---

148 Ibid.
149 Ibid.
150 Ibid.

> It was their first time in a Catholic evangelistic setting. They [the Promise Keepers' representatives] were impressed. When they were leaving, we invited them to go through our bookstore and take out any books that they wanted. They went home with all kinds of theology books, Vatican II teachings.[151]

Both men returned to Steubenville for the 1996 men's conference, where Sengenberger took them to a Eucharist Holy Hour. Yet in spite of this apparent melding together of the Catholic-customized version of Promise Keepers with the Promise Keepers, there were still some very profound differences that needed to be resolved between the evangelicals of Promise Keepers and the Catholics who were sympathetic. As *Our Sunday Visitor* reported:

> Last year [1996] Promise Keepers published a "statement of faith" with a line that seemed to be crafted to exclude Catholics – or force them to reject their Catholic faith. Section five of the Promise Keepers credo read: "We believe that man was created in the image of God, but because of sin, was alienated from God. That alienation can be removed only by accepting, through faith alone, God's gift of salvation, which was made possible by Christ's death."[152]

One final statement taken from *Our Sunday Visitor* will explain clearly why the appointment of Michael Timmis to the Promise Keepers board in 1997 was so significant. Completely denying the basis for the Protestant Reformation, in three short paragraphs the article stated:

> ***"Faith alone"*** is a key doctrine of the Protestant Reformation. Though that phrase appears nowhere in Scripture, it was inserted by Martin Luther into his German translation of the Bible. Concerned about this development at Promise Keepers, Sengenberger had several Catholic theologians review the statement and present their objections to Wagner last summer. Early this year, Promise Keepers revised the statement in a

[151] Ibid.
[152] Ibid.

way that passed theological muster with those Catholics: "*Only through faith,* trusting in Christ alone for salvation, which was made possible by His death, and resurrection, can that alienation be removed."[153] [Emphasis mine]

Awake, Sleeper!

These statements that I have quoted from a Catholic newspaper, explain what is happening to Christianity today. No longer is the silent agenda, silent. According to the words of Paul, we are to be awake and alert in the last days. As he stated:

> Let no one deceive you with empty words, for because of these things the wrath of God comes upon the sons of disobedience. Therefore do not be partakers with them. For you were once darkness, but now you are light in the Lord. Walk as children of light (for the fruit of the Spirit is in all goodness, righteousness, and truth), finding out what is acceptable to the Lord. And have no fellowship with the unfruitful works of darkness, but rather expose them. For it is shameful even to speak of those things which are done by them in secret. But all things that are exposed are made manifest by the light, for whatever makes manifest is light. Therefore He says: "Awake, you who sleep, Arise from the dead, And Christ will give you light." See then that you walk circumspectly, not as fools but as wise, redeeming the time, because the days are evil.[154]

Although few may recognize the difference between the Promise Keepers "old" statement of faith to the "new" Catholic seeker-friendly version, there is a huge difference. As Albert James Dagger pointed out is his article called "Promise Keepers Sells Out To Vatican," this difference is paramount. He stated:

> So when Promise Keepers changed their statement from "through faith alone" to "only through faith," the difference is not readily apparent. But the meaning is huge in terms of doctrinal purity. The new statement means that through faith in

---

[153] Ibid.

[154] Ephesians 5:6-16

> the papacy, instituted by Christ to guide the Church on its course in history, one may believe in Christ alone for salvation. The faith is not in Christ alone, but in the papacy along with Christ! Yet the quislings of Promise Keepers consider this of no concern.[155]

In this chapter I have attempted to show how Christianity is moving towards a "one" church concept. Such an ecumenical unity would never have been considered possible just a decade ago. After doing the research for this chapter I have found that the lily pond illustration is far more relevant than I had ever imagined. We see that this geometrical progression of changes within the church is now completely out of hand.

But there is one more major question that needs to be answered. Although we can now see how Christians could unite together as one body, what about the ecumenical imperative that requires Christianity to unite together with other world religions? How could the meaning of Christianity ever be modified enough so that it could become the common ground for other religions?

---

[155] Albert James Dagger, "Promise Keepers Sells Out To Vatican," *Media Spotlight*, Volume 20, No. 2, 7.

8

REDEFINING JESUS

The gospel, by definition, means good news. This good news can only be understood when one realizes who Jesus Christ is and what He has done. Jesus was born of a virgin. Jesus lived a sinless life here on earth. Jesus died upon the cross at Calvary as a living sacrifice for the sins of mankind. Jesus was resurrected from the dead as living proof that He is the Messiah of the world. No other person who has ever lived can equal these claims attributed to Jesus of Nazareth.

The New Testament teaches that these foundational tenants are all essential in order to understand the gospel. However we know that ever since Jesus was here on earth some two thousand years ago, there have been many man-made additions or deletions to this important message.

An analysis of Christian history will show there have been many trends or movements that have influenced the way people interpret the claims the Bible makes about Jesus Christ. However today, it seems there are more and more people and organizations that claim to be followers of Jesus Christ who are accepting ideas about Jesus that have no biblical basis. This trend to abandon the sufficiency of the Word of God for the teachings and the philosophies of men has left many people confused.

Some have asked the question — If Jesus is really God, what about the validity of other religions? Would God limit His Holy

Spirit to just one group of religious faithful? Shouldn't we just accept there are many ways to God and agree to lay down our differences and be more tolerant of the beliefs of others?

Who is Jesus?

The Rev. Bill Phipps was elected as moderator of the United Church of Canada in 1997. *Maclean's,* a popular secular Canadian weekly periodical, published a major article in its December 15, 1997, issue that was centered on the controversial election of Rev. Phipps. According to Sharon Doyle Dreidger who wrote the article called "Is Jesus Really God?" Bill Phipps's controversial views about Jesus Christ have created the flash point for a religious debate that is "as hot as hellfire."[156]

As the moderator of Canada's largest Protestant denomination and pastor of the Scarboro United Church in Calgary, Alberta, Canada, Bill Phipps placed himself at the cutting edge of Christian reform. By publicly denying that Jesus is the Son of God and making the claim that Jesus never physically rose from the dead, he challenged the very foundation of Christianity. Expanding on his views in an interview with *Maclean's,* Rev. Phipps stated:

> I believe that God is more than Jesus. God is huge; mysterious, wholly beyond our comprehension and beyond our total understanding. Jesus therefore does not represent or embody all of God, but embodies as much of God as can be in a person. Jesus is unique and special and the Christian makes the leap of faith that such divine revelation has not happened in this way in any other place, in any other historical figure.[157]

Not only did Moderator Phipps deny the deity of Jesus Christ; he also made it clear in the interview that he did not believe that the Resurrection of Jesus ever happened. Although he stated the Resurrection was not just a "hallucination" experienced by the followers of Jesus, he believes that the Resurrection

---

[156] Sharon Doyle Dreidger, "Is Jesus Really God?," *Macleans*, Dec. 15, 1997, 40.

[157] Ibid., 43.

was a "mysterious" idea that "cannot be reduced to a provable event." Further clarifying this point, he stated:

> But the body that he was crucified with – dying and coming back and walking around the earth and then ascending into heaven in a three-story universe – that doesn't make sense. If I have to put it in those terms, it loses its power because it's not credible to me. Jesus did not want us to make a confession of faith so that we would follow him into heaven somewhere. His call was always into the world, to feed the hungry, free the captives, shelter the homeless and on and on.[158]

Some For, Some Against

The controversy surrounding the question of whether or not Jesus is God is not new. Ever since Jesus walked this earth, there have always been an abundance of skeptical inquirers who have denied His divinity. However, over the past few years, a myriad of skeptics who call themselves Christian have joined the ranks. Protestant denominations like the United Church of Canada, once grounded on the literal teachings of the Bible, now are among the leading detractors. As Ariel O'Neil, a longtime member of Bill Phipps's Scarboro United Church in Calgary stated:

> If Jesus was not raised from the dead, we're just wasting our time following the Christian faith. It seems that the liberal theologians are taking over. I'm really upset because the church is not being true to its origins.[159]

There are other members of Rev. Phipps's church who are much more complimentary. Ralph Garret, another regular attendee at Scarboro, supported his pastor in an interview by stating: "Everybody loves Bill. He's stimulated our spiritual lives."[160] Then commenting on the foundations of the faith such as the divinity of Christ, the Resurrection, and the existence of heaven and hell, he added: "The answers are unknowable, so why waste

---

[158] Ibid.
[159] Ibid., 44.
[160] Ibid., 43.

our energy? Instead we should put every effort into making this a better world."[161]

There are a number of other clergy, from different denominations, who are willing to go on record and support Moderator Phipps's position that Jesus is not God. Some seek to substantiate the idea that Christians should abandon the view there is only one true faith. For example, another Canadian, Anglican Bishop Michael Ingram, author of the book *Mansions of the Spirit,* has called for a new vision of God who reveals himself to all religions. "We don't have a monopoly on God's truth," he stated. Then further expounding on the view that Christians should be setting new goals for the future, he added: "The task of Christianity today is to remove some of its inflated claims for itself."[162]

Rethinking Jesus

Throughout this book, there has been an emphasis on the fact that the Bible teaches there will be an end-times delusion that will take place in Jesus' name. It would seem that if the Bible warns that this would take place, Bible believers would want to do all they could to warn those who were being deceived. Unfortunately, this is not the case. Even those concerned about the direction Christianity is headed are often reluctant to make a stand for fear they will be considered critical or divisive. For example, when Rev. James Crighton, pastor of the Westboro United Church in Ottawa was asked to comment on the direction the moderator of his fellowship had chosen to represent, he commented: "We try to be as inclusive as possible. Nobody wants a witch-hunt. The Christian thing to do would be to pray for his conversion."[163]

Although praying for Moderator Phipps's conversion would be an appropriate Christian thing to do, it would also seem appropriate to pose a very important question. How can a person who denies the deity of Christ become the moderator of a large

---

[161] Ibid.
[162] Ibid.
[163] Ibid., 44.

fellowship of Christians when a Canada-wide survey revealed that eight out of ten members said they believed in the deity of Jesus Christ?[164]

It becomes apparent that the beliefs of the chief shepherd of some denominations may not reflect the beliefs of the sheep that they oversee. But given the fact that people are more and more reluctant to be outspoken about the truth, it will only be a matter of time before the majority of the sheep will have the wool completely pulled over their eyes.

In November of 1997, the executive general council, the governing body of the United Church of Canada, voted to support Bill Phipps's right to express his beliefs. Expounding on this position, Peter Wyatt, the United Church general secretary for theology, faith and ecumenism commented: "Our strength is in our diversity and the freedom we give people. But the shadow side of this is that people wonder whether there are boundaries."[165]

The Bible teaches there are boundaries and that there are absolutes. The doctrines that have been embraced in the post-Christian era by modern day theologians shows how far we have strayed from biblical foundations that were embraced in the past. According to Thomas Bardy, head of the United Church's evangelization ministry, "everybody is trying to make Christianity more relevant to contemporary culture."[166] Or as Sally McFague, author of *Super, Natural Christians: How We Should Love Nature*, stated:

> Every age has to answer the question Jesus posed to Peter in the gospels, "Who do you say that I am?" That means reframing the question in terms of the most pressing issues of our day. Is Jesus Christ important for the planet or just for human beings?[167]

---

164 Ibid.
165 Ibid.
166 Ibid., 42.
167 Ibid.

Finally, consider the remarks made by Michael McAteer, co-author of *The Man in the Scarlet Robe: 2000 Years of Searching for Jesus.* McAteer, another Canadian who dismisses Jesus Christ as nothing more than religious fiction, stated:

> I don't believe in the Resurrection. I would accept that somebody like Jesus existed. That's as far as I can go. Anybody who has a definitive answer, I think is either dishonest or disillusioned.[168]

Jesus' own words recorded in the seventh chapter of Matthew seem appropriate to conclude this chapter. Although these verses have been quoted before in this book, repetition will only help emphasize the urgency of the days in which we live. As part of His famous Sermon on the Mount, He stated:

> Enter by the narrow gate; for wide is the gate and broad is the way that leads to destruction, and there are many who go in by it. Because narrow is the gate and difficult is the way which leads to life, and there are few who find it. Beware of false prophets, who come to you in sheep's clothing, but inwardly they are ravenous wolves.[169]

So what is really behind this present movement which seems bent on redefining the meaning of Jesus and making the narrow way wide? What form of Christianity will this propaganda produce? Will Jesus Christ be the chief cornerstone of the Christian faith in the 21st century, or will another christ replace Him? Is it possible the world is being set up for a global religion that comes under the banner of Christianity but instead is the religion of the Antichrist?

---

[168] Ibid.

[169] Matthew 7:13-15

9

ECUMENICAL JIHAD

Even the most casual observer of current events can see there is a major shift going on today in the arena of religious discussion. While Christians are busily redefining what it means to be Christian, other world religions are expanding their boundaries in order to embrace the new Christian that is being redefined. As we begin a new millennium, there seems to be an organized effort uniting the religions of the world in a common hope that global peace can be attained here on earth.

While unifying all the religions of the world seems to be far more utopian than reality permits, there are definite signs that we are headed down this path. However there is a question many are asking - How could religious unity ever occur when we know that religious strife has never been successfully resolved? Throughout the centuries past, nations have warred against each other and much blood has been shed because of religious unrest. What would ever give us the idea that this highly emotional issue could be laid to rest? How could the religions of the world ever be willing to shake hands and join together and become brothers and sisters under one common God?

In order to answer this question, it is important to reconsider what the Bible teaches about Satan's plan for man, particularly in the last days. As we have mentioned earlier in this book, we know that Satan is a master schemer. Ever since the fall of man in the Garden of Eden he has been orchestrating his plan. While in the past he has used religious differences as the incentive for humans to eliminate each other from the face of this earth, in the last days, we can expect that his agenda will be reversed.

Rather than using religious differences as a means of agitating people to kill each other off, religion will actually become the means he uses to seduce the world into embracing the greatest delusion of all time. Consider the statements made by contemporary leaders from a variety of religious viewpoints and we can get a glimpse of a scenario that demonstrates Satan's final solution for delusion is currently underway.

Happy Holidays

For years when the calendar changes from November to December North Americans know that Christmas is just around the corner. December 25th has always been the day we have associated with the birth of Jesus. Although this day was not the exact day of the year that Jesus was born, Christians, both Catholics and Protestants have chosen the day as a reminder that Jesus was born as a human here on earth some 2000 years ago.

Over the last several years it has become increasingly more apparent that a special Christian Holy Day in celebration of Jesus' birthday is no longer acceptable in our global pluralistic society that tolerates anything and everything. No one religious group can be given special status above any another group, we have often been told.

As a result of this spiritual sensitivity that pluralism demands, the Christmas season has been renamed to reflect how open-minded our western society has become. Now instead of using the term "Merry Christmas," public school teachers and other employees who hold secular jobs have been instructed to use "Happy Holidays." Taking the Christ out of Christmas is just one of the necessities required to prove we are all spiritually equal in the "global village" we call planet earth.

The Holy Days

On December 21, 1997 the *Orange County Register* published an article called "Gifts of the Spirit" which helps demonstrate the point at hand. Under a subheading called "The Holy Days," the following statement was made:

> Hanukah, Christmas and Ramadan, holy days of three of the world's major religions, are bunched unusually close together this year – December 23, 25, and 31, respectively. The proximity of the holidays changes from year to year because of the differing calendars used by Judaism, Christianity and Islam. Christmas of course always occurs on December 25, but Hanukah can begin anytime between late November and late December, and Ramadan falls near Christmas once every thirty-five years or so.[170]

The article then went on to clarify the significance of these three separate religious Holy Days for Jews, Christians and Muslims by stating the following:

> Hanukah commemorates the victory of the Jews led by Judah Maccabee, over the Syrian Greeks and the rededication of the temple in Jerusalem in 165 B.C.E. Christmas marks the birth of Jesus Christ, the faith's Messiah. Ramadan marks when Islam's founder, the prophet Muhammad, is said to have begun to receive the divine revelations that became the Qur'an.[171]

In order to illustrate the new level of tolerance that has already been attained, we can examine four articles written by Southern California religious leaders about their individual meditations regarding the meaning of the Holy Days. Rabbi King from Irvine presented his view from a Jewish perspective. Norman McFarland, bishop of the Diocese in Orange represented the Roman Catholic position. The Rev. Robert Schuller, pastor of the Crystal Cathedral in Garden Grove was the

---

[170] "Gifts of the Spirit," Commentary Section, *Orange County Register*, December 21, 1997, 4.

[171] Ibid.

spokesperson for Protestants. The fourth representative was Shabbir Mansuri, director of the Council on Islamic Education in Fountain Valley.[172]

Each one of the articles presented personal thoughts regarding the significance of the Holiday Season. I found the one written by the Islamic representative particularly important in light of the subject matter of this chapter. Mr. Mansuri introduced his article by stating: "The prophet Jesus affirms the oneness of God that unites all believers."[173]

This statement that was made by the representative for the Islamic faith is rather provocative. While it is common knowledge that Muslims believe that Jesus was a prophet, the statement that Jesus may be a factor in uniting religions is quite profound. In order for anyone to embrace such a statement would mean that Jesus' own words as recorded in the Bible would have to be completely ignored. In fact, after making this initial statement about unity of believers through Jesus, the writer seems to head off in a completely different direction. He stated:

> For Muslims, the purity of Mary, the miraculous birth of Jesus and his role as the Messiah and an eminent prophet are fundamental articles of faith. Jesus' teachings affirm the oneness of God, a message reiterated by a long historical line of prophets beginning with Adam, and including Noah, Abraham, Moses, David, and Solomon, culminating with the prophet Muhammad. The honor intended for Jesus during the holiday season accords well with Muslims' own love for Jesus and his mother Mary. Certainly the prominence of the Blessed Virgin as one who is favored by God is reflected in the fact that one of the 114 chapters of the Qur'an is entitled "Mary."[174]

Although we will deal with the importance of Mary and her ecumenical ability to draw the religions of the world together in a later chapter, it is appropriate to make mention of the signifi-

---

[172] Ibid., 1.

[173] Shabbir Mansuri, "Gifts of the Spirit," Commentary Section, *Orange County Register*, December 21, 1997, 1.

[174] Ibid.

cance of Mary to the Islamic faith at this point. There are various other factors besides Mary that we want to discuss to show how Christianity could someday merge with the Muslim worldview.

Holy War

Author and speaker Peter Kreeft is also excited about the possibility of all "believers" being united as one. As a Boston College philosophy professor, a convert to Catholicism and one of its chief apologists, Kreeft authored a book called *Ecumenical Jihad.* Kreeft has an objective to morally transform society by encouraging a coalition with all the religions of the world. In order for this to happen, Kreeft believes "God is raising an army, forging a new alliance of all who hate evil."[175] In his book he states:

> This new alliance may prove to be more unifying than anything else in the history of religions. Perhaps all the world's religions will eventually be united in this cause; but so far, in the West, we can see this army being made up of five religious groups who have not bought into the sexual revolution and its offspring, abortion: orthodox Catholics, Evangelical and Fundamental Protestants, Muslims, religious Jews, and eastern Orthodox.[176]

The diversity of the coalition that Kreeft is advocating is much greater than Protestants, Catholics, Jews and the Orthodox coming together. In his book *Ecumenical Jihad,* Kreeft praised the pope for organizing a special prayer vigil in Assisi, Italy on October of 1986 when he brought together a wide variety of religious representatives. Gathered at Assisi were Muslims, Hindus, Buddhists, spiritists, snake worshipers, animists, and native witch doctors. Positively commenting on this gathering Kreeft stated:

---

[175] Peter Kreeft, *Ecumenical Jihad: Ecumenism and the Culture War,* (Ignatius Press, San Francisco, 1996), 49.
[176] Ibid.

> Representatives of all the major religions of the world met and prayed together for peace at Assisi... *such a thing had never happened before in the history of the world.*[177]

Although it can be clearly documented that Allah, the God of the Muslims, is the moon-god and not the God of the Bible,[178] Peter Kreeft believes he has discovered why the Muslims have become so successful in the expansion of their faith over the past several years. Asking why Islam is expanding so spectacularly, Kreeft answers his own question by saying: "To any Christian familiar with the Bible, the answer is obvious: because God keeps his promises and blesses those who obey His laws and fear Him."[179]

If Kreeft's justification of the Muslim faith is not strange enough, consider what Peter Kreeft has to say about the reunification of Catholics with Protestants. In an earlier book he authored called *Fundamentals of the Faith: Essays in Christian Apologetics,* Kreeft claimed that the time has come for Protestants to repent and come back to the Catholic Church. He wrote:

> And what do Protestants have to repent of? Doctrinally, whatever they left behind in the Reformation that was not a perversion – like selling indulgences or ecclesiastical politicking – but part of the apostolic tradition. I believe this includes the teaching authority of the Church, the inerrancy of her creeds, sacramentalism, apostolic succession, prayers to saints, Purgatory, transubstantiation, and even a definite papal primacy – all suitably defined, suitable not first of all to Catholics but to the Spirit of Christ.[180]

Peter Kreeft's book is an apologetic against biblical Christianity and is written to support Roman Catholicism that is based on many man-made, extrabiblical ideas. If Peter Kreeft's ideas

---

[177] Ibid., 37. [emphasis his]

[178] Robert A. Morey, *Islam Unveiled: The True Desert Storm*, (The Scholars Press, Shermans Dale, PA, 1991), 49,

[179] Peter Kreeft, 38.

[180] Peter Kreeft, *Fundamentals of the Faith: Essays in Christian Apologetics*, (Ignatius Press, San Francisco), 297.

were unique, I suppose we could overlook him entirely and say that the majority of Protestants would never be duped by such extrabiblical theology. However, this is not the case. His book, *Ecumenical Jihad* is endorsed by well-known evangelical leaders like Chuck Colson and J. I. Packer who have stated:

> Peter Kreeft is one of the premier apologists in America today, witty, incisive and powerful. On the front lines in today's culture war, Kreeft is one of our most valiant intellectual warriors.[181]

> This racy little book opens up a far-reaching theme. With entertaining insight, Kreeft looks into the attitudes, alliances and strategies that today's state of affairs requires of believers. Catholics, Protestants and Orthodox alike need to ponder Peter Kreeft's vision of things – preferably in discussion together. What if he is right?[182]

Pope Asks Forgiveness

In an unprecedented moment in the history of the Catholic Church, Pope John Paul II made a statement for the whole world to hear. He asked for God's forgiveness for the sins of Roman Catholics through the ages. "We forgive and ask forgiveness," the pope solemnly said at several points during the Day of Pardon Mass at St. Peter's Basilica in Rome.[183]

Historians have documented a record of social atrocities that have been committed throughout the centuries, all apparently endorsed by the Catholic Church. Thousands of Protestant heretics were burned at the stake during the Inquisition. Armies made up of God's chosen faithful slaughtered Muslims and Jews by the masses during the Crusades.

While the pontiff did not specifically mention in his speech how the Catholic Church treated Protestants, Muslims and Jews

---

[181] Kreeft, *Evangelical Jihad*, back cover, endorsement by Chuck Colson.

[182] Ibid., endorsement by J.I. Packer.

[183] Candice Hughes, "Pope asks forgiveness," *The Orange County Register*, March 13, 2000, 1.

in the past, the references were clear enough so that everyone should get the point. "It's extraordinary, heroic and unprecedented," said Monsignor Lawrence Baird of the Diocese of Orange. "It's really an invitation to all faiths to take responsibility for errors of the past and to work together with all of God's people."[184]

The pope delivered his message of repentance on behalf of the whole church. The apology he made was taken from a more extensive 31-page treatise by the International Theological Commission, a document approved by the Vatican that outlined the theological precedents for the apology.[185]

Bishop Piero Marini who was in charge of the papal ceremony, commented before the mass: "Given the number of sins committed in the course of 20 centuries, it (the apology) must necessarily be rather summary."[186]

While the document produced by the Theological Commission may excite all those who are enthusiastic about ecumenical unity with the Catholic Church, there is still reason to express some concern. According to the Theological Commission, the Catholic Church is still holy. While the sins of its children have stained the reputation of the Church, "constant purification" is still attainable. As well, no statement was made to clarify how past popes can still be viewed as infallible even though responsibility was assumed for their past sins.

The Pope in the Holy Land

While Pope John Paul's plea for forgiveness was historic, it was only the beginning. On March 26, 2000, just two weeks after the Day of Pardon Mass in Rome, the same pope inserted a request for forgiveness between two large blocks at the Western Wall in Jerusalem. This gesture by the pontiff took place on the final day of his whirlwind tour of the Holy Land. The head of

---

[184] Ibid.

[185] Alessandra Stanley, "Apology a marker of pope's legacy," *The Orange County Register*, March 13, 2000, 17.

[186] Ibid.

the Catholic Church was making a final plea for peace by visiting the sacred sites of Judaism, Christianity and Islam, all within the disputed confines of Jerusalem's walled Old City.

At the Church of the Holy Sepulcher, he knelt at the site where Catholics believe Jesus was buried. Later at the Haram as-Sharif, the hilltop where Muslims say Mohammed ascended to heaven, he met with Jerusalem's top Islamic cleric.[187]

While it was apparent that the pope's visit had little immediate effect in bringing about reconciliation between Jews and Muslims, his efforts were not unnoticed. As *Time* magazine reported:

> The situation in the Middle East is delicate but promising. A former Israeli commando is looking for his opening; an American president is circling in search of a legacy. It would not be surprising, a few years down the road, to hear from an Arafat, a Barak, a Clinton or even an Assad that one of the things that kept them on track in the fateful spring of 2000 had been a bent old man who dropped by the neighborhood and suggested, by word and deed, what strong will, good faith and leadership were all about.[188]

But there is more to the pope's plan for peace in the Middle East. In another article titled "What More Can He Hope To Accomplish?" that appeared in the same April 3, 2000, *Time* the following statement was made:

> In May the Pope will visit in Portugal to beatify two shepherd children to whom the Virgin Mary is said to have appeared there in 1917. For John Paul, the visit will have a mystical significance: his personal *Totus tuus* (All yours – giving himself to Mary). When he survived the 1981 assassination attempt by Mehmet Ali Agca, the Pope noted that the attack oc-

[187] Jocelyn Noveck, "Pope leaves Holy Land after final dramatic gesture," *Orange County Register*," March 27, 2000, 1.
[188] Jamil Hamad and Aharon Klein, "A Pilgrim's Progress," *Time*, April 3, 2000, 36.

curred on the anniversary of the Fatima apparition, and he credited his survival to intercession by the Blessed Virgin.[189]

In this chapter I have attempted to present the dangers that can occur when we refuse to build our theology on the Word of God alone. Joining together in a world ecumenical movement in the name of Christ is exactly what the Bible teaches will take place in the last days.

While documentation shows that this is already happening, it seems there is still some distance to go before all of the world's religions will be prepared to greet the false messiah, whom the Bible calls the Antichrist. In the following sections, we will look at a possible scenario that could play an important role in paving the way.

---

[189] Greg Burke, "What More Can He Hope To Accomplish," *Time*, April 3, 2000, 38.

Figure 16: Pope John Paul II has a special interest in "The Queen of Heaven," also known as "Our Lady of Fatima." An attempt to assassinate the pope occurred on May 13, 1981, the same date as the anniversary of the apparition of Fatima. Pope John Paul II believes that "Mary" saved his life.

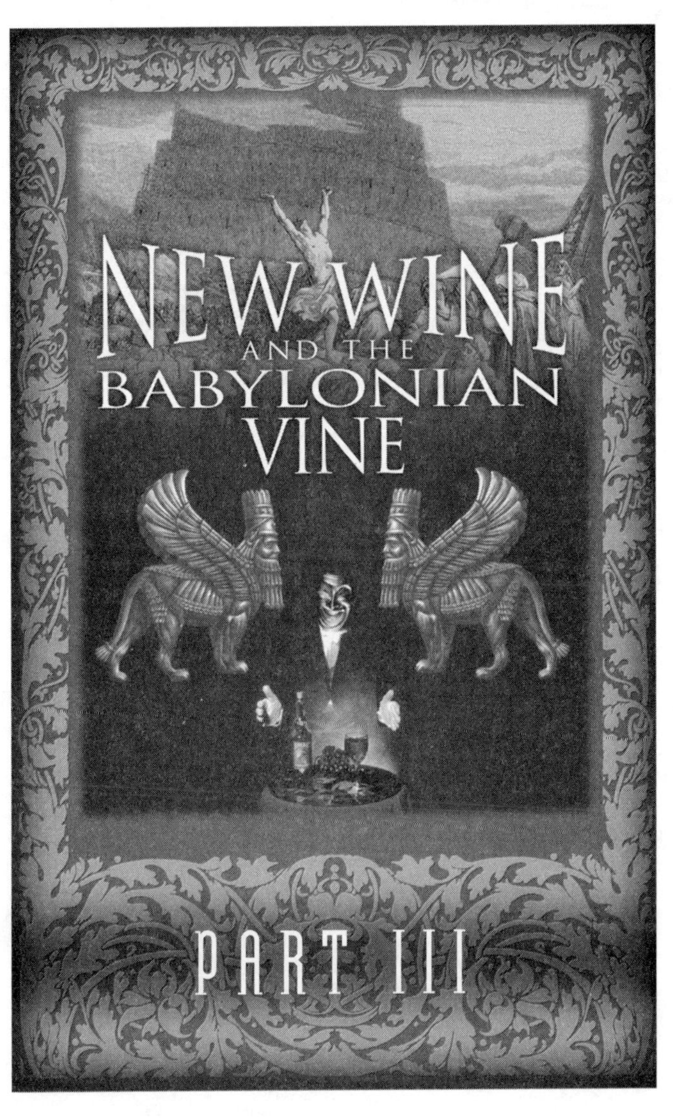

CREATION SPIRITUALITY

10

BUILDING A BRIDGE TO BABYLON

Is it possible to establish a global religion based upon a unity that is so diverse that it would provide room for all religions? If this were possible, what good would it do? Even if a religious holy alliance between Catholics, Protestants, Jews, Muslims and Orthodox Christians could be accomplished, how would this rectify the global crisis situations that threaten the future of our planet?

It has become increasingly apparent that an "ecumenical jihad" may play an important role in man's efforts to bring about the Kingdom of God here on the earth. A great religious alliance is now in the process of being established. While this new global religion or global ethic that many are espousing often makes reference to the name Christ, there are some that claim this united religious effort may actually become the religion of the Antichrist. The purpose of this chapter is to examine current trends in light of the Bible to see if such a claim has any credibility.

An International Symposium

The Bible states that if we commit our works unto the Lord, our paths will be established.[190] During my life as a Christian, I

[190] Proverbs 16:3

have seen this biblical truth demonstrated over and over again. On numerous occasions I have seen events unfold before me that I had no part in orchestrating. In retrospect, it was obvious that God's hand was the guiding factor that implemented whatever had been accomplished.

One such event occurred while I was in the process of writing this book. An unexpected invitation came for me to present a lecture at the Second Annual International Symposium on Energy and the Environment that was to be held in Southern California at the Long Beach Hilton. Three speakers, including myself, had been asked to give presentations during the opening day. Each speaker was asked to present thoughts on the important issue of the environment by presenting a spiritual perspective. My responsibility was to speak on a Christian worldview.

Although I do not consider myself to be an authority on the subject of the environment, and while there would have been others far more qualified to speak on this issue than I, there were a few areas where I felt that I was able to contribute. First, I am a Christian. I have been a Christian for over twenty years -- my conversion to Christianity coming at the age of thirty. Second, because I have a background in biology and agriculture I have always had a keen interest in environmental issues. And third, as a Christian, I believe it is the responsibility of every human being to be concerned about our planet and the ecological relationship we have with all living creatures that God has created. As well, throughout my life I have made a number of observations relating to the environment based upon a biblical perspective that indicates society is headed towards a catastrophic future.

I was educated during the '50s and '60s through the Canadian public school system, then later at the University of Saskatoon in Saskatchewan. During those years I, like my colleagues, was brought up in the educational mindset that our world could be understood from a purely natural and mechanistic worldview. The concept that God was dead and that science and technology would bring utopia to the earth, were two foundational ideas in my belief system during that time.

By the '70s and '80s it became obvious to many that a paradigm shift in thinking was underway. It was apparent that many of the byproducts of our technology had the potential of destroying us – the pollution of the atmosphere, our lakes, rivers, oceans, and the soil. Not only was our planet being threatened, our bodies were being pumped full of molecular time bombs that silently tick away. Even more significant was the fact that humans had developed the potential to completely annihilate the entire planet through weapons of mass destruction.

By the early '80s it became clear to many there needed to be a solution to the overwhelming problems we were facing as a global community. Crisis situations such as global warming and the ozone depletion affected the entire planet. These problems, if they were going to be resolved, needed solutions that would have to be implemented internationally.

A Biblical Christian Perspective

As part of my presentation to the symposium, I felt it was important to clear up some misunderstandings regarding the Christian perspective on the environment. Based upon Genesis 1:26-27, (two verses in which God instructed mankind to have "dominion over the creation") some say the Bible gives man the mandate to do whatever he wants, in whatever way he wants, thus having no respect for the planet and the ecosystem. This argument has often been used to blame the Christian worldview for our ecological problems.

In response to this, one only needs to take a trip to the former Soviet Union where atheism was encouraged and Christianity outlawed for over seven decades. The disregard for the environment in these areas has been deplorable. Christianity should not be blamed for environmental genocide -- the problem has been created by mankind's selfish lust for power and greed.

The Christian worldview on the environment is very simple: God, the Creator of all things, did indeed create all things. Although there are some who would try to say that God used evolution as a process to create, such a view is a contradiction of terms. Evolution, by definition is a natural process that does not require supernatural intervention. Naturalistic evolution is based upon time and chance – natural selection by natural direction rather than supernatural intervention that required an intelligent Creator Designer God. In no way can the complexity seen within nature be explained by fortuitous events that accumulate over vast periods of time driven by random chance.

The Christian view is that creation reveals the handiwork of the Creator. Although the original creation was perfect, we now live in an imperfect world. When man allows his greed to supersede environmental need, this degeneration and contamination accelerates further.

As well, the Christian view is that the Creator is sovereign and eternal, while man is not. Although God is the Creator of all things, He is separate from His creation and is not to be worshipped as the creation. In other words, God created everything, but everything is not God.

The Psalmist in the Bible wrote, "I will praise You, for I am fearfully and wonderfully made; Marvelous are Your works, And that my soul knows very well."[191] A Christian who truly believes that God is the Creator of all things has a reverence and awe for God and the creation. Because of this reverence and accountability there comes a responsibility. This responsibility should reflect the way we treat other people, the environment, and all things that exist.

Christians should be concerned about the environment and be good stewards of the creation that God has given us. If left alone, the environmental problems we face will only continue to follow the path we all understand based upon the Second Law of Thermodynamics. Positive programs and initiatives need to be presented and discussed by scientists and concerned citizens who gather the facts, and politicians who can develop legislation for the betterment of our world and all life that lives here. Wise intelligent decisions will need to be made in the future, so that we can indeed have a future.

---

[191] Psalms 139:14

Christian Pantheism

The invitation for me to speak at the International Symposium on Energy and the Environment came at a very important time in the formulation of the outline of this book. For the past two decades I have been tracking the environmental movement and the role it plays in the fulfillment of Bible prophecy. For some unknown reason, I had not included this important topic in the *New Wine and the Babylonian Vine* outline. After I heard the other speakers present their perspectives from a New Age pantheistic worldview, I was reminded that another major area needed to be added to this book in order to make the prophetic jigsaw puzzle complete.

During the discussion period that followed my lecture, the speaker who had represented a New Age perspective on the environment asked me if I was familiar with the writings of Catholic theologian and author Pierre Teilhard de Chardin. It was interesting that in the preparation for my lecture I had actually reviewed some of de Chardin's writings that I had in my library. At one point in my life I had embraced many of de Chardin's ideas.

Teilhard de Chardin was born in France on May 1, 1881. He was educated at Jesuit schools in France and England and then later studied at the Sorbonne in Paris, where he received his doctorate in paleontology in 1922. Teilhard's teaching career at the Catholic Institute in Paris was terminated because the Vatican hierarchy regarded his views as unorthodox. The Darwinian evolutionary theory was the key to Teilhard's thought. He interpreted evolution as a purposeful process in which the matter-energy of the universe was in the process of continual change in the direction of increased complexity. With the emergence of humanity, he argued, evolutionary development had entered a new dimension. Ultimately, he believed the evolutionary process would culminate in the convergence of the material and the spiritual realms into a superconsciousness that Teilhard called the Omega Point.[192]

Figure 17: Teilhard de Chardin, a Jesuit Catholic priest, was a strong promoter of the Darwinian evolution worldview. He is known for the theory that man is presently evolving, mentally, spiritually and socially, toward a final spiritual unity.

Pierre Teilhard de Chardin popularized the idea that human history can only be understood by accepting the key role that Darwinian evolution has played. His writings clearly reject the

[192] "de Chardin," *Microsoft Encarta Encyclopedia*, 1998, CD-ROM.

Bible as an accurate historical record of human origins. For example de Chardin stated in one of his writings:

> The truth is that it is so impossible to include Adam and the earthy paradise (taken literally) in our scientific outlook, that I wonder whether a single person today can at the same time focus his mind on the geological world presented by science, and on the world commonly described by sacred history. We cannot retain both pictures without moving alternatively from one to the other. Their association clashes, it rings false. In combining them on one and the same plane we are certainly victims of an error in perspective.[193]

While de Chardin's teachings did much to demote the Genesis account of creation to nothing more than a myth, he is best known for his ideas that supported Christian pantheism. By relegating God to an absentee landlord, he suggested that it was possible for one to be a Christian and still embrace the Eastern religious perspective that God is everything. As de Chardin stated in his essay called "Pantheism and Christianity":

> What I am proposing to do is to narrow that gap between pantheism and Christianity by bringing out what one might call the Christian soul of pantheism or the pantheistic aspect of Christianity.[194]

Then in another essay titled "How I Believe," de Chardin presented his strong conviction that some day in the future there would be an ecumenical union of all religions that would form an alliance based upon the idea of a universal Christ. He stated:

> In the great river of mankind, the three currents (Eastern, human and Christian) are still at cross-purposes. Nevertheless there are sure indications which make it clear that they are coming to run together. The East seems already almost to have forgotten the original passivity of pantheism. The cult of progress is continually opening up its cosmogonies ever more

[193] Pierre Teilhard de Chardin, *Christianity and Evolution,* (Hartcourt Brace and Company, San Diego, CA), 47.
[194] Ibid., 56.

> widely to the forces of spirit and emancipation. Christianity is beginning to accept man's effort. In these three branches the same spirit which made me what I am is obscurely at work.[195]

The New Genesis

While Pierre Teilhard de Chardin was a Catholic free thinker, his was not endorsed by leaders of the Catholic Church during the time that he wrote. However, a study of recent religious history will reveal that his writings have had a huge impact on other free thinkers, both Catholics and non-Catholics, many of whom have been influential in shaping the thoughts of educators worldwide.

Robert Muller is one such individual. As an assistant to three former secretary-generals of the United Nations, he is well respected for the achievements he has attained. In his book *New Genesis,* Muller explained that his spiritual journey started at the age of forty-six when he took the position of director for Secretary-General U Thant's office.[196] While U Thant's Buddhist beliefs were influential in helping Muller shape his religious worldview, most of the credit should be given to Pierre Teilhard de Chardin. Muller stated:

> In 1970, the year of the twenty-fifth anniversary of the UN, I was appointed director of the Secretary-General's Office. From then on I had to have a total view and I often heard myself being described as "Teilhardian." Father Emmanuel de Breuvery, a companion of Teilhard de Chardin, had already exposed me to the ideas and philosophy of Teilhard when I was working on the Natural Resources Division of the United States. With Secretary-General U Thant this exposure became even more frequent, and now after a third of a century of service with the UN I can say unequivocally that much of what I have observed in the world bears out the all-encompassing,

---

[195] Ibid., 130.

[196] Robert Muller, *New Genesis: Shaping a New Global Spirituality,* (World Happiness and Cooperation, Anacortes), 169.

global, forward-looking philosophy of Pierre Teilhard de Chardin.[197]

While "Teilhardianism" was once looked down upon by the Catholic leadership, men like Robert Muller have done a magnificent job of bringing his ideas back into the religious mainstream. However this time there seems to be very little opposition from the Catholic Church. Although Mr. Muller is now retired from his position with the United Nations he spends his time promoting a World Core Curriculum that he would like to see taught in classrooms all over the world.

Although Mr. Muller is a Catholic, he wants to see people of all religions come together in a common faith. "My great personal dream is to get a tremendous alliance between all major religions and the UN," he has stated.[198]

As well, Mr. Muller sees that the Catholic Church and the United Nations are quite similar in the goals they both desire to achieve. He sees that both are worldwide in scope, prize human life, and seek what is ultimately good for humanity. While critics often dismiss the Catholic Church and the United Nations as lofty, unrealistic and ineffective in achieving their goals of peace and brotherhood, Mr. Muller disagrees. He has stated: "In my opinion, they are both extremely effective – in the long run. They are part of building the ethics and evolution of humanity."[199]

The Evolution of Humanity

There is no doubt that Teilhardianism is alive and well and that it is not just being promoted from the United Nations based in New York. While Muller has described the UN as "the place of a thousand bridges" and "the cradle of the future of world destiny,"[200] the methods that he has advocated are an abomination to the God of the Bible. For example, Muller has stated:

---

[197] Ibid., 160.
[198] Ibid., xiii.
[199] Ibid., xiv.
[200] Ibid.

> Little by little, a planetary prayer book is thus being composed by an increasingly united humanity seeking its oneness, its happiness, its consciousness, its peace, its justice and its full participation in the continuous process of creation and the miracle of life. Once again, but this time on a universal scale, humankind is seeking no less than its reunion with the "divine," its transcendence into ever higher forms of life. Hindus call our earth Brahma, or God, for they rightly see no difference between the earth and the divine. The ancient simple truth is slowly dawning again upon humanity. Its full flowering will be the real, great new story of humanity, as we are about to enter our cosmic age and to become what we were always meant to be: the planet of God.[201]

Although Muller believes these new ideals will cause "our children to know a better future, a more peaceful world, an unprecedented fulfillment of individual human life and consciousness,"[202] the Bible reveals that what Muller and others are striving to accomplish will not only fail, it will bring God's wrath.

The idea that evolution is a guiding force that brings about peace and prosperity here on this planet is foreign to the Bible. In fact, from God's perspective this is "the lie."[203]

While there may be some who read this book who are not familiar with Teilhard de Chardin or Robert Muller, there are now plenty of others who are effectively propagating the same ideas. It seems in the last days, the whole world will be willing to believe this lie.[204] Shouldn't we be willing to do something to warn people about this deception?

---

[201] Ibid., 49.
[202] Ibid.
[203] Genesis 3:5
[204] Romans 1:25

11

ENVIRONMENTAL JIHAD

There is no doubt that our planet faces many global life-threatening problems. As everyone knows problems are never resolved by time alone. Global problems require global solutions. These global solutions require the cooperative efforts of policy-makers who can make laws. In the past, political leaders were given the responsibility to come up with the answers. However, the problems we now face in the world seem to demand spiritual solutions as well. Rather than turning to the God of the Bible, man, because of his rebellious nature, believes that he can come up with alternative methods to establish utopia here on planet earth.

This collective approach that is presently underway eliminates God from the equation and is similar to what mankind was attempting at Babylon following the Flood of Noah. For the descendants of those who survived the Flood, human reasoning was considered to be far more important than God's revelation. They decided to do what they wanted, rather than what God wanted. As a result of their rebellion they established a political-religious system that angered God and brought about their demise and their geographical division.

Today we see a similar pattern being repeated, only this time it is global in nature. In order to keep in line with twenty-first century culture and standards, science and religion are being united with the objective of establishing a messianic global religion that promises peace and prosperity.

It is this end-times "Christian pantheism" that the apostle Paul was warning about in the New Testament. For example, in Romans chapter one Paul made it very clear that when man chooses to reject the overwhelming evidence there is a Creator who has made all things, he will eventually become very spiritual and worship the creation instead.[205]

This chapter documents a number of recent events that demonstrate this is exactly what is happening today. A new environmental ethic based upon an old religious lie is in the process of being established. While many are saying this is an evolutionary imperative that is necessary for the future survival of mankind, the Bible perspective is completely opposite.

Earth in the Balance

Al Gore, is a devout advocate for global environmental reform. While holding a position as a United States senator, Mr. Gore published his views on the environment in a book titled *Earth in the Balance: Ecology and the Human Spirit*.[206]

Mr. Gore's book has become a classic for anyone who is interested in the environment. The book not only defines the global ecological problems, it also attempts to provide political and spiritual resolutions that could be implemented as possible solutions.

Although Gore claims to be a Christian, his views differ drastically from the foundational principles of Christianity that were clearly annunciated by Jesus Christ. While Jesus said that He alone was the truth and the way,[207] Mr. Gore believes that it is important to "investigate the wisdom found in all religions" in order to find truth. As he stated in his book, "this panreligious

---

[205] Romans 1:18-25

[206] Al Gore, *Earth in the Balance: Ecology and the Human Spirit,* (Houghton Mifflin Company, Boston, MA).

[207] John 14:6

perspective may prove especially important where our global civilization's responsibility for the earth is concerned."[208]

According to Gore, the world should investigate the "rich tapestry of ideas about our relationship with the earth" that can only be learned by "studying western native Indian beliefs." For example, Gore positively endorsed a statement made by Chief Seattle in 1855, who stated: "Will you teach your children what we have taught our children? That the earth is our mother?"[209] Also quoting a modern day prayer of the Onondaga tribe from Upstate New York (O great Spirit, whose breath gives life and breath to the world and whose voice is heard in the soft breeze) Gore suggests native spirituality teaches us a lot about man's connection to the earth.[210]

Mr. Gore also advocates that goddess worship should be reconsidered in our quest for environmental enlightenment. Hinting that Christianity unnecessarily eliminated organized goddess worship in the past, he suggests that it would be profitable for society if goddess worship could be encouraged to make a comeback. He stated:

> A growing number of anthropologists and archaeologists, such as Marija Gimbutus and Riane Eisler, argue that the prevailing ideology of belief in prehistoric Europe and much of the world was based on the worship of a single earth goddess, who was assumed to be the fount of all life and who radiated harmony among all things. Much of the evidence for this primitive religion comes from the many thousands of artifacts uncovered in ceremonial sites. These sites are so widespread that they seem to confirm the notion that a goddess religion was ubiquitous throughout much of the world until the antecedents of today's religions – most of which still have a distinctly masculine orientation – swept out of India and the Near East, almost obliterating belief in the goddess.[211]

---

[208] Gore, 258-259.
[209] Ibid., 259.
[210] Ibid.
[211] Ibid., 260.

Another position that Gore supports in his book, is the idea that many common truths can be found in the diverse religious views found all over the world. For example, he states that there is a "common religious thread" that can be found surrounding the "sacred quality of water."[212] While Christians are "baptized in water as a sign of purification," Muslims also "believe that everything has been created from water," Mr. Gore explained. As well, according to Gore, Hinduism and Sikhism also embrace the view that water is the source of the "life force."[213]

Mr. Gore also encourages his readers to support the Vatican's position on the environment. He quoted directly from a speech made by Pope John Paul II on December 8, 1989 in which he said:

> Faced with the widespread destruction of the environment, people everywhere are coming to understand that we cannot continue to use the goods of the earth we have in the past...a *new ecological awareness* is beginning to emerge, and rather than be downplayed, ought to be encouraged to develop into concrete programs and initiatives.[214]

Mr. Gore also pointed out in his book that Christians who have a "prophetic view of a coming apocalypse," are guilty of ignoring "their responsibility to be good stewards of God's creation." "Not only is this idea heretical in terms of Christian teachings," he stated, "it is an appalling self-fulfilling prophecy of doom."[215] Then developing this point further, Mr. Gore called for the establishment of a new faith for the future. He stated:

> Nevertheless, there is no doubt that many believers and non-believers alike share a deep uneasiness about the future, sensing that our civilization may be running out of time. The religious ethic of stewardship is indeed harder to accept if one believes the world is in danger of being destroyed – by either God or humankind. This point was made by Catholic theolo-

---

[212] Ibid., 261.
[213] Ibid.
[214] Ibid., 262. [emphasis not mine]
[215] Ibid.,. 263.

gian Teilhard de Chardin when he said, "The fate of mankind, as well of religion, depends on the emergence of a *new faith in the future.*"[216]

A New Faith for the Future

The current events that are unfolding show that a major shift in thinking is taking place regarding resolutions to global environmental problems. We now know that world political leaders are proposing a new global ethic as an attempt to save our planet from the possibility of human destruction. While such an effort may seem appropriate to many, those who have studied the Bible from a prophetic perspective have reason to be concerned.

The Bible clearly warns there will be serious consequences when man chooses to worship the creation rather than the Creator. According to the words written by the apostle Paul to the Romans:

> For the wrath of God is revealed from heaven against all ungodliness and unrighteousness of men, who suppress the truth in unrighteousness, because what may be known of God is manifest in them, for God has shown it to them. For since the creation of the world His invisible attributes are clearly seen, being understood by the things that are made, even His eternal power and Godhead, so that they are without excuse.[217]

It is apparent that world leaders who are pushing the new spirituality do not take the words of the apostle Paul seriously. Rather than acknowledging God as the Creator, these spiritual promoters of the New Age, like Al Gore, have chosen to proclaim the mystical view that evolution is God. For example in *Earth in the Balance,* Gore elevates evolution to the status of God by stating:

> The long and intricate process by which evolution helped to shape the complex interrelationship of all living and nonliving things may be explicable in purely scientific terms,

---

[216] Ibid. [emphasis mine]
[217] Romans 1:18-20

> but the simple fact of the living world and our place on it evokes awe, wonder, a sense of mystery – a spiritual response – when one reflects on its deeper meaning.[218]

This spiritual response that Mr. Gore writes about is dependent upon mankind acknowledging evolution as the force responsible for bringing about the "complex interrelationship of all living and nonliving things." Developing this point further he stated:

> And if we could find a way to understand our own connection to the earth – all the earth – we might recognize the danger of destroying so many living species and disrupting the climate balance. James Lovelock, the originator of the Gaia hypothesis, maintains that the entire complex earth system behaves in a self-regulating manner characteristic of something alive, that it has managed to maintain critical components of the earth's life support systems in perfect balance over eons of time.[219]

A New Look at an Old Lie

Although Mr. Gore may make the claim that the Gaia hypothesis has scientific credibility, insight from ancient history will show the idea is deeply rooted in pagan idolatry. The word *gaia* was coined by the Greeks to describe their religious view that the earth was the mother of all life. James Lovelock, a British scientist, came up with his Gaia hypothesis, based upon the Darwinian view that evolution proves that the earth is the mother of all life. As anyone can see, the idea is not new at all. It is the same old Babylonian belief that has been around ever since man willfully rebelled against God shortly after the Flood of Noah as recorded in Genesis chapter eleven.

However, there is one important change that has taken place since Babel was constructed. Modern day supporters of the Mother Earth hypothesis are the religious and political leaders of

---

[218] Gore, 264.
[219] Ibid.

the entire world. Scattered all over this planet since the dispersal of mankind from Babylon, it appears that mankind is on the final end-times spiritual pilgrimage that is embracing the very lie that triggered God's anger when the Tower of Babel was built. Claiming that the earth is a "superorganism" where life has "co-evolved," these spiritual high priests are calling for the nations of the world to come together in an environmental jihad. The new Babylon that must be established, they say, will be dependent upon the unification of a one world political and religious system that will be the only thing that will save the planet from disaster.

Under New Management

While the doctrine of evolution may have prepared the way for the Gaia comeback, politicians and scientists are also instrumental in playing a key role. Faced by numerous global crisis situations that are in the news continually, these leaders are challenged to come up with innovative ideas that have practical applications. Mankind has been aggressive, prolific and greedy for resources and must now repent from its evil ways, we are being told. Now is a time for the world to realize ecological limits, trade in assertiveness for cooperation, and express self-regulation as the golden rule.

Along with the new global spiritual awakening, there will need to be those who are willing to take definite action by providing leadership beyond national boundaries. Mr. Gore is one example of such a leader. Recognizing that the problems the world faces will require a consensus by an international consortium of nations, Mr. Gore has called for a "Global Marshall Plan" similar to the plan that was formulated in Europe after the Second World War. Calling for a unified global response to the environmental problems the world faces, Gore stated:

> Improbable or not, something like the Marshall Plan, if you will – is now urgently needed. The scope and complexity of this plan will far exceed those of the original; what's required now is a plan that combines large-scale, long-term, carefully targeted financial aid to developing nations, massive efforts to

> design and then transfer to poor nations the new technologies needed for sustainable economic progress, a worldwide program to stabilize world population, and binding commitments by industrial nations to accelerate their own transition to an environmentally responsible pattern of life.[220]

Such a noble effort proposed by Al Gore is no longer an idea. Called "an evolutionary imperative," the Global Marshall Plan suggested by Gore is becoming more and more of a reality with each passing year.

Earth Conference One

They came from around the world. Some came from parliaments, senates and assemblies. Others came from laboratories, universities and boardrooms. It was the first time that spiritual and parliamentary leaders had come together with the scientific experts to confront the threats of the environmental crisis, nuclear war, famine and disease. After five days of dialogue and contemplation the participants pledged to join forces to care for and protect the earth with all its interdependent forms of life.

This unprecedented meeting, the Global Survival Conference held at Oxford, England in April of 1988 was extremely significant. It was the first time in the entire history of the planet that such a meeting had taken place between the leaders of historically hostile realms, the spiritual and the temporal.

While Earth Conference One may have been the first time that the world's political and religious leaders joined forces for the common good of planet earth, it was not the first time that the religions of the world had come together for an ecumenical peace party. Two years before in Assisi, Italy, Pope John Paul II had hosted a similar conference for world peace. Over 140 spiritual leaders representing over a dozen religions of the world had gathered together by invitation of the pope. Included in the gathering were witch doctors, shamans, Anglican priests, and even the Dalai Lama.

---

[220] Ibid., 297.

Figure 18: Political and religious leaders from around the world met in Oxford, England to discuss global solutions for global problems.

This god-man from Tibet was one of the main speakers at Oxford. Addressing the members of the conference as "brothers and sisters," he stated that although the religions of the world have special roles, "all religions emphasize forgiveness, tolerance, brotherhood and sisterhood." He continued, "we need to realize the oneness of human beings. Lovingkindness is the universal religion."[221]

Evolution and the Pope

"The Pope Rehabilitates Darwin," one headline read. "The Pope Says We May Descend From Monkeys," another stated. According to an announcement made by John Paul II, evolution is not just a hypothesis - but that there is scientific evidence supporting the theory[222] While some claimed that the pope's statement was made to "facilitate a greater reconciliation between science and faith,"[223] there were others that were extremely upset.

A computer search will show that the word *evolution* is not found anywhere in the entire Bible. So why would the leader of the Catholic Church come up with the idea that evolution and God are compatible?

The pope's statement came nearly a century and a half after Charles Darwin wrote *The Origin of Species* and places the authority of the Roman Catholic Church firmly behind the teaching of evolution. The evolutionary view supports the idea that life is not the handiwork of a Creator, but instead is the product of a gradual process of accumulated change that has involved nothing more than chance and time. Regarding the pope's announcement, Antonino Zichichi, a well known Italian physicist stated: "As he has done many times in the past, the Holy Father recognizes science as a depository of values that are on the same plane as those of faith."[224]

Ever since the time of Charles Darwin, the scientific community has done its best to promote the idea that evolution is the only credible way to understand where we came from and why we are here. With the pope's formal statement to the Pontifical

---

[221] Anuradha Vittachi, *Earth Conference One: Sharing a Vision for Our Planet*, (New Science Library, Boston, MA, 1989), 73.

[222] John Taglibue, "Pope: Evolution Not just an Hypothesis," *Orange County Register*, Oct. 29, 1996, 18.

[223] Ibid., 1.

[224] Ibid., 18.

Academy of Sciences on October 23, 1996, Pope John Paul acknowledged the idea of evolution as a credible means by which God could have created. According to Pope John Paul II "fresh knowledge has led to the recognition of the theory of evolution as more than just a hypothesis."[225]

A review of history will show that the Catholic Church has never formally condemned the theory of evolution. However, there was a strong statement of concern expressed in an encyclical letter "Humani Generis" issued by Pope Pius XII in 1950. This document cautioned that evolution played into the hands of the materialists and atheists who sought to remove God from the act of creation. Evolution, as history reveals, has had a major role to play in advancing an atheistic Marxist worldview in many countries.

Although the pope did not elaborate upon how "fresh knowledge" compelled him to publicly endorse evolution as a viable theory, one thing we know for sure is that there will be major ramifications from his decision to back Charles Darwin's theory. Although the pope seems to think that evolution is just good science and is compatible with Christianity, Darwin, who popularized the idea of evolution disagreed. Evolution was purely a natural process that did not require the supernatural at all, he insisted. In fact Charles Darwin wrote in his autobiography that Christianity was "a damnable doctrine."[226] Evolution was his way of distancing himself from God.

Is Evolution God?

Although the leader of the Catholic Church may have indicated he believes that it is permissible to place God into the evolutionary formula, the very idea is a contradiction of terms. Evolution, by definition is a natural process that does not require the supernatural. It is a dog-eat-dog and a survival of the fittest scenario. No intelligent designer is required -- only matter, time

---

[225] Ibid., 1.

[226] Nora Barton, editor, *The Autobiography of Charles Darwin*, (W.W. Norton & Company, New York, 1958), 87.

and chance. Creation requires the handiwork of a Creator. According to the Bible, it was this intelligent Designer who brought about all things. In the beginning all things were created by Him and for Him.[227] As well, according to the Bible, God's creation from the beginning was perfect.

Moreover, the pope's announcement that promotes the metaphysical idea of evolution to give it scientific respectability will have a profound impact on the way people think about spiritual things. For example, consider the fact that so many people today are reviving the ideas and teachings of Pierre Teilhard de Chardin, the Catholic Jesuit philosopher that has already been mentioned in this book. As one of the most widely read Roman Catholic thinkers of his time, de Chardin advanced the controversial view that combined evolution with eastern mysticism. Although the Vatican once banned his works from Catholic bookstores, his influence still touches millions of lives within and without the Catholic Church.

Creation Spirituality

Matthew Fox is a present-day Catholic theologian. His writings show a strong influence from Teilhard de Chardin's ideas. Like de Chardin, at one time Fox's teachings were considered to be outside the blessing of the Vatican authorities. However, now that the pope has made a bold endorsement of evolution, we can expect to see Matthew Fox's ideas gaining a lot more credibility.

Matthew Fox, like Pope John Paul II, is a strong advocate of ecumenical unity. Two of his books that reflect this theme include *The Coming of the Cosmic Christ: The Healing of Mother Earth and the Birth of a Global Renaissance* and *Creation Spirituality: Liberating Gifts for the Peoples of the Earth.* He is a Dominican priest, theologian, educator and founding director of the Institute in Culture and Creation Spirituality at Holy Names College in Oakland, California.[228]

---

[227] Colossians 1:16

[228] Matthew Fox, *Creation Spirituality: Liberating Gifts for the Peoples of the*

Fox's books reveal what he describes as a future renaissance that will take place in the Christian church. In *The Cosmic Christ* he predicted that a major shift in religious thinking would affect the entire world in the future. He wrote:

> I foresee a renaissance, a rebirth based on a spiritual initiative, as the result of the outpouring of the Spirit. This new birth will cut through all cultures and all religions and indeed will draw forth the wisdom common to all vital mystical traditions in a global religious awakening I call "deep ecumenism."[229]

What is this "new renaissance" that Fox is talking about? How can you combine a belief in Christ with paganism? Where in the Bible are we instructed to call the earth our mother? Where in the Bible do we find instructions that would permit mankind to draw from the wisdom of all of the world's religions? Certainly this is not Christianity; this is apostasy in its most obvious form.

In his book *Creation Spirituality,* Fox clarifies his position regarding where he believes the ecumenical movement is headed -- a melting pot of Christian mysticism with a contemporary struggle for social justice, feminism and environmentalism. In short, it is Fox's hope that people of every religious and political persuasion will unite in a new vision through which we will learn to honor earth bringing about a global transformation.[230]

Similar to Al Gore's "earth in the balance" approach, Fox believes that the people of the earth are in the process of being prepared for a coming ecological utopia, a time when it will be necessary to "cease looking *up* for deity and start looking *around.*"[231] He calls for what he terms a "panentheistic spirituality" which he claims will become the spirituality of the future

---

Earth, Harper and Row, San Francisco), back cover.

[229] Matthew Fox, *The Coming of the Cosmic Christ,* (Harper and Row, San Francisco, 1988), 5.

[230] Fox, *Creation Spirituality*, back cover.

[231] Ibid., 41.

that allows worshippers to see "all things in God and God in all things."[232]

Figure 19: The illustration on the front cover of Matthew Fox's book *Creation Spirituality* illustrates Fox's view of a coming one-world religion. The serpent represents the oneness of life. The three women represent the female trinity of God. Notice the woman at the top giving birth to planet earth.

It is this movement towards universal panentheistic spirituality that Matthew Fox calls "creation spirituality." By removing

[232] Ibid.

God as a personal Creator and transposing Him to "her" (that is, an impersonal "force" that permeates all things in the name of Christ), suddenly we have the basis for a global religion that could easily produce a counterfeit bride for the Antichrist. As Fox has boasted:

> As a movement, creation spirituality becomes an amazing gathering place, a kind of watering hole for persons who have been touched by the issues of our day – deep ecologists, ecumenists, artists, native peoples, justice activists, feminists, male liberationists, gay and lesbian peoples, animal liberationists, scientists seeking to connect science and wisdom, people of all prophetic faith tradition – all of these groups find in the creation spirituality movement a common ground on which to stand.[233]

So what about this idea of "creation spirituality" that Fox believes will be the new spirituality of the future? Is he merely promoting a radical belief supported by a fringe group of New Age radicals? Or has Fox accurately laid out the basis for a religiosity of the future that will be given scientific credibility by those who are proclaiming that evolution is God?

In addition, Matthew Fox suggests that biologist Rupert Sheldrake has come up with a credible scientific hypothesis to understand our evolutionary roots and explain why twenty-first century intellectuals are returning to their spiritual Babylonian roots. He states:

> If biologist Rupert Sheldrake is correct in his hypothesis that a "morphic field" is created by a kind of cumulative memory from the past, then perhaps the creation spirituality movement, because it awakens ancient memories, is an example of an ongoing "morphic resonance" that is resurfacing in human consciousness today. Psychologist June Singer believes that Sheldrake's theory explains how new archetypes emerge in the human collective consciousness: "At first a change in attitude or behavior is difficult, but as more and more individu-

[233] Ibid., 17-18.

als change, it becomes progressively easier for other people to do so, and not just through direct influence."[234]

Although this may sound absurd to the average person who goes about his daily task of living, unaware that current events are falling in place that complete a biblical prophetic jigsaw puzzle, the reality is Fox's "creation spirituality" is here to stay. The Cosmic Christ that Fox is promoting can be accepted by all religions as the perfect answer for global ecumenism. As Fox has stated:

> Every theologian must embark on these pathways and awaken them if the theological enterprise is to accomplish its task in our time. This will require a deep letting go of the old paradigms of education and theology. The old wineskins of an anthropocentric, rationalistic, antimystical, antimaterial world view can not contain the new wine of creativity that is exploding wherever minds, and hearts and bodies are being baptized into a cosmology, into the living Cosmic Christ. Perhaps it is time to back huge moving vans up to seminaries, load up the immense theological paraphernalia that has accumulated around the theme of the historical Jesus, and channel religion's resources in another direction - the quest for the Cosmic Christ.[235]

And what will this "new wine" of creativity produce? How will the historical Jesus be transformed into a Cosmic Christ so that all of the world's religions will be able to participate in a "deep ecumenism" that Fox and others are saying holds out our last hope for world peace? Fox provides the answer:

> The Cosmic Christ and the living cosmology that the Cosmic Christ ushers into society and the psyche have the power to launch an era of what I call deep ecumenism. Deep ecumenism is the movement that will unleash the wisdom of *all* the world religions – Hinduism and Buddhism, Islam, Judaism, Taoism, Shintoism, Christianity in all its forms, and native

[234] Ibid., 18.
[235] Ibid., 78-79.

> religions and goddess religions throughout the world. This unleashing of wisdom holds the last hope of the survival of the planet we call home. For there is no such thing as a Lutheran sun and a Taoist moon and a Jewish ocean and a Roman Catholic forest. When humanity learns this we will have learned a way out of our anthropocentric dilemma that is boring our young, killing our souls, trivializing our worship, and all the traditions of the Cosmic Christ in the Scriptures and in Western history that we have considered above.[236]

Who could have predicted that the twentieth century would end with scientists, educators and politicians coming to the common realization that the sun, the moon and mother earth could be called "the Christ"? The answer: only those who have believed and followed the teachings of Jesus Christ.

When His disciples questioned Him about what to expect before the end of the age, Jesus stated: "See to it that no one misleads you. For many will come in My name, saying, 'I am the Christ,' and will mislead many."[237]

However, there are many that call themselves Christian who are completely unaware that an environmental jihad in the name of Christ is already underway. These people are going about their daily living oblivious to the fact that the Babylonian vine is creeping throughout every aspect of our global society.

Is it reasonable to conclude that we are living at a time when the world is being prepared for the greatest delusion in history? It seems when environmentalism, evolutionism and pagan mysticism unite to become a revival of ancient Babylonianism in the name of Christ, it is time to heed the warnings from God's Word. As we will in subsequent chapters, such is not the case.

---

[236] Fox, *The Cosmic Christ*, 228.

[237] Matthew 24:4-5

12

PEACE, PEACE

Ask anyone the question: If a third world war was to break out, what would be the most likely place in the world for this to happen? Political and religious differences that have been taking place for the past several decades make it clear that the Middle East is the most likely location. In fact, leaders of countries throughout the world are always concerned about the ongoing struggle over Jerusalem.

While the conflict we see featured in the daily news in the Middle East is usually centered on the problems between the Jewish and Islamic faiths, everyone knows there are far reaching effects for all the world. Throughout history there have been wars over religious differences in the Middle East. However, given the technology of our day and the weapons of destruction that mankind has been able to design, a skirmish over religious differences has the potential to trigger off a nuclear holocaust.

The Dome of the Rock

The Dome of the Rock is a Muslim shrine in Jerusalem. The building stands on the traditional site of the Temple of Solomon. It was here, it is believed, Abraham offered the sacrifice of his son Isaac to God. For Muslims, it is the second holiest site of pilgrimage after Mecca. Muslim legend claims that it was on the Temple Mount that the prophet Muhammad ascended into heaven to receive the commandments of God. The Dome of the

Rock remains essentially as it was when completed in 692 by the Muslims. The roof has been renewed several times and other minor changes have been made to the surface decoration. The Dome of the Rock was built not only to commemorate Muhammad's ascension to heaven, but also to rival the splendor of Christian and Jewish sanctuaries already in Jerusalem. The building is octagonal in plan, with a large golden dome on top. The surfaces, both inside and out, are covered in marble and mosaic patterning, much of it on the interior being highlighted with precious stones and gold.[238]

Figure 20: The Dome of the Rock on the Temple Mount.

A Time Bomb

The Dome of the Rock is considered to be a fuse that could set off a third world war. Deep-rooted religious animosity has been brewing over this site for years. An Associated Press article that appeared in the January 1, 1998 edition of the *Orange County Register* tells the story:

> Hours after Israeli soldiers captured Jerusalem's Old City in 1967, the army's chief rabbi urged that the golden Dome of the Rock mosque be blown up, according to a newspaper re-

[238] "Dome of the Rock," *Microsoft Encarta Encyclopedia*, 1998, CD-ROM.

> port Wednesday. The landmark mosque is atop the Temple Mount, the last remnant of the ancient Jewish Temples and a flash point for conflicts between Jews and Muslims. Arabs have long been suspicious that Jews want to destroy the mosque, a move that would inflame the Muslim world.[239]

The reason for the release of this information to the public some thirty years after the event was also mentioned in the article titled "Report: Dome of Rock's destruction urged in '67." These remarks made by Rabbi Shlomo Goren had been quoted in an interview with retired Major General Uzi Narkiss with the *Haaretz* newspaper in May of 1997. Narkiss had stipulated that nothing be published until everyone present at the discussion had died. Major General Narkiss who had led the capture of the Old City of Jerusalem in 1967 died on December 17, 1997. Rabbi Goren died in 1994.[240]

Obviously the Dome of the Rock was not blown up. The golden-domed eight-sided building takes precedence above all other objects on the Temple Mount to this day. Jewish people are forbidden by the government of Israel to enter through the Temple gates. The location where their former Holy Temple once stood, today is "holy ground" for people who belong to the Islamic faith.

The Temple Institute

The Temple Institute, located in the Jewish Quarter of the Old City of Jerusalem, is a non-profit apolitical organization. One of the major objectives of the Temple Institute is to create authentic temple vessels and priestly garments according to biblical specifications. This has been an ongoing process for some years. By 1996, over sixty sacred objects had been created from gold, silver and copper. The Institute operates a permanent exhi-

---

[239] The Associated Press, "Report: Dome of the Rock's destruction urged in '67," *Orange County Register*, January 1, 1998, 20.

[240] Ibid.

bition, "The Treasure of the Temple," which has attracted over 200,000 visitors from around the world.[241]

According to the first newsletter published by the Temple Institute, one of the main goals of the organization is to "attempt to raise the consciousness of the Jewish people and the whole world to the realization that mankind's spiritual vacuum can only be filled by the Holy Temple." As well, the following statement is made: "The epoch of the Third Temple is promised, by our Prophets, to be a period of peace, compassion and human understanding. How and when this will come about, especially in light of the current state of affairs, we do not profess to know."[242]

While the Temple Institute may not represent the general desires or wishes of the majority of the Jewish people, these statements made by the newsletter are very interesting in light of Bible prophecy. This enthusiastic group also believes the Third Temple will be the secret to world peace. The newsletter continues:

> The Holy Temple is the unifying factor for all humanity... 'For My House shall be called a House of Prayer for all nations,' the Prophet Isaiah declares. This universal harmony, this all-encompassing unity, is brought about by nothing less than the resting of the *Divine Presence.*[243]

Temple Institute supporters are open to the idea that the Temple Mount area could be a common location for this "Divine Presence." Asking a question and then answering this question the Temple Institute newsletter stated:

> Why are the eyes of the world riveted on the Temple Mount? Because it is truly the nerve center of mankind, the concentration of the world's holiness; the very birthplace of the first Man – Adam. We are taught that the prayers of each and

---

241 *On The Altar,* The Temple Institute newsletter, Summer 1996, Volume 1.1, 1.

242 Ibid.

243 Ibid. [emphasis mine]

> every person, before ascending into Heaven, gather at the Foundation Stone on the Mount, from whence all of humanity was hewn, and from there the prayers make their way to G-d, like a cosmic switchboard. This process continues even today.[244]

Such a statement is interesting in light of the fact that the Jewish people are not in control of the Temple Mount. Muslims consider the Temple Mount to be a sacred Holy Spot for their Islamic faith. Could this mean that the Temple Mount is perceived as a holy "transmitter" for Muslims as well?

The Eye of the Universe

While visiting the Temple Institute in February of 1997, I noticed a book for sale in their bookstore. The author of the book was Rabbi Aryeh Kaplan. The title of the book was *Jerusalem: The Eye of the Universe.*

There were a number of questions asked on the back cover of the book that caught my interest. These questions included:

> What is the significance of Jerusalem? Why is it the most important place on the earth? What is its uniqueness? Why is it the only city mentioned in our prayers? What is the source of its holiness? Why can the Temple be located only in one spot? Why is its status so important so significant to its friends and enemies?[245]

Another statement on the back cover of the book said the author would answer these questions. I purchased the book and read through it in the next few days. Rabbi Kaplan added more insight to the information than what I had read in the Temple Institute newsletter *On the Altar.* On page 40 of Rabbi Kaplan's book the following statement was made:

---

244 Ibid.

245 Aryeh Kaplan, *Jerusalem: The Eye of the Universe,* (Published by the National Conference of the Synagogue, New York, 1976).

> Jacob called Jerusalem "the gate of heaven" (Genesis 28: 17). On a simple level this means that it is a gate which prayer ascends on high. In a deeper sense, this also means that it is a gate through which one enters heaven by means of mystical or prophetic experience.[246]

Then building upon the idea of the "Divine Presence" in another portion of the book, Rabbi Kaplan clarified further what he believed was meant by the "gate of heaven." He stated:

> This again brings us to the location of the Foundation Stone, the focus of all spiritual forces. It was set on the crossroads of civilization, so that all peoples should interact with these forces and throughout history, be influenced by them. In this manner all mankind is gradually elevated by these forces, paving the way for the ultimate rectification of the world. This will be realized in the Messianic Age, when Jerusalem becomes a center for God's teaching for all mankind: "Out of Zion shall come forth the Torah, and God's word from Jerusalem."

Rabbi Kaplan made the point that the Temple Mount in Jerusalem is a very significant piece of property, especially in the last days. As well, we know that the Bible indicates the same. A temple must be rebuilt in order to prepare the way for the coming Antichrist. It seems that current events are unfolding that line up with Bible prophecy indicating that we are living in very important days.

A Formula for Peace

When it comes to resolving any dispute there must always be the willingness to give and take. Never do we see religious disagreements between opposing groups resolved by time alone. Treaties or peace agreements are usually drawn up before peace can ever be attained. Religious tension between Jews and Muslims through the years has caused much bloodshed and pain in the Middle East. Today there appears to be few signs that a

---

[246] Ibid., 40.

peaceful resolution could ever come about without a concentrated effort by many world leaders.

In his 1998 Easter Sunday address to the world from the steps of St. Peter's Basilica in Rome, Pope John Paul II brought up this very issue. He urged humanity not to repeat the tragic errors of the 20th century and warned that the world was being sown with new "seeds of death" as it neared the year 2000. He also prayed for the Middle East and made reference to Israel's building of settlements in Arab East Jerusalem as a major stumbling block that was "putting the holy city at risk."[247]

The pope's words of warning came just two days after the historic Irish "Good Friday Agreement" that proposed the beginning of a new era of hope for religious strife-torn Ireland. Two religious factions that both professed the name of Christ had hammered out a preliminary agreement endeavored to provide a basis for ending hostility and bloodshed. Mayor of Belfast, Alban Maginness summed up the agreement by saying: "We are now moving from the politics of strife and violence into the politics of inclusiveness and reconciliation."[248]

For decades, the world has watched with horror the bloody sectarian battle that has been going on in Northern Ireland where at least 3400 people have been killed over the past several decades. Although the initial agreement did not come with any guarantees, at the very least, a resolution to make amends for the sake of peace is commendable.

Whether or not peace will be established on a permanent basis, only time will tell. However, one thing has been established; peace is attainable when leaders of opposing groups agree to a mediation process by neutral authorities. So what about the possibility that a peaceful resolution could be mediated between Jews and Muslims? Some have suggested that the pope, the

---

[247] Phillip Pullella, "Pope warns not to repeat tragic errors," *USA Today*, April 13, 1998, 1.

[248] Stryker Mc Qune, "A Clean Shot at Peace," *Newsweek*, European Edition, April 20, 1998, 11.

leader of the Catholic Church would be a good candidate for mediator.

Guiding the Ship

He has been called the "man of the century." Pope John Paul II, a man millions of people believe represents Jesus as the head of the Catholic Church, has left quite a legacy behind him. Although it is obvious that his health has been failing, the pope still demands respect. World leaders like President Bush of the United States, Prime Minister John Chretien of Canada, and Palestinian leader Yasar Arafat all have paid him a visit.

On February 11, 1998 the president of Russia, Boris Yeltsin, dropped by the Vatican to greet the pope. John Paul II, the first Polish pope, and Yeltsin, a former Communist who became Russia's first elected leader, had a fifty minute private conversation in which they discussed among other things, the celebration of year 2000. According to a *New York Times* article John Paul II, in his conversation with Yeltsin stated: "Let us hope we will go together toward the third millennium."[249]

Ten days after the meeting with Yeltsin, the pope held another special meeting. This time it was a ceremony to recruit twenty-two new cardinals to assist him with his responsibilities as the 20th century drew to a close. In an Associated Press article titled "Pope Elevates 22 Cardinals to Help Him 'Guide the Ship'" the following statement was made:

> Sitting in his golden chair, Pope John Paul II elevated 22 new cardinals Saturday, placing on their heads the red, three-cornered hats that symbolize their role as the "princes" of the church. The pontiff summoned the men – dressed in crimson cassocks, capes and socks – to lead the Roman Catholic Church into Christianity's third millennium. "You are called, along with the other members of the College of Cardinals, to help the

[249] Celestine Bohlen, "Pope and Yeltsin Meet at Vatican, Looking Toward Year 2000," New York *Times*, February 11, 1998, Online posting.

> pope guide the ship of St Peter to this historic goal," the pope told them.[250]

The article also reported that several of the new cardinals are seen as "papabile," a term which means "a potential pope." One of them, a man by the name of Schoenborn, is a highly respected theologian to whom John Paul gave the important job of preparing the church's new catechism.[251]

I obtained a copy of the new Catholic Catechism for my library. The next section will explain some very interesting things that I discovered as I read through it.

Catechism of the Catholic Church

The *Catechism of the Catholic Church* is a large book that officially presents the Vatican's position on all teachings that are deemed part of the Catholic Church's theology. While it is beyond the scope of this book to present all of these theological positions, there is one portion of the catechism that needs to be presented in order to document Catholic teaching regarding salvation.

Two sections will be quoted exactly as they appear in the official *Catechism of the Catholic Church.* These sections are called "Who Belongs to the Catholic Church" and "The Church and non-Christians."

Who Belongs to the Catholic Church?

> 836 All men called to this catholic unity of the People of God. And to it, in different ways, belong or are ordered: the Catholic faithful, others who believe in Christ, and finally all mankind, called by God's grace of salvation.
>
> 837 Fully incorporated into the society of the Church are those who, possessing the Spirit of Christ, accept all the means of salvation given by the church together with her entire orga-

[250] Ibid.

[251] Ibid.

nization, and who – by the bonds constituted by the profession of faith, the sacraments, ecclesiastical government, and communion – are joined in the physical structure of the Church of Christ, who rules her through the Supreme Pontiff and the bishops. Even though incorporated into the Church one who does not however persevere in charity is not saved. He remains indeed in the bosom of the Church, but "in body" not "in heart."[252]

The Church and Non-Christians

839 Those who have not received the Gospel are related to the People of God in various ways. *The relationship of the Church with the Jewish People:* When she delves into her own mystery, the Church, the People of God in the New Covenant, discovers her link with the Jewish People, the first to hear the Word of God. The Jewish faith, unlike other non-Christian religions is already a response to God's revelation in the Old Covenant. To the Jews belong the sonship, the glory, the covenants, the giving of the law, the worship, and the promises; to them belong the patriarchs, and of their race, according to the flesh, is the Christ, for the gifts and the call of God are irrevocable.

840 And when one considers the future, God's People of the Old Covenant and the new People of God tend towards similar goals; expectation of the coming (or the return) of the Messiah. But one awaits the return of the Messiah who died and rose from the dead and is recognized as Lord and Son of God; the other awaits the coming of the Messiah, whose features remain hidden till the end of time; and the latter waiting is accompanied by the drama of not knowing or misunderstanding Christ Jesus.

841 *The Church's relationship with Muslims.* The plan of salvation also includes those who acknowledge the Creator, in the first place amongst who are the Muslims; these profess to hold

[252] *Catechism of the Catholic Church*, (Liberia Editrice Vaticana, Liguoria Publications, Liguoria, MO), 222.

> the faith of Abraham, and together with us they adore the one, merciful God, mankind's judge on the last day.

These two sections quoted from the Catholic Catechism present an interesting foundation upon which an ecumenical movement headed by the Catholic Church could provide the way for a worldwide religion to be established in the name of Christ. However, it is obvious that this scenario is not according to the gospel of Jesus Christ. The "gospel" that is being presented by the catechism is clearly not the gospel that Jesus of Nazareth proclaimed.

Not only has the Christian gospel been redefined to permit the Roman Catholic Church the authority to determine who can go to heaven and who cannot, a possible scenario is unfolding that provides a way so that the Jewish Messiah and the Christian Second Coming of Jesus could be the same event. Finally, this Catholic dogma allows Muslims to be embraced as brothers and sisters in Christ. Surely such teachings are not only extrabiblical and heretical; they provide the foundation for a religion in the name of Christ that may well be the religion of the Antichrist.

Keys to the Kingdom

It is well known that the Catholic Church is built upon the idea that Jesus handed the "keys to the kingdom" to Peter and that Peter then became the first pope. This dogma is based upon a portion of Scripture that is incorrectly interpreted. In Matthew chapter 16, the Bible records:

> When Jesus came into the region of Caesarea Philippi, He asked His disciples, saying, "Who do men say that I, the Son of Man, am?" So they said, "Some say John the Baptist, some Elijah, and others Jeremiah or one of the prophets." He said to them, "But who do you say that I am?" Simon Peter answered and said, "You are the Christ, the Son of the living God. Jesus answered and said to him, "Blessed are you, Simon Bar-Jonah, for flesh and blood has not revealed this to you, but My Father who is in heaven. And I also say to you that you are Peter, and on this rock I will build My church, and the gates of Hades

> shall not prevail against it. And I will give you the keys of the kingdom of heaven, and whatever you bind on earth will be bound in heaven, and whatever you loose on earth will be loosed in heaven."[253]

When we take Jesus' question in context, we see that Jesus was asking His disciples to tell Him what people were saying about Him. After hearing them report various answers, Jesus then asked the disciples personally, "Who do you say that I am?" Peter responded with the confession of faith that leads to eternal life: "Thou art the Christ, the Son of the living God." Jesus then acknowledged that what Peter had stated was God inspired.

Following this, Jesus made the important statement that the Catholic Church claims they have interpreted correctly. Jesus said: "And I also say to you that you are Peter, and on this rock I will build My church, and the gates of Hades shall not prevail against it. And I will give you the keys of the kingdom of heaven, and whatever you bind on earth will be bound in heaven, and whatever you loose on earth will be loosed in heaven."

So what was Jesus saying? Did He mean that He was going to hand over the keys of the Kingdom of God to a mere man such as Peter? Or was Jesus saying that the only true key to the Kingdom of God is when one recognizes who Jesus Christ is and what He has done? If Jesus meant that Peter was to become the first pope, the first in a long line of God-appointed "Vicars of Christ" who could declare infallible teachings outside of biblical parameters, then a serious error had been made. A few verses later in Matthew 16 we read that Jesus rebuked Peter by saying: "Get behind Me, Satan! You are an offense to Me, for you are not mindful of the things of God, but the things of men."[254]

The problem that Jesus pointed out to Peter is the same problem that many professing Christians have today. They listen to what men are saying rather than to what God has already said. We must always base our doctrines on Scripture. If we do

---

[253] Matthew 16:13-19
[254] Matthew 16:23

not, then we are guilty of the same thing that Peter was guilty of doing. There is only one narrow way by which one can enter into the Kingdom of God – through acknowledging the finished work of Jesus on the cross.

It is disturbing to me that the Catholic Church promotes the doctrine that they are the only true church through which God has chosen to establish His Kingdom. There are many Protestants who believe that the Catholic Church has changed their point of view and that they are now willing to be co-partners in evangelism. However, as I have already pointed out, this is not true. People are being deceived.

Feeling the Presence

The April 1996 *National Geographic* contains an article on Jerusalem that provides us with a graphic illustration of the ecumenical brand of Christianity that the Catholic Church embraces. A two-page color spread shows three Catholics who are on a pilgrimage from Brazil to Jerusalem during Easter of 1995. Talo Santos, the leader of the group is shown walking down Via Dolorosa. She has a large wooden cross, draped over her right shoulder. Hanging around her neck is a medallion that represents the sun and the moon god. From her right hand is suspended another medallion that is inscribed with a pyramid. A Catholic rosary hangs from her left hand. "My faith became gigantic," reported Santos. And further she stated, "We felt Him walking among us."[255]

Christian Babylonianism! There is no other term that more adequately describes experiential Christianity that seeks after the presence of Christ without seeking after His Word. Someday, just as the Bible predicts, a man who claims that he is the Christ will emerge with a perfect plan for peace. A Jewish Temple will be built, but it will not be exclusively for Jewish worshippers.

All religions will be able to worship in this Temple and all the people will believe that the Messianic Age has arrived. How-

---

[255] Alan Mainson, "The Three Faces of Jerusalem," *National Geographic*, April 1996, 4.

ever, before this can happen there will have to be more signs and wonders of the lying variety that draw the world into an end-times delusion in the name of Christ.

I believe we are living in a period of time that will see lying signs and wonders materialize and intensify. The only way that we can be protected from this delusion is to have a God-given discernment that comes from knowing the Word of God.

In the next two sections we will examine the signs and wonders movement promoted by both Protestants and Catholics. We will examine the claims that are being made by Christians. Although their experiences cannot be supported by Scripture, we will see that these experiences can be understood in light of Scripture.

Figure 21: An experienced-based Christian feels the "presence" of Christ in Jerusalem. The illustration is a reproduction taken from a photo that appeared in *National Geographic,* April 1996.

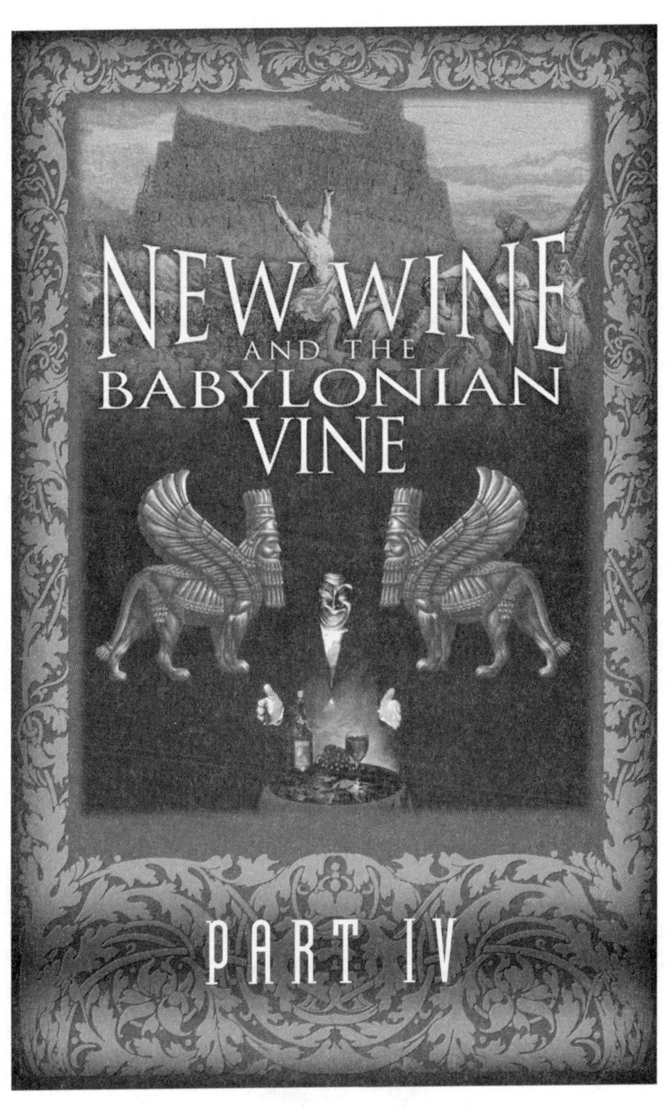

NEW WINE

13

NEW WINE OR OLD DECEPTION?

It is happening around the world. Many are saying we are living in the midst of a spiritual awakening. God is pouring out His Spirit on believers and unbelievers, and we are about to see the greatest revival in history, many are proclaiming. Now is the time to "catch the wave" and renounce old religious ideas, they insist. We have arrived. This is the new era that so many have been predicting for decades. You must embrace the Holy Spirit's new strategies for revival or you will be left behind.

The December 1999 *Charisma* magazine featured a major article that foretold the future of the body of Christ. On the front cover, the following statement was made: "Fasten your seat belt. A Christian revival could sweep the world in the next 25 years."[256] Like others who espouse the final end-times great revival, *Charisma* has been promoting this idea that God is pouring out a new anointing to prepare an army of God to win the world for Jesus in these last days. Experiencing God's power by imbibing the new wine is proof you have enlisted as a member of God's army, some are also saying. The more unity there is in the body of Christ, the more signs and wonders will occur. The more signs and wonders that are demonstrated, the more people will

[256] *Charisma*, December 1999, front cover.

come to Christ, proponents of the New Wine Movement are claiming.

The Fire Is Spreading

The July 1997 issue of *Charisma* contained a feature article called "The Blessing Spreads Worldwide." The lead paragraph stated: "Since an unusual spiritual renewal movement erupted in 1994, many Christian leaders have become convinced that a global revival is on the way."[257]

According to this New Wine theology, a "fire" that was lit at the Toronto Airport Vineyard (now the Airport Christian Fellowship) in January of 1994 is now being transferred worldwide. Proponents say the Toronto "blessing" is transferable and contagious. Once you get "it," you can give "it" away to others.[258]

In this article writer Marcia Ford retraced the origin of the blessing back to it's sources: Pastor John Arnott and his wife Carol picked up their anointing from Claudio Freidzon while in South America.[259] Claudio Freidzon had received his anointing from Benny Hinn. Benny Hinn claims he received a special empowerment when he came in close contact with the bones of Kathryn Kuhlman.[260]

Another source of this New Wine anointing for the Toronto church came from St. Louis Vineyard pastor Randy Clark.[261] He received an "anointing" from self-proclaimed "Holy Spirit bartender" Rodney Howard-Browne.[262] Howard-Browne claims

---

[257] Marcia Ford, "The Blessing Spreads Worldwide," *Charisma*, July 1997, 54.
[258] Ibid., 55.
[259] John Arnott, *The Father's Blessing,* (Creation House, Orlando, FL, 1995), 58.
[260] Benny Hinn, "Double Portion Anointing, Part #3" (Orlando Christian Center, n.d.), audiotape #A031791-3. This sermon was also aired on TBN April 7, 1991
[261] Arnott, 59.
[262] Paul Carden, "Toronto Blessing Stirs Worldwide Controversy," *Christian Research Journal* (Winter 1995), p. 5

that God appointed him to light the fire of revival around the world.[263]

From Toronto this "blessing" has spread to many countries throughout the world. Recipients have taken it back to their homes in England, South Africa, Australia and even Mainland China.[264] The Brownsville Assemblies of God in Pensacola Florida also got a double-dose of the blessing. Senior pastor John Kilpatrick's wife brought it from the Toronto Airport Christian Fellowship.[265] Evangelist Steve Hill received his "anointing" while attending the Holy Trinity Brompton church in London, England and then brought it to Florida.[266] Now the Pensacola Assemblies of God church promotes a variation of the Toronto Blessing called "the river of God."[267]

The Anointing

The New Wine Movement and the new "anointing" go hand in hand. When you "catch the fire" you get "it." Nearly everyone who has received this experience has his own personal story. The following is an account given by John Arnott, senior pastor of the Toronto Airport Christian Fellowship:

> We heard about the revival in Argentina so we traveled there in November of 1993, hoping that God's anointing would rub off on us somehow. We were powerfully touched in a meeting led by Claudio Freidzon, a leader of the Assemblies of God in Argentina.[268]

According to Arnott, this "power encounter" occurred when Claudio Freidzon prayed and then touched John and Carol Arnott. John fell over and then stood up. At first he questioned whether or not this experience was his own flesh or from God.

---

[263] Rodney Howard-Browne, *Manifesting the Holy Ghost* (R.H.B. E.A Publications, 1992), 16.
[264] Ford, 54-59.
[265] Albert James Dagger, "Pensacola: Revival or Reveling?" *Media Spotlight,* June 1997, 2.
[266] Ibid., 1.
[267] Ford, 56.
[268] Arnott, 58.

Then something else happened. Freidzon asked John Arnott if he wanted the "anointing." As Arnott described:

> "Oh yes, I want *it* all right," I answered. "Then take *it!*" He slapped my outstretched hands. "I will. I will take *it*," I said. Something clicked in my heart at that moment. It was as though I heard the Lord say, "For goodness sake, will you take *this?* Take *it, it's* yours." And I received by faith.[269]

The Transferable Anointing

One of the central themes of the New Wine Movement is the idea that the Spirit of God is a transferable anointing. Once received, it is commonly believed, this anointing can be given away to others. Often the word *impartation* is used by those who believe they have this God-given ability to transfer the "anointing."

However, it can easily be documented that the concept of impartation is not new. During the late 1940's, this doctrine was promoted by an aberrant group of experience-focused Christians from North Battleford, Saskatchewan, Canada known as the Latter Rain Movement. This concept that certain individuals are capable of receiving and then imparting an anointing was one of the main reasons many church leaders declared the Latter Rain teachings heretical. While this and other Latter Rain teachings had a major impact throughout North America and some parts of Europe, strong opposition by Bible teachers who supported sound biblical doctrine, forced the "manifest sons of God" belief underground. Richard Riss, a staunch supporter of the Latter Rain Movement, writes about this in his book called *The Latter Rain.*[270]

At a General Council meeting held by the Assemblies of God in Seattle, Washington in the fall of 1949 a resolution was adopted disapproving the practices of what was termed "The New Order of the Latter Rain." A number of specific concerns

---

[269] Ibid [emphasis mine]

[270] Richard Riss, *The Latter Rain,* (Honeycomb Visual Productions, Ontario, 1987).

were listed in this document. Among these were "the overemphasis to the imparting, identifying, bestowing and confirming of gifts by laying on of hands and prophecy," and "the erroneous teaching that the Church is built upon the foundation of the present-day apostles and prophets." The official disapproval concluded by stating:

> For it be further resolved, that we recommend following those things which make for peace among us, and those doctrines and practices whereby we may edify one another, endeavoring to keep the unity of the Spirit until we all come into the reality of faith.[271]

Although the Assemblies of God General Council rebuked the New Order of Latter Rain in 1949, time has a way of deleting memories. Fifty years and a few generations later, it is apparent that things have changed. Impartations, the "transferable anointing" and the apostle and prophet movement all are right back in style. Only now, very few are concerned. While in the past, most evangelical Protestants would have considered such ideas heretical and the earmark of a cult, there is a large trend underway today that indicates many evangelicals are embracing a similar view.

A myriad of well-known Christian leaders are claiming that God is raising up an elite group of supernatural prophets and apostles, reminiscent of the claims of the Latter Rain Movement of the 1940s and '50s.[272] Called the Apostolic Movement or the New Apostolic Reformation, this mighty end-times army of God, consisting of saints who have been trained by specially commissioned apostles, has been called to establish the Kingdom of God here on planet earth, they say. Dr. Bill Hamon, a noted bishop, an apostle and a modern-day prophet has written a book on this

---

[271] Assemblies of God in the U.S.A., 23rd General Council Minutes, Seattle, WA, 1949, 26-27.

[272] For a comprehensive look at the history and doctrines of the Latter Rain Movement, refer to: Roger Oakland, *New Wine or Old Deception: A Biblical View of Experience Based Christianity,* (Word for Today, Costa Mesa, CA, 1995) and also, Roger Oakland, *When New Wine Makes a Man Divine: True Revival or Last Days Deception,* (Understand the Times, Santa Ana, CA 1997).

subject. *Apostles, Prophets and the Coming Moves of God: God's End-Time Plans for His Church and Planet Earth.* In the dedication of this book we read:

> May it be enlightening and enabling to all those who are called and chosen to co-labor with Christ in fulfilling the coming moves of God. It is for all those who are committed to making ready a people, preparing the way by restoring all things. This will enable Christ Jesus to be released from heaven to return for His Church and establish His kingdom over all the earth.[273]

The New Apostles

The apostle John Eckhardt, pastor and overseer of Crusaders Ministries in Chicago, has traveled throughout the U.S. and around the world imparting spiritual truths. He sees it as his job to be about the business of "perfecting the saints." He discusses his role in a chapter of the book, *The New Apostolic Churches*, compiled by C. Peter Wagner. Eckhardt states:

> It was never the will of God for the Church to go without the apostolic dimension. Because of tradition and unbelief, this dynamic did not continue from generation to generation. The good news is, though, that we are now living in times of restoration. We view ourselves as being a part of prophetic fulfillment.[274]

Eckhardt goes on to explain how vital this newly recognized office is to God's plan for the world in the last days:

> One of the first truths the Lord taught us is that the saints could not be fully perfected without the ministry of the apostle. The five ministry gifts given for equipping the saints (see Eph. 4:11) include apostles and prophets. It takes all five of

---

[273] Bill Hamon, *Apostles Prophets and the Coming Moves of God: God's End-Time Plans for His Church and Planet Earth*, (Destiny Image Publishers, Inc., Shippensbrug, PA, 1997), v.

[274] Apostle John Eckhardt, "Crusaders Church and International Ministries of Prophetic and Apostolic Churches," *The New Apostolic Churches*, C. Peter Wagner, editor, (Regal Books, Ventura, CA, 1998), 51.

> these ministry gifts operating in the church to properly mature God's people for the work of the ministry. When the apostle is absent, the saints will lack the apostolic character they need to fulfill the Great Commission.[275]

When most Christians hear the title "apostle" they most commonly think of the apostle Paul or Peter, pillars of the Christian faith. Leaders of the New Apostolic Reformation believe this title is bestowed upon some today based on such concepts as "calling," "revelation," and "gifting." They say that today's apostle has the responsibility to establish new churches, correct error and oversee other ministries. Dr. Bill Hamon adds to this description:

> The apostle has a revelatory anointing. Some major characteristics are great patience and manifestation of signs and wonders and miracles. We will know more and see greater manifestations concerning the apostle during the peak of the Apostolic Movement.[276]

And the Apostolic Movement is growing. With signs and wonders, and meetings characterized by prophetic utterances, these apostles and prophets are militant in urging others to leave behind the encumbrances of traditional Christianity and go where the Spirit takes them. Gathering at well-organized and well-attended conferences, they have a strategy for spreading their theology around the world.

Fire and Rain

The "Catch The Fire: The Release of the Apostolic and the Prophetic Conference" was held at the Harvest Rock Church in Pasadena, California, November 12-16, 1997, and hosted by Pastor Ché and Sue Ahn. According to the brochure that was sent out to announce these meetings, the host pastors have a heart for evangelism and "a vision to see a new generation

---

[275] Ibid., 47.
[276] Hamon, 279.

saved, empowered, trained, and released to the nations for the coming harvest."[277]

The roster of speakers over this five-day conference included Paul Cain, John Arnott, Gerald Coates, Rick Joyner, Mike Bickle and Frank Damazio. The brochure gave background information and several reasons why the conference was going to be held. It stated:

> Revival fires are burning in hot spots around America and the world. There is hardly a day that passes when our email lines do not report a new outbreak of God's power somewhere. The Church of Jesus Christ is uniting in unprecedented ways for global prayer, fasting, and world evangelism initiatives. The zeal of God is crushing His enemies and His people are bursting with millennial expectation that a great worldwide awakening, the dawning of a new era of a church full of the glory of God, and a blazing revelation of Jesus Christ.[278]

The brochure then offered an explanation for the "worldwide awakening" that is supposedly underway by stating:

> The Apostles and the Prophets, of whom the Book of Ephesians speaks, are arising as the foundation of the church, Jesus Christ Himself being the Chief Cornerstone. There used to be a day when little hope was offered for the fulfillment of the vision of the Ephesian Magna Carte of the Church. But God has spoken and a manifestation of true prophets and apostles will come forth to cause His church to reveal Christ in fullness to the world.[279]

The *Catch the Fire* brochure also presented a brief biography for each of the conference speakers. Regarding Paul Cain the brochure stated:

> With a life marked by the supernatural since he was in the womb, Paul Cain has been used of God since he was a boy; ful-

---

[277] *Catch The Fire,* Harvest Rock Church, Pasadena, CA, Aug. 1997, brochure.
[278] Ibid.
[279] Ibid.

> filling the call of his life to "preach the gospel as the apostle Paul of old." After an almost thirty year hiddenness with the Lord, Paul emerged in 1988 with a message of holiness and revival; proclaiming the gospel of the Lord Jesus Christ to unbelievers and calling the church back to the New Testament standards of purity and power. In 1992, the Lord began to use Paul to minister prophetically to both national and international leaders at the highest levels of government. He has since been invited to meet with the Heads of State from several nations.

Paul Cain's biography mentioned that his ministry had emerged from a "hiddenness" with the Lord for over thirty years. This "hiddenness" seems to correspond to a period of time in his life when he was also embarrassed. In a message called "The Latter Rain" that Cain delivered at the Toronto Airport Vineyard on May 28, 1995,[280] he mentioned that for a long time "he was embarrassed" to talk about the topic of "latter rain" in "certain evangelical circles." Apparently he is no longer embarrassed to talk about this latter rain doctrine since the new awakening made popular by the Toronto Blessing has been embraced worldwide.

Spread the Fire is the bimonthly newsletter published by the Toronto Airport Christian Fellowship. The purpose of this newsletter is to inform interested supporters of what God is doing through the Toronto Blessing. In the December 1996 issue, an article was written summarizing a Paul Cain prophecy called "From Appetizer to Main Course."[281]

The article in this issue updated supporters of the Toronto Blessing with a prophecy Paul Cain had recently given. Cain, a former associate of William Branham and a bold supporter of the questionable doctrines of the Latter Rain Movement, claimed that God had now given him some new insight regarding the

---

[280] Paul Cain, "The Latter Rain," transcription of message given at the Toronto Airport Vineyard, May 28, 1995.

[281] "From Appetizer to Main Course," *Spread The Fire*, December 1996, Volume 2 Issue 6, 5.

future of the Toronto Blessing. According to Cain another visitation in Toronto was in the making and the next thing of the "new thing" would soon be on its way. Quoting directly from the article:

> On September 14th the prophet, Paul Cain, delivered the following prophetic words to John and Carol Arnott according to the following main points. The Lord has initiated the Toronto Blessing, not man… He has refreshed His people in order to prepare them for the next level of visitation… We are now at the place of the Lord's threshing floor. The Toronto Blessing has gathered the wheat and the chaff during this visitation... God is preparing the wheat to go on to the next level.[282]

It's this "next level" or the "next wave" that so many supporters of experience-based Christianity are waiting for today. Cain and others believe that only those whom he calls the "wheat" will be able to go on to the "next level." As he stated in his prophecy: "Others (the chaff) will be blown away by the next wind, or fall. You are to lead the people on to the next level, from appetizer to main course… the days ahead should be employed for preparation for the next thing God will do."[283]

Church historians who have studied the Latter Rain Movement will immediately recall that this same kind of terminology was used once before. The "new level" or the "main course" that Cain is talking about is supposed to birth the "new breed" of Christian that Latter-Rainers believed would be manifested. In the '40s and '50s they were called the "overcomers" or the "manifested sons of God."

The elitist attitude that emerged from the "overcomer" and "manifested sons of God" doctrines during the Latter Rain Movement produced divisions within families and church splits. Is this what will happen when the New Wine Movement adds the "full meal deal" to the menu?

---

[282] Ibid.
[283] Ibid.

Test the Spirits

Even New Wine promoters like John Arnott preach and teach that spiritual experiences need to be tested biblically. But it is apparent that he is confused on this issue. It is easy to say that you stand upon the Word of God. But it is quite another thing to understand what the Word of God actually teaches. Again, consider John Arnott's own words:

> These questions need to be asked when evaluating a spiritual experience: Is this in the Word of God? Is something similar in the Word? Does the Word of God prohibit this? Is it within the character of God as revealed through the Bible? When we ask if something is biblical, we're really asking if it is from God, aren't we? We don't want to be deceived. And we have the Bible to show us who God is, what He is like and what kinds of things He does. So we evaluate things according to the Bible, as we should. Yet as we see the Spirit of God doing more and more, we may see some things that no chapter and verse in the Bible specifically describes. Why? God did not intend to describe every act He would ever do in the Bible.[284]

This statement by John Arnott is the typical defense made by New Wine promoters. I am convinced this brand of apologetics is based upon a desire to justify anything and everything in the name of God even though "it" cannot be found in the Word of God. It seems to me that it is very possible that genuine sincere Christians who follow this kind of teaching could easily be led astray. If we are not willing to be consistent about what we believe, then we will be inconsistent. Inconsistency can easily lead to apostasy. As Paul warned, apostasy is a key factor in preparing the way for the Antichrist.[285]

I am convinced that a spiritual delusion is presently underway in the name of Christ. The apostle Paul stated this would happen[286] and the current trend indicates that this is exactly

---

[284] Arnott, 61.

[285] 2 Thessalonians 2:3-12

[286] Ibid.

what is happening. And according to the Bible, if Christians are being deluded now, we can expect the delusion will intensify.

John Arnott, of course, would disagree. He stated: "When we first experienced the increase of the Holy Spirit's power, the Lord told us, 'I am going easy on you now so that when the real power shows up, you will not be terrified.'"[287]

Although Arnott and his colleagues believe they have heard the voice of the Lord, I am not so sure. Many voices are being heard today. Do we need to be reminded that there is another spirit, another gospel, and another christ?[288] Wouldn't it be wiser to be cautious knowing that strong delusion is predicted for the end of the age? To this John Arnott argues: "Comparatively speaking, we have not really seen anything yet. If we can't participate when the power is low, what are we going to do when the real power shows up? Realize that God is awesome, and don't be surprised if His power overwhelms you."[289]

The River of God

The "river of God" has been the central focus of the teachings that have emerged from the Brownsville Assemblies of God in Pensacola, Florida. According to a full-page advertisement in the December 1996 issue of *Charisma* magazine, over one million people have traveled to Pensacola to receive a "touch from God." Afterwards they return home and "spread the fire" to their own churches.[290]

The fire that is being transferred according to these enthusiasts does not come from a burning flame. The method of receiving the "fire" comes by letting "the river of God surround, uphold, refresh and at times overwhelm you."[291] The biblical basis for this new doctrine, supporters say, can be found in Ezekiel chapter 47. According to this interpretation of the Scriptures,

---

[287] Arnott, 82.
[288] 2 Corinthians 12:3-5
[289] Arnott.
[290] *Charisma*, Dec. 1996, 55.
[291] Ibid., 60.

Ezekiel saw a vision of a river that flowed from the temple of God. This river is supposed to be the river that is now flowing in churches where people are open to the "new thing" God is doing.

Portal in Pensacola

Renee DeLoriea is the editor of *Feast of Fire,* a magazine focused on revival, published by the Brownsville Assemblies of God Church. Her articles, reports and stories have appeared in numerous Christian publications around the world.[292] In her book *Portal in Pensacola,* she documents many of the events she personally experienced during what is commonly called the Pensacola Awakening.

DeLoriea, a student of revivals of the past, believes that God revealed to her in advance a great revival that was to take place in Pensacola. She sold all of her possessions, uprooted her family and moved to Florida. Her book is a firsthand account of what she believes is a miraculous move of God that is happening at the Brownsville Assemblies of God and around the world.[293]

In the first chapter of her book, "The Assembling of God's Last-Days Army," DeLoriea described what happened at the November 26, 1996, Pastors' Conference held at the Brownsville Assemblies of God Church. Over 2000 pastors and their spouses had gathered there from throughout the United States and around the world anticipating some kind of encounter with God. DeLoriea writes:

> At last, there seemed to be hope for a real move of God - the kind of move they dreamed about in history books and in Scripture. A portal, a grand opening in the heavens, had sovereignly opened over Pensacola, and the shekinah glory of God was streaming down upon His people like rays of brilliant sunshine piercing the clouds of an abating thunderstorm. The men and women of God seemed to be wondering if it might be

---

[292] Rene DeLoriea, *Portal in Pensacola,* (Revival Press, Shippensburg, PA, 1997), back cover.
[293] Ibid.

> possible that God would actually give them just a bit of the anointing they had heard God was pouring out at Brownsville.[294]

DeLoriea gave a detailed account of the message made by senior pastor John Kilpatrick at the Pastors' Conference. According to her, he opened his address by saying: "God has sovereignly decided to once again replenish the parched dry places of our hearts and lives. By His grace and mercy, He has sent in a river, and in that river is the glory, His manifest presence and the things of God that we, for such a long time, have longed for and cried for."[295]

Kilpatrick's comment is typical of many Christians today who are genuinely seeking to know God and the power of God in their lives. While enthusiasm and sincerity are important qualities of the Christian life, it is also important that believers always balance their feelings and emotions with the Word of God. However, as we have seen, there are many Christians today who place experience above the Word. Such a decision can lead down a path that actually leads away from God.

Pastor Kilpatrick's message seems to open a door to that very thing. Suggesting that participants of the conference would be experiencing God in a new and miraculous way, he further stated: "The anointing God has poured out here is a transferable anointing. God sees your hunger and thirst for Him. Your hunger and thirst is evidenced by the fact that you have made the pilgrimage here, and God will most assuredly fill you."[296]

Doctrinal Differences

Bible doctrine is based on the idea that a particular tenet of faith must be established by the support of the whole council of God. Scripture must always provide the basis for biblical doc-

---

294 Ibid., 4.
295 Ibid., 5.
296 Ibid.

trine. The Bible teaches that Scripture has been given by the inspiration of God.[297]

Today, there are many church leaders who are saying that Bible doctrine is not as important as we once thought. Holding firm to biblical doctrine can divide the body and hold back revival, some are saying. Others have claimed that not everything that God has ever done is in the Bible. It is important that we not judge the new things God is doing, some leaders of the New Wine Movement have said. Let God be God, and just go along with the flow.

Supporters of this brand of experience-based Christianity often use the Book of Acts to support their views that strange behavior and chaos occur in the church as God pours out His Spirit. For example, Dick Reuben, a regular speaker at the Brownsville Assemblies of God in Pensacola, Florida, has stated:

> If you read the book of Acts, you will discover some pretty strange and abnormal things going on. People looked on and marveled. Let me tell you, the church through the years, [has] become organized, and we've learned how to do church and we've depended on the hand of the flesh, and we've devised programs. But listen, when God shows up, it gets kind of chaotic. Did you know that?[298]

Then admonishing his critics and proposing a new doctrine based on what the Bible does *not* say, Reuben continued:

> You say, "Well I don't see some of this happening in the book of Acts." Listen – the Holy Spirit couldn't put everything that He did in the book of Acts. If God did everything - if He reported everything He did on the day of Pentecost in the Bible, you'd have to have a wheelbarrow just to carry Acts 2 around. And so God didn't put everything in the Bible that happened![299]

---

[297] 2 Timothy 3:16
[298] Dagger, 18.
[299] Ibid.

So how about this new doctrine that has been designed to justify strange behavior in the church? Is it biblically accurate to teach that new doctrines can be fabricated to justify our feelings and beliefs? What about the Berean style of Bible study mentioned in the Book of Acts? Why did Luke commend them for their diligence to check out the Scriptures daily to see that Paul was not feeding them a line?[300]

Of course it would take a wheelbarrow to carry around the Book of Acts if everything that God did on the day of Pentecost was recorded. But God only inspired Luke to write down all that He wanted us to know. The Bible indicates that Christians should be more concerned about what the Bible teaches, rather than what the Bible does not teach. However, as we have been able to document in this chapter, the very opposite is happening within the New Wine Movement. God's Word is not only being ignored, it is being completely reinterpreted to justify the signs and wonders that are touted as a necessary prerequisite for revival.

We have looked at some of the extrabiblical doctrines that are a part of the New Wine theology. In the next chapter we will examine some of the supposedly new experiences that are attracting the sincere, the curious and the skeptical to the movement.

---

[300] Acts 17:11

14

IMBIBE THE NEW WINE

Something is definitely happening to the body of Christ. Although followers of Jesus have always been open to new movements, the current trend is quite unique. A global phenomenon is underway. People worldwide are experiencing the same kinds of things. The communication network provided by satellite television and the Internet now make it possible for everyone to be members in our global spiritual village.

The general consensus is that something big is just around the corner. When it comes to making predictions about the future based on the current trends, there are many who are willing to stake their claims. For example, consider the December 1999 issue of *Charisma* magazine where author Robert Stearns writes: "As we move into the new millennium, we must renounce old religious ideas and embrace the Holy Spirit's new strategies."[301]

Robert Stearns is not alone in his assessment. Standard theology and sound doctrine once widely accepted, is now considered by many to be too narrow and culturally unacceptable for the Christian Church of the third millennium.

The Bible teaches, however, that God's Word never changes. If this is the case, then how can Bible believers adapt to this teaching that we are in the midst of a spiritual awakening and

---

[301] Robert Stearns, "A Church for the 21st Century", *Charisma*, December 1999, 47.

that stale religion must be replaced by a vibrant faith? What is this vibrant faith all about? Is it a biblical faith or is it a faith that can be understood in light of the Bible?

According to Robert Stearns this is the time for mankind to get on with God's program for the 21st century. He writes:

> But I believe this generation will rise up with new anointing and authority in the creative domain. It will bring forth anointed sounds and sights that will glorify God and draw men to Jesus. Casting off restraints of the spirit of religion, a torrent of creative power will break through the dam of fear and brittle dryness. Let dancers dance! Let singers sing! Let the writers write! Let the artisans create! Be released! We must allow the yearning of our hearts to express love and adoration for Him. We cannot be restrained any longer.[302]

Holy Laughter

I will never forget my first impression of the so-called gift of holy laughter. Surfing through the cable channels, my attention was drawn to a program that was being broadcast over the Trinity Broadcasting Network. A very large man was speaking. The people who were in a church service were laughing hysterically and uncontrollably. He seemed to be enjoying himself. He told the people not to pray. Instead, he said they should let laughter "bubble up" from their bellies. He kept yelling, "more Lord, more Lord, more Lord."

At first I thought this must be someone making fun of Christianity. However the more I watched, it became apparent that this self-proclaimed "Holy Spirit Bartender" was serious about what he was doing. Later I discovered the man's name was Rodney Howard-Browne. He had come to the United States from South Africa. Apparently God had told him that he was to light the fires for revival.

A few weeks later I was in Australia participating in a speaking tour that included Sydney, Adelaide and Perth. Just

---

302 Ibid., 50.

before my arrival, Howard-Browne had toured the country. A number of people who attended several of the churches where I had been invited to speak told me Australia was in the midst of revival. But this revival they were talking about was focused on manifestations such as laughing, shaking and twitching. They didn't seem too excited about coming to know Jesus as their Savior.

Near the end of this trip, I had a day off to spend some time resting at the beach in Perth. While I was sitting there contemplating what I had been observing something happened that had an impact on my thinking. I noticed a family throwing scraps of bread up in the air for sea gulls to eat. The gulls had voracious appetites.

A man who was sitting nearby was also watching the gulls. He took his Styrofoam coffee cup, crumpled it up in his hand, and tossed the pieces up in the air. A number of the gulls left the people who were feeding them with the pieces of bread and went for the Styrofoam chunks.

In a moment, God spoke to my heart. The illustration powerfully confirmed my thoughts about what is happening and what will continue to happen in the body of Christ. Christians are putting aside the pure Word of God that is our spiritual bread and instead are gravitating toward the new and sensational to the detriment of their own spiritual health.

Upon returning to America, my thoughts were consumed with this trend that seemed so clearly underway. For the next year it seemed as though God was leading me on a journey. I made more observations, not only in the United States and Canada but also around the world. In June of 1995 I had the opportunity to be in Toronto and make observations at the Toronto Airport Vineyard (now called Toronto Airport Christian Fellowship). While there I purchased several videotapes promoting the usual manifestations that were occurring in Toronto under the pastoral leadership of John Arnott.

About one month later, on my way back from Russia to the United States, I spent several days in the United Kingdom. One of the churches I visited was a Baptist church in the London suburb of Wimbledon. It was there that I talked with church leaders who said they were capable of giving "it" away. I was told that this was a "transferable anointing." In other words, once you got "it" you could give "it" away.

After returning to my home base in California I completed my first book on experience-based Christianity called *New Wine or Old Deception?* My heart was troubled because of what I had observed. I was appalled by what people were embracing in the name of Christ. And I was shocked to discover that many church leaders I knew and respected were not only embracing unbiblical manifestations as evidence of the Holy Spirit, they were promoting the idea that God was doing something new.

One day, as I was reading through the Book of Ezekiel, God spoke to me clearly through His Word. Ezekiel had been appointed to be a watchman to warn his people about embracing ideas that would lead them astray. I sensed God was warning His church about the very same thing. Although Ezekiel knew there was a cost for proclaiming the truth, he proclaimed the truth anyway.

Drunk in the Holy Ghost

Seattle, Washington is one of the numerous locations where the New Wine Renewal Movement has had an impact. According to *Charisma* July 1997 issue, spiritual renewal has swept Seattle, bringing a newfound emphasis on unity among churches and pastors.[303] Evidence of this "new unity" is found at the Seattle Revival Center where three suburban churches hold joint weekend meetings. In two years of what has been called ongoing revival services, the church has seen thousands of visitors leave with a "fresh anointing" and a "renewed passion for Christ," the *Charisma* article stated.[304]

---

303 Brian O'Connell and Jeff King, "Renewal Movement Sweeps Seattle," *Charisma*, April 1997, 31.
304 Ibid.

The three pastors who pioneered the Seattle Revival Center claimed they each received a fresh infusion of faith when they visited the Toronto Airport Christian Fellowship church in Toronto, Canada. Before making their spiritual pilgrimages to Toronto, they had been in competition with each other. But the Toronto experience was a major turning point for all of them. As one of the pastors said, "We got drunk in the Holy Ghost. We were blitzed from the outside with such power." Before going to Toronto this same pastor had considered abandoning the ministry due to burnout. Since the Toronto visit, he said he had been "drunk in the Holy Spirit for 2 1/2 years."[305]

All three founding pastors of the Seattle Revival Center were "convinced that holding renewal meetings is God's plan to push down denominational walls and allow [them] to work together to reach [their] city."[306] One pastor stated he believed revival was about to explode. Since January of 1997, the "anointing seems to be increasing," he said.[307]

Throughout the world today, there are a number of "new wine drinking holes" similar to the Seattle Revival Center. All seem to be characterized by this strange anointing that is associated with what is called being "drunk in the Spirit." While supporters of this experience say this kind of behavior is from God, there is biblical evidence to the contrary.

In Jeremiah we read about God's warning of coming judgment to the children of Israel because they had not observed His word:

> And I will make drunk Her princes and wise men, her governors, her deputies, and her mighty men. And they shall sleep a perpetual sleep and not awake, says the King, whose name is the LORD of hosts. Thus says the LORD of hosts: The broad walls of Babylon shall be utterly broken, and her high gates

---

[305] Ibid.
[306] Ibid., 32.
[307] Ibid.

> shall be burned with fire; the people will labor in vain, and the nations, because of the fire; and they shall be weary.[308]

The New Wine Drinking Song

Richard and Kathryn Riss are faculty members at Zarephath Bible Institute located in New Jersey. Prior to joining Zarephath Bible College both Richard and Kathryn taught at Chicago Bible College and at Christian Life College in Mt. Prospect, Illinois. Richard is the author of five books and has contributed over thirty articles to three different encyclopedias, including the *Zondervan Dictionary of Pentecostal and Charismatic Movements.* Kathryn did her undergraduate work at UCLA and completed her Master of Divinity at Trinity Evangelical Divinity School in Deerfield, Illinois.[309]

Richard and Kathryn are both enthusiastic supporters of the idea that a worldwide last days revival is presently underway. They believe God is "blessing" Christians with unusual experiences that can be interpreted as manifestations of the power of God. They believe these experiences which commonly occur as part of the New Wine Movement, prove that God is pouring out His Spirit in the last days as prophesied by the Prophet Joel.

Awakening List, a newsletter for new wine supporters is available on the Internet. The purpose of this ongoing electronic update is to keep subscribers informed on the New Wine Movement as it grows around the world. On April 19, 1997, Kathryn Riss posted a song she had written called "The Drinking Song." In a letter addressed to "Dear Winos," Kathryn stated:

> I am not a songwriter, neither the son of a songwriter, but the Lord gave me a "New Winos Drinking Song Number One." The verses sound like the verses for "When the Roll," except that instead of holding out the last note you continue

---

[308] Jeremiah 51:37-39

[309] Bio for Richard and Kathryn Riss, Online posting, www.grmi.org/renewal/Richard_Riss/bio, April 2000.

the bouncy rhythm and do a little turn to fit in the words. It's easy![310]

Kathryn Riss gave permission in her letter for her song to be duplicated and widely distributed. She stated: "I told the Lord if He ever gave me any music, I would give it away."[311] However, Kathryn Riss stipulated the following rules for the public release of her song: "Everybody sing it as much as you want and get as drunk as you can! Pass it on to as many other New Winos as you want. Post any new verses you make up to the New Wine List, so we can all enjoy them. Give God ALL the glory, and DON'T MERCHANDISE IT. Just give it away![312] The following are the words to the "New Wine Drinking Song":

If you feel too serious and kind of blue,
I've got a suggestion, just the thing for you!
It's a little unconventional, but so much fun,
That you won't even mind when people think you're dumb!

Just come to the party God is throwing right now,
We can all lighten up and show the pagans how
Christians have more fun and keep everyone guessing
Since the Holy Ghost sent us the Toronto blessing!

I used to think life was serious stuff;
I didn't dare cry, so I acted kind of tough
'Til the Spirit of God put laughter in my soul,
Now the Holy Ghost's got me, and I'm out of control!

Now I'm just a party animal grazing at God's trough,
I'm a Jesus junkie, and I can't get enough!
I'm an alcoholic for that great New Wine,
'Cause the Holy Ghost is pouring, and I'm drinking all the time!

Now I roar like a lioness who's on the prowl,
I laugh and shake, maybe hoot like an owl!

---

310 "Kathryn's Drinking Song," April 19, 1997, owner-awakening@list.listserver.com

311 Ibid.

312 Ibid.

Since God's Holy River started bubbling up in me,
It spills outside, and it's setting me free!

I laugh like an idiot and bark like a dog,
If I don't sober up, I'll hop like a frog!
And I'll crow like a rooster 'til the break of day,
'Cause the Holy Ghost is moving, and I can't stay away!

So, I'll crunch and I'll dip and I'll dance round and round,
'Cause the pew was fine, but it's more fun on the ground!
So I'll jump like a pogo stick, then fall on the floor,
'Cause the Holy Ghost is moving, and I just want MORE![313]

Although some may argue that the "New Wine Drinking Song" should not be taken seriously, I believe the nature of the New Wine Movement demands that we examine the song seriously in light of Bible prophecy. Although the words Kathryn Riss has chosen to describe how people behave when they have tasted of the "new wine" may sound bizarre to some, what she has written is not an exaggeration. Her song provides an accurate description of what is happening to people in many churches, conferences and revival services as they are being asked to "let go" and "let God."

Barnyard Behavior

Mona Johnian is a supporter of the New Wine Movement and the author of several books including *Fresh Anointing* and *Revival 2000*. In her third book called *Signs and Wonders*, Mona Johnian relates that besides uncontrollable laughter and exhibitions of drunkenness, sometimes people will respond to a "touch of God" by crawling around on the floor and behaving like some animal. She describes one such example:

> On New Year's Day, 1995, which happened to fall on Sunday, we were in great worship when one of our members got down on her hands and knees and began to crawl among the worshipers who were standing around the altar. As she went

[313] Ibid., 2.

near each of the people, she began to purr like a cat. Some people stood still, some snickered, some pulled away. After this demonstration of God's love, the woman stood and said, *"The Spirit of God is being poured out upon the Church – most people do not know how to respond. Some are standing, some are snickering, some are pulling away. But God is calling us to enter in, to flow with what He wills to do in this hour."*

Another member of the congregation followed the prophetic word with this understanding. *"The cats that meow will now become the lions that roar!"* Some contend that such manifestations are foolishness. They often will remark, "What is spiritual about roaring like a lion?" Roaring like a lion is a sign from God. It has occurred in various Christian denominations in England, Canada and the United States, since the new outpouring of the Holy Spirit began in 1993. As one of many signs, it is teaching us truths from the Scriptures about the day in which we live.[314]

John Arnott, the senior pastor of the Toronto Airport Christian Fellowship has fully endorsed animal behavior as part of regular church services. In his book, *The Father's Blessing,* Arnott stated:

It is no coincidence that we have seen people prophetically acting like lions, oxen, eagles and even warriors. In Steve Witt's church in St. John's New Brunswick, I saw all four of those manifestations happening at the same time – the ox, the eagle, the lion, and the man (warrior)... The people who were doing this were mostly credible pastors or leaders. I was astonished but sensed the awesome presence of God.[315]

Yes, many pastors and church leaders have succumbed to these "astonishing manifestations of the presence of God." Some

---

[314] Mona Johnian, *Signs and Wonders: Amazing Evidence as the Boston Revival Gains Momentum,* (Superior Books, Woburn, MA, 1995), 66 .

[315] John Arnott, *The Father's Blessing,* (Creation House, Lake Mary, FL, 1995), 178.

attended the meetings initially as skeptics but were won over when it happened to them.

Coming to Believe in "It"

Che Ahn is the senior pastor of Harvest Rock Church in Pasadena, California, a multiethnic church that has been hosting renewal meetings since 1995. Ahn is also founder and president of Harvest International Ministries, a worldwide network of more than 140 churches and ministries with a common goal to fulfill the Great Commission.[316]

Pastor Ahn has written a book titled *Into The Fire.* This book gives an extensive overview of the historical aspect of the New Wine Movement as well as insight into the direction this movement will be headed in the future. In the introduction of the book a long list of endorsements by a number of well-known leaders of the New Wine Movement is included. The first endorsement is given by Mike Bickle, pastor of Metro Christian Fellowship, Kansas City, Missouri who said: "Che Ahn is a voice God has raised up in this hour to help bring together the diversity of God's bride across the face of the earth."[317]

While often participants and proponents of the New Wine Movement will admit they were initially skeptical about certain aspects of the movement, it is quite common for them to change their opinion after they have had a personal encounter with what they believe is the Holy Spirit. Che Ahn described in detail what happened to him while attending the 1994 Vineyard Annual Conference. He stated:

> Lou Engle and I had registered for the conference and had no clue that a fresh revival was beginning in the Vineyard movement. That quickly changed the first day of the conference as we saw with our own eyes the Holy Spirit falling on people producing unusual manifestations of laughter, shaking and other loud cries and noises. Initially, I was cynical about what was occurring. I had read about Rodney Howard-Browne

[316] Che Ahn, *Into The Fire,* (Renew, Ventura, CA, 1998), book cover.
[317] Ibid., 1.

> and "holy laughter" in *Charisma* magazine, but had never experienced it. I thought the people were laughing through mass suggestion and hysteria and not through a genuine move of the Holy Spirit. One day during the conference, however, people seated in separate sections of the auditorium all laughed at one time as the Holy Spirit swept through the hall like a fresh wind.[318]

Che Ahn's description of what happened to him at this point is very intriguing. He was transformed from a skeptic to a believer in a moment. He continued by saying:

> My friend Lou poked me with his elbow and excitedly yelled, "It's coming toward us!" I remember saying, "Well, I'm not going to laugh." When the Holy Spirit hit our section, though, I felt myself becoming inebriated. I could not stop laughing. It lasted at least 20 minutes. Everything was funny... even though no one was saying anything funny. A bald man was sitting in front of me, and for whatever reason, his bald head looked funny to me. I leaned over and began to message his head. He didn't care; he was laughing too. It was a wonderful refreshing experience that seemed to invigorate every part of my being. I didn't notice until later that my depression was gone.[319]

Che Ahn's comment regarding his deliverance from depression is quite common among those who have encountered the various manifestations related to the New Wine Movement. For example, John Arnott has also made statements that confirm this. He has stated: "We had been praying for God to move, and our assumption was that we would see more people saved and healed, along with the excitement that this would generate. It never occurred to us that God would throw a massive party where people would laugh, roll, cry and become so empowered that emotional hurts from childhood were just lifted off of them.

---

[318] Ibid., 36.
[319] Ibid.

The phenomena may be strange, but the fruit this is producing is extremely good."[320]

How To Get "It"

Everyone who has experienced the manifestations associated with the New Wine Movement has a testimony about the experience. Some say they were skeptical before the "anointing" happened. Others were "burned out," ready to give up on ministry or even Christianity. Then others say they were just seeking more of God.

Ken Gott and his wife Lois founded Sunderland Christian Center in Sunderland, England, and also Revival Now! International Ministries. Their vision is to reap the harvest around the world, and plant and financially support churches that reach out to the poor and needy. In addition the Gotts have formed S.T.O.R.M. teams (short-term outreach missions) that go into Eastern Europe and Third World countries.[321]

Ken Gott, a Pentecostal Assemblies of God preacher, has written a book called *Anointed or Annoying: Searching for the Truth of Revival.* In his book he describes in vivid detail three separate encounters with what he believed was the Holy Spirit. Each of these experiences provides interesting insight into the New Wine Movement.

The first encounter describes what happened to Ken and his wife Lois when they visited the Toronto Airport Christian Fellowship during the summer of 1994. He wrote:

> When John Arnott of Toronto Airport Christian Fellowship said, "I'd like to pray for you," my response was, "Well, that would be wonderful." And I gently pushed my wife, Lois, in front of me. As he prayed for her, I watched Lois do things I'd never, ever, seen her do before. Although no one was touching her, she bounced up and down like a puppet on a string until she finally collapsed in a heap on the floor. "Has she ever done

---

[320] Arnott, 59.

[321] Ken Gott, *Anointed or Annoying: Searching for the Fruit of Revival,* (Revival Press, Shippensburg, PA, 1998), back cover.

> this before?" John asked. I just shook my head and said, "No she has never done *that* before."[322]

Then Pastor Gott explained what happened when John Arnott prayed for him. He was overcome by a spiritual experience he believed was a vision. He saw fires in clusters all over England with his hometown of Sunderland right in the middle. Then he gave the following account of what happened to his physical body:

> Then it seemed as though I felt the Lord put His hands inside me and pull. I know it sounds odd, but I literally felt like my spirit man was being *stretched* by God. I bent over at the waist with my arms extended out to the side in an exaggerated way – I'd never done anything like that in my life. Then I moaned with a loud voice, "O-h-h-h-h, o-h-h-h-h."[323]

The second supernatural encounter described by Gott occurred while attending a meeting at an Anglican church in London, England. In June of 1994, a few weeks before Ken and Lois had gone to Toronto, a friend invited him to attend a meeting at Holy Trinity Brompton. At first, the offer was rejected. As he stated in his book:

> An Anglican church in London was the last place I ever wanted to be. After all, I was a dyed-in-the-wool Pentecostal Assemblies of God man. Pridefully I wondered, *What could the Anglicans know about the Holy Spirit? After all, aren't we Pentecostals the ones who "own" the Holy Spirit? We know our doctrine don't we? Weren't we the ones who tarried for the baptism of the Holy Spirit when everyone else wanted to bury it? Weren't we the ones who got out there on a limb? We embraced the "full gospel" and went through all the bad times of ridicule and persecution, but now that it is "respectable" it seems like everybody wants to jump on the bandwagon.*[324]

---

[322] Ibid., 1.
[323] Ibid., 2.
[324] Ibid., 8. [italics in the original]

Gott said he did not want to go at first, but he eventually went as the result of what he called a "Holy Ghost setup." Although initially he was quite reluctant to participate in the Holy Trinity Brompton pastors' meeting, his attitude suddenly changed. In his own words:

> Once we got through the Vineyard music, Bishop David Pytches, the vicar of St. Andrews Anglican Church in Chorleywood, told us what would happen when the Holy Spirit came upon us. (That really irked me. We knew what would happen! We would speak in tongues, for goodness' sake.) He said, "Some of you may laugh, and some may fall on the floor. Some of you will find yourselves doing all kinds of things that you have never done before."[325]

Gott further described his reluctance to being led by an Anglican bishop, holding back because of what he calls his "Pentecostal pride." But eventually he gave in. Then two seconds after Bishop Pytches prayed "Father, come and get them. Come and get them," something amazing happened. Gott explained:

> I spent the next one and a half hours on my back, under the font of an Anglican church with my Pentecostal friends. It was like the Holy Spirit had dropped a bomb in the middle of our circle. Not only were we on our backs, we managed to shed every shred of dignity! We were laughing uncontrollably. We were getting absolutely falling-down drunk. One time I looked up to see the baptismal font overhead and I started laughing. *I don't even believe in that!* I thought, and laughed all the more.[326]

The third encounter described by Gott occurred when he went "looking for a fire at a conference."[327] This occurred at a Reinhard Bonnke signs and wonders meeting held at Frankfurt, Germany when Benny Hinn took his turn on the platform. Just like the previous two encounters, Ken Gott explained how he was at first reluctant to subject himself to the "transferable

[325] Ibid., 9-10.
[326] Ibid., 11-12.
[327] Ibid., 75.

anointing." Although he was especially annoyed with Hinn's style of prolonged repetitive worship, when Hinn called for the British pastors in the audience to come forward, he was overcome with an enthusiastic response. He stated:

> You wouldn't believe what happened the minute he said it. English pastors ran to the platform from every part of that building! They ran from the top corner, and from the left and the right. They even ran over the chairs like idiots in a mad rush to get to the front. And I beat the lot of them.[328]

Then something amazing happened. According to Gott:

> Since I got there first, I took my position in the corner of the platform. My eyes were closed in good Pentecostal fashion, but I could hear Benny Hinn saying to the men as he passed them, "Take it, take it, take it, take it." And I was thinking, *I'm offended, I'm offended, I'm offended, I'm offended. I'm offended.* Suddenly everything became quiet for some reason. There wasn't a sound in the place. Then I heard Benny say, "Young man." I opened my eyes and noticed with a shock that he was looking right at me and standing about ten yards away. "Are you an English pastor?" he asked. "Yes I am," I replied.[329]

It was at this point in the encounter that something happened to Ken Gott. In his book he stated that he felt something that he had never felt before. As he approached Benny Hinn he was hit by what he called a "field of anointing" that measured about one meter off the floor. As he approached Hinn the power became stronger and he started "vibrating like a leaf." Then Hinn said to Gott: "Take it. Take it."

Ken Gott then fell down on the floor. He stated: "I was standing up, but when I fell down, I was 'baptized' in it."[330] Then the following explanation of an additional experience:

---

[328] Ibid.

[329] Ibid., 78-79.

[330] Ibid., 79.

> Benny Hinn captured my attention all over again when he said, "Okay, pick him up again." There were some large well-built men standing on each side of me, and they moved closer as Benny did exactly what I hoped he wouldn't – he blew right in my face. I was about to get really offended, but Benny's breath just went all over my body and I fell down again! It got worse. I heard him tell the muscular men towering over me, "Pick him up again." By this time I was shaking like a leaf, my hair was on end, and I was vibrating under the power of God. He looked right at me and said "Young man, from this moment on you will never be the same again. Take it." And I fell down for the count. [331]

Signs and Wonders

Monia Johnian, in her book *Signs and Wonders* has stated: "As we approach the turn of another century, and the beginning of a brand new millennium, our hearts rise in anticipation of the signs and wonders God is preparing to give to his people," [332] As an apologist for the Signs and Wonders Movement, Johnian is not willing to accept constructive criticism. She has written:

> Some warn us, "You are going to get carried off-base with these signs." This cannot happen however, because true signs are the voice of God – this new word to His people. For far too long, God's people have been robbed. As soon as God begins to do something extraordinary in the Church, people who are locked up into old forms and traditions will begin to spray their words like weed-killers by saying, "It may be God, but you do not want to get carried away by signs." My response to these well-meaning folks is to point out the fact that these signs from God represent the voice of God. Therefore, I surely want to get carried along with the voice of God. [333]

So how should we evaluate a statement like this? Should we ignore it saying, "let's just agree to disagree?" Or should we ex-

331 Ibid.
332 Johnian, xiv.
333 Ibid., 8.

amine the statement in light of the full council of God? What about the idea that it is possible to get carried off base with signs and wonders? What if the "signs" people are seeking after are like weeds? Weeds left uncontrolled will become uncontrollable. What it someone really believes they have heard the voice of God but it was actually the voice of the "god of this world"?

As has been already pointed out in this book, there will be signs and wonders in the last days that will be deceiving. With this in mind, consider another statement that Mona Johnian makes in her book:

> The Word, in fact tells us that signs will increase as the day of restitution draws near. Instead of exercising a poor attitude toward signs, Jesus sternly rebuked the religious people for failing to "discern the signs of the times" (Matt. 16:3). Hypocrites can discern what is going on in the world, but they cannot discern what is going on in the Church. We should be careful about speaking against the signs of God because such speaking can easily turn into blasphemy. If, in sincerity, we cannot discern the signs and moves of the Holy Spirit, then we should get on our knees and ask God to open our eyes of our understanding. If God is speaking and I do not hear His voice, something is wrong with me, not the signs.[334]

This statement by Mona Johnian is typical of the New Wine Movement. On numerous occasions I have been rebuked by these same words that have come from other sincere Christian leaders who have told me that I have blasphemed the Holy Spirit. I do not take their accusations lightly. I do not want to spend eternity in hell, as some are saying that I will. What if my Christian brothers and sisters are embracing something they believe is from the Holy Spirit when it is not? What if they are playing a role in deceiving others?

[334] Ibid., 10.

The Berean Call

Christians who say they believe in Jesus do not always take the words attributed to Jesus as seriously as they should. For example, consider Jesus' statement as recorded in the Book of John: "If you abide in Me, and My words abide in you, you will ask what you desire, and it shall be done for you. By this My Father is glorified, that you bear much fruit; so you will be My disciples."[335] It is apparent from Scripture that to be a follower of Jesus it is important to pay attention to His Word. In the Book of Acts, Luke commended the Bereans who diligently checked out Paul's teachings to see if they corresponded to Scripture.[336]

This principal that is so clearly laid out in the Bible apparently is not well understood by many that promote the New Wine theology. John Arnott, in his book *The Father's Blessing* claims that we should place no limits on what he believes are manifestations of the Holy Spirit. He states:

> Some have argued that people who laugh and shake, unable to stop, are "out of control"; therefore, they say, it cannot be from God. But the scripture in Galatians is referring to the fruit of the Holy Spirit in a person's life – the results of an encounter with God, not the encounter itself.[337]

John Arnott and others seem to be convinced that God is pouring out His Holy Spirit upon people, even though there is no biblical precedent to support the behavior they claim is a gift from God. The Bible still demands that we always check things out. Although New Wine seekers are sincere, there are no guarantees that sincerity will prevent people from being deceived. But to this line of reasoning John Arnott states:

> It is amazing how the fear of deception will short-circuit the faith of many who desperately need a fresh touch from heaven. Attributing the works of the Holy Spirit to Satan is a very serious offense... God loves us, is faithful, and He will not

---

[335] John 15:7-8
[336] Acts 17:11
[337] Arnott, 106.

> give something false to us. We have to come to Him in faith. We are not coming expecting a counterfeit. We are not coming expecting to be deceived. We are coming to God and expecting to receive more of the Holy Spirit![338]

In the next chapter we will further examine the manifestations that so many are saying can be attributed to the Holy Spirit. Indeed, as John Arnott states, it is a serious offense to blaspheme the Holy Spirit. But there is also another side to this issue that needs to be examined. What if people are attributing behavior to the Holy Spirit when it really is not the Holy Spirit? Is it possible people could be deceived and then as a result spend eternity in hell?

---

[338] Ibid. 112-113.

15

THE SERPENT POWER

In the sixteenth chapter of the Book of Proverbs, Solomon declared a very important biblical principle that should be foundational to everyone who proclaims to be a follower of Christ. He stated: "Commit thy works unto the LORD and thy thoughts shall be established."[339] Ever since becoming a believer I have been on a spiritual journey. It has been clear to me there has been a path that I have been called to follow. Not always have I stayed on the path. There have been some tough times, a few deep valleys.

This journey has led me on a search for the truth. While this search has been driven by a passion for the love of the Word of God, God has also given me a heart for the deceived. All of us are deceived to some extent. The Bible states that "the heart is deceitful above all things, and desperately wicked; Who can know it?"[340]

For the first fifteen years of my ministry it was apparent that my calling was to build up Christians in the faith so they could reach out and share the gospel with others. My desire to promote biblical truth was directed in an evangelistic way. Strong sheep have the potential to reach the lost sheep, I thought.

---

[339] Proverbs 16:3

[340] Jeremiah 17:9

But then a number of events and circumstances caused me to look at my calling from another perspective. Wherever I traveled I could see that Christianity was being seduced and undermined. Christianity was fast becoming a faith based upon extrabiblical ideas and experiences. It seemed like an epidemic was underway. Individuals, churches and organizations, although Christian by name, were not always Bible based. In fact the trend that was developing seemed to be in line with what the Bible predicted would occur in the last days in relation to a great falling away.[341]

Although I knew other individuals and ministries that were playing the Berean role by calling Christians back to a Bible-based faith, I sensed God speaking to my own heart about the importance of being a watchman. Although I knew it would not be easy, I also knew that I did not have a choice. Christianity to me, since I had become a believer, was an all or nothing kind of faith. Our relationship with Jesus must be number one in our life. If Christians are compromising, then they must be warned.

Traveling The Globe

Over the past two decades, God has given me the opportunity to travel the world. Not only have I been able to see Christianity in action in numerous countries, I have also been able to see how unbiblical ideas and teachings have spread around the world like wildfire. Without planning any particular agenda I was placed in circumstances and situations that exposed me to a wide variety of ideas and beliefs that were being embraced in the name of Jesus. Whether in Australia, North America, South America, Russia, Eastern Europe, Western Europe, China, Japan, or the United Kingdom, my eyes were being opened. I could see that a spiritual awakening was definitely underway. However, the question that I needed to answer was – what was happening in light of a biblical perspective?

What is it that makes people laugh and shake uncontrollably when they are prayed for or touched on the head? What is going

---

[341] 2 Thessalonians 2:3

on when some claim they sense a burning feeling, groan with pain as if they are giving birth to a child or behave like some wild animal that has just been released from a cage? Although I searched the Scriptures I failed to see that there was any biblical basis for this kind of behavior as something that is caused by the Holy Spirit. While proponents of the New Wine Movement argued otherwise, I was fully convinced time would show they were wrong. Nowhere in the Bible could I find that Spirit-filled believers behave in this manner. Therefore I believed it was important to look for another explanation that might answer the question we have been pursuing in the previous chapters – what is this "it" so many are talking about? What is going on?

Nothing New

When I attended university, history was not one of my favorite subjects. In fact, rather than take history as a required class, I decided to take philosophy instead. Later in life when I became a Christian I regretted that I had not studied history. Now whenever I travel, I make every effort to find out about the history of each country. If you want to understand the present and the future it is important to check out the past.

The Bible is God's revelation to man, given to man, inspired by God. When you study the Bible from this view you will have God's perspective about history. Unfortunately for mankind, humans are not real keen about learning from this inspired "His story" book. Certainly the children of Israel were a perfect example of this. Even though God demonstrated His power to the chosen people, they just did not seem to get the message.

God said that if they were obedient to Him, He would bless them. But He also made it clear that if they were disobedient there would be serious consequences. For example in the Book of Deuteronomy we read:

> See, I have set before you today life and good, death and evil, in that I command you today to love the LORD your God, to walk in His ways, and to keep His commandments, His statutes, and His judgments, that you may live and multiply;

> and the LORD your God will bless you in the land which you go to possess. But if your heart turns away so that you do not hear, and are drawn away, and worship other gods and serve them, I announce to you today that you shall surely perish; you shall not prolong your days in the land which you cross over the Jordan to go in and possess. I call heaven and earth as witnesses today against you, that I have set before you life and death, blessing and cursing; therefore choose life, that both you and your descendants may live.[342]

A casual reading of the Bible will make it clear that God's chosen people chose disobedience rather than obedience. In the Book of Judges we read:

> Then the children of Israel did evil in the sight of the LORD, and served the Baals; and they forsook the LORD God of their fathers, who had brought them out of the land of Egypt; and they followed other gods from among the gods of the people who were all around them, and they bowed down to them; and they provoked the LORD to anger. They forsook the LORD and served Baal and the Ashtoreths. And the anger of the LORD was hot against Israel. So He delivered them into the hands of plunderers who despoiled them; and He sold them into the hands of their enemies all around, so that they could no longer stand before their enemies.[343]

In order to remind His people that their sin would bring about their destruction, God sent His prophets to warn His people. But the people did not want to listen to the prophets of God either. In fact as you read through the various Old Testament books, you will see that the children of Israel were more inclined to listen to the false prophets who were preaching a message contrary to the message of the prophets. The Book of Jeremiah was a perfect example of this. While the false prophets were predicting peace and safety for the future, Jeremiah was pleading that his countrymen would repent and turn back to God. In the eleventh chapter we read:

---

[342] Deuteronomy 30:15-19
[343] Judges 2:11-14

> And the LORD said to me, a conspiracy has been found among the men of Judah and among the inhabitants of Jerusalem. They have turned back to the iniquities of their forefathers who refused to hear My words, and they have gone after other gods to serve them; the house of Israel and the house of Judah have broken My covenant which I made with their fathers. Therefore thus says the LORD: Behold, I will surely bring calamity on them which they will not be able to escape; and though they cry out to Me, I will not listen to them. Then the cities of Judah and the inhabitants of Jerusalem will go and cry out to the gods to whom they offer incense, but they will not save them at all in the time of their trouble. For according to the number of your cities were your gods, O Judah; and according to the number of the streets of Jerusalem you have set up altars to that shameful thing, altars to burn incense to Baal. So do not pray for this people, or lift up a cry or prayer for them; for I will not hear them in the time that they cry out to Me because of their trouble.[344]

Although Jeremiah was a prophet that lived before Jesus Christ and his message was to the Jews and not to Christians, the same message applies to Bible professing Christians today. We need to pay attention to this biblical principle. Has there been a conspiracy found among us? Is the master deceiver still duping people today? Is it possible to believe that you are enlightened spiritually when in reality you are deceived? Again, we need to remind ourselves that no one is immune from Satan's devices. If the serpent has manipulated people in the past, then certainly it is not beyond him to do the same today.

Abide in Him

Education is the process by which our minds are programmed with information. As Christians, we have the advantage over those who do not believe that the Holy Spirit can guide and direct our thoughts according to the Word of God. The Bible teaches we are to take all our thoughts captive. In other words

---

[344] Jeremiah 11:9-14

we should always make choices that will draw us closer to God and avoid choices that will lead us away from a close relationship with God.

Satan the deceiver knows exactly how our minds work. He did not create us, but he is certainly intelligent enough to know how we can be manipulated. Since the fall of man, we live in a world where our flesh desires to be king. Although we may become new creations in Christ, we still have to battle the flesh. Paul wrote about this in the Book of Galatians. He stated:

> I say then: Walk in the Spirit, and you shall not fulfill the lust of the flesh. For the flesh lusts against the Spirit, and the Spirit against the flesh; and these are contrary to one another, so that you do not do the things that you wish. But if you are led by the Spirit, you are not under the law. Now the works of the flesh are evident, which are: adultery, fornication, uncleanness, lewdness, idolatry, sorcery, hatred, contentions, jealousies, outbursts of wrath, selfish ambitions, dissensions, heresies, envy, murders, drunkenness, revelries, and the like; of which I tell you beforehand, just as I also told you in time past, that those who practice such things will not inherit the kingdom of God. But the fruit of the Spirit is love, joy, peace, longsuffering, kindness, goodness, faithfulness, gentleness, self-control. Against such there is no law. And those who are Christ's have crucified the flesh with its passions and desires.[345]

Paul's list of the works of the flesh is familiar to us. As we read through this list we can see that the flesh is corrupt and carnal. Christians are supposed to crucify the flesh. However that is not completely possible. There is always a battle going on between the flesh and the spirit. In the Book of Romans Paul wrote: "For we know that the law is spiritual, but I am carnal, sold under sin. For what I am doing, I do not understand. For what I will to do, that I do not practice; but what I hate, that I do."[346]

---

[345] Galatians 5:16-24

[346] Romans 7:14-15

In the list from Galatians chapter five that depicts fallen human behavior, we recognize that Christians have the capability and the ability not only to be carnal, but also to participate in practices that are outright demonic. Some Christians may deny that this is possible, but it can be well documented this is the case.

Satan, the master deceiver, is the father of lies. Not only does he want people to spend eternity in hell, he wants them to be deceived in the name of the deliverer, Jesus Christ. The serpent's power to deceive should never be underestimated. Although Christians know that "greater is He that is in you than he who is in the world"[347] we still do not have the license to sin willingly. Christians must be obedient to the Word of God. As Jesus said:

> If anyone loves Me, he will keep My word; and My Father will love him, and We will come to him and make Our home with him. He who does not love Me does not keep My words; and the word which you hear is not Mine but the Father's who sent Me.[348]

From Christianity to Mysticism

We are experiencing the dawning of a New Age. As one New Age book states: "Many people are undergoing a profound personal transformation associated with a spiritual enlightenment. Under certain circumstances, this process results in emotional healing, a radical shift in values, and a profound awareness of the mystical dimension of existence."[349]

The Stormy Search for Self is a book written by Christina and Stanislav Grof, the world's foremost authorities on the subject of spiritual emergence. In the introduction of their book they state that they believe spiritual development is the innate evolutionary capacity of all human beings. The purpose for writing their

---

[347] 1 John 4:4

[348] John 14:23-24

[349] Christiana and Stanislav Grof, *The Stormy Search for the Self: A Guide to Personal Growth through Transformational Crisis*, (G.P Putman and Sons, New York, 1990), back cover.

book was to help people who are experiencing spiritual transformation to reach their full potential.[350]

Christina Grof grew up in Honolulu during the 1940s and the 1950s. She describes herself as a typical baby boomer who relied on conventional values, doing what was expected and remaining very much in control of her life. When she was ten, she attended an Episcopal church near her house and developed "a passion for Jesus." Two years later she was confirmed into the church. By her own words she describes herself as a dedicated committed Christian: "To me, Jesus was not some historical figure who lived two thousand years ago. His death and resurrection were vivid experiences in which I could participate. He was real, present and available to me here and now."[351]

However Christina's Christian story changes dramatically later in her life. According to her testimony, an interest in yoga led her to a guru from South India by the name of Swami Muktananda. This man claimed to have attained "self-realization and the ability to be what is called a *shaktipat* master – a person who is able, through a look, a touch, or a word, to awaken spiritual impulses and energies in people beginning in a process of spiritual development."[352]

Christina's meeting with Swami Muktananda at a retreat completely altered the course of her life. She states: "Although I knew little about Muktananda and his world, on the second day of the retreat (I) received *shaktipat* entirely unexpectedly. During a meditation period, he first looked at me and then with some force, slapped me several times on the forehead with his hand." Following this experience she described further what happened to her:

> Suddenly I felt as though I had been plugged into a high-voltage socket as I started to shake uncontrollably. My breathing fell into an automatic, rapid rhythm that seemed beyond my control, and a multitude of visions flooded my conscious-

---

[350] Ibid., 1.
[351] Ibid., 9.
[352] Ibid., 11.

> ness. I wept as I felt myself being born; I experienced death; I plunged into pain and ecstasy, strength and gentleness, love and fear, depths and heights. I was on an experiential roller coaster, and I knew I could no longer contain it. The genie was out of the bottle.[353]

This experience that is usually initiated by a person touching another person on the forehead is quite common among those who have encountered the touch of a spiritual master. Often when this power is transferred the recipient will fall over backwards. Lying flat on his back, the person will feel as if his life has been switched into rapid motion. He may describe a mystical sensation that provides him with an awareness of a deep connection with a new spirituality that fills his inner being with joy and peace. From that point on he is driven to pursue a spiritual journey. As well, once a recipient has received "shaktipat," this same person now has the ability to become a shaktipat master.

Christian Shaktipat?

When researching my first book on experience-based Christianity, *New Wine or Old Deception?*, I came across a book written by Rodney Howard-Browne. Pastor Rodney claims he has the ability to transfer what is called the gift of holy laughter and the gift of drunkenness to others. He received his ability to transfer this "anointing" after he had a power encounter with what he believes was God.

This "anointing" that Howard-Browne received, according to New Wine proponents is transferable. Once you get "it" you can give "it" to others. They believe that God has appointed certain men and women to be conduits for this new anointing. They also believe this power is presently being poured out all over planet earth to induce a great revival, they believe must take place before Jesus returns.

Howard-Browne, like many of the other leaders and promoters of this spiritual movement, claims he received this power

---

353 Ibid.

to administer the "anointing" when God personally appeared to him. In his own words he stated:

> It felt like liquid fire - like someone poured gasoline over me and set me on fire... the best way I can describe it is that it was as shocking as if I had unscrewed a light bulb from a lamp and put my finger into the socket. I knew it was of God.[354]

The gifts of holy laughter and the gifts of drunkenness that Rodney Howard-Browne and others have become so famous for distributing are only two of the many outward manifestations professed to be the evidence that God is pouring out a new wave of His Spirit as part of a worldwide revival before the return of Jesus. The uncontrollable and often hysterical laughter that is being experienced, it is said, is God's way of expressing His intimate love for us during this time.

From Atheism to Mysticism

Stanislav Grof is the husband of Christina Grof. He also has an interesting story that explains his journey from atheism to the world of spiritual enlightenment. Dr. Stanislav Grof's book titled *Realms of the Human Unconscious* is based on Dr. Grof's twenty years of research with LSD. He documents many of the same experiences his wife Christina encountered in her spiritual journey from Christianity to eastern mysticism.

Stanislav was born in Prague, Czechoslovakia in 1931. Brought up as an atheist, he became interested in psychology after reading Sigmund Freud's *Introductory Lectures on Psychoanalysis.* According to Grof, reading this book turned out to be one of the most influential experiences in his life. He was deeply impressed with what he calls "Freud's penetrating mind, his unrelenting logic, and his ability to bring rational understanding to such obscure areas such as symbolism and language of dreams."[355]

---

[354] Rodney Howard-Browne, *Manifesting The Holy Ghost,* (R.H.B.E. Publications, 1992), 16.
[355] Grof, 18.

In *The Stormy Search for the Self,* Stanislav Grof writes about his spiritual journey from an atheist to a mystic:

> In my childhood I was not exposed to religious programming of any kind. My parents had decided not to commit me and my younger brother to a specific church affiliation, wanting us to make our own choice when we came of age. Although I was intellectually interested in religions and Oriental philosophy, I was basically an atheist. Six years of study at the Charles University School of Medicine in Prague furthered strengthened my atheistic worldview. A materialistic orientation and mechanistic thinking are characteristic of Western medical training anywhere in the world. Furthermore, in Prague and other Eastern European countries at that time, the education system was dominated by Marxist ideology, which was particularly hostile to any departures from pure materialistic doctrine. Any concepts that would point in the direction of idealism and mysticism were either carefully screened from the curriculum or subjected to ridicule.[356]

During the late fifties Stanislav Grof worked as a medical researcher with the hallucinogenic drug LSD in Basel, Switzerland. In 1956, he became one of the early experimental subjects. In his first LSD session, in an event he described as "a royal road into the unconscious," Stanislav had an experience that marked the beginning of a radical departure from the traditional view he had held of psychiatry. He wrote:

> I found myself in the middle of a cosmic drama of unimaginable proportions. I experienced the Big Bang, passed through black and white holes in the universe, identified with exploding supernovas, and witnessed many other strange phenomena that seemed to be pulsars, quasars, and other major cosmic events. There was no doubt that the experience I was having was very close to those I knew from reading the great mystical scriptures of the world.[357]

---

[356] Ibid., 19.
[357] Ibid., 22.

Grof's experiments continued and so did his mystical encounters. He started to have experiences that were indistinguishable from those described in the ancient mystical traditions and spiritual philosophies of the East. Some of them were powerful sequences of death and rebirth; others involved feelings of oneness with humanity, nature and the cosmos. Many of his clients also reported visions of deities and demons from different cultures and visits to various mythological realms.[358]

So what was happening to Stanislav Grof? Was he encountering an actual supernatural spirit world or can all of these experiences be understood purely through a naturalistic materialistic worldview? In order to provide further insight, Grof's own explanation is helpful. He stated:

> I had discovered what Aldus Huxley called "perennial philosophy," an understanding of the universe and the existence that has emerged with some minor variations again and again in different countries and historical periods. Similar maps have existed in various cultures for centuries or even millennia. The different systems of yoga, Buddhist teachings, the Tibetan Varjrayana, Kasmir Shaivism, Taoism, Sufism, Kabala, and Christian mysticism are just a few examples.[359]

It is apparent from the testimonies of Christina and Stanislav Grof that religious power encounters are possible whether one is a Christian or an atheist. The door to Nirvana can be quite wide and the experiences can be varied. It's possible to open the door to enlightenment whether one uses the key of Karl Marx, Jesus Christ, mysticism, religion or drugs.

But what is behind this enlightenment? Paul, as part of his warning to the church at Corinth wrote: "For Satan himself transforms himself into an angel of light. Therefore it is no great thing if his ministers also transform themselves into ministers of righteousness, whose end will be according to their works."[360]

---

[358] Ibid., 23.

[359] Ibid., 24-25.

[360] 2 Corinthians 11: 14-15

The Kundalini

Stanislav and Christina Grof both have the ability to transfer a spiritual energy. Descriptions of this form of spiritual energy can be found in ancient Indian literature and are given the term *Kundalini.* Another term that is used for the Kundalini is the serpent power. Dormant Kundalini is commonly represented as a serpent coiled three and a half times around the phallic symbol. Among the practices that can lead to the awakening of the Kundalini are meditation practices, contact with an advanced spiritual teacher or guru, and certain types of exercises associated with Eastern religion. In some instances people have reported the spontaneous arousal of Kundalini unexpectedly without an obvious trigger.

The Kundalini, or serpent power is also commonly represented by the depiction of fire. Kundalini when activated, participants say, changes into a fiery form called Shakti that rises up the spine. Individuals who claim to experience the Kundalini awakening often describe ecstatic states as they attain a higher level of consciousness. While this is happening individuals experience a rich spectrum of emotional and bodily manifestations. According to Grof and Grof:

> They have intense sensations of energy and heat streaming up their spines, and their bodies are overcome by violent shaking, spasms, and twisting movements. Their psyche can be unexpectedly flooded by powerful waves of emotions, such as anxiety, anger, sadness, or joy and ecstatic rapture. Individuals involved in this process might find it difficult to control their behavior during powerful rushes of Kundalini energy. They often emit various involuntary sounds and their bodies move in strange and unexpected patterns. Among the most common manifestations of this kind are unmotivated and unnatural laughter or crying, talking in tongues, singing previously unknown songs and spiritual chants, assuming yogic postures

and gestures and imitating a variety of animal sounds and movements.[361]

What Has God Said?

The behavior described and attributed to the serpent power by Grof and Grof is very disturbing for anyone who has researched the current New Wine Movement. *The Stormy Search for the Self* was written and published in 1990. The New Wine Movement and the behavior associated with it did not become known worldwide until the latter part of 1994.

When it comes to examining any new teaching or trend within the body of Christ, it is imperative that we take all the Scriptures into account. Based upon a study of the Word of God there is absolutely no basis for attributing to the Holy Spirit behaviors that are characteristic of the serpent power.

On several occasions, when I have pointed out to sincere Christians my concerns about the Kundalini behavior and its similarity to this "new thing" that God is supposedly doing, I have been told that I am walking in dangerous territory and risk the chance of blaspheming the Holy Spirit. Of course, no Christian in their right mind would want to be guilty of such a terrible offense. But what if the New Wine Movement is embracing teachings and behavior that is not the Holy Spirit, in the name of the Holy Spirit? What if you knew this was happening but just remained silent? Would God hold you responsible for this? As a researcher and a writer, I have pondered these questions and searched the Bible for the answers. My heart is troubled. Paul warned the early New Testament church because he was troubled about what Christians were doing in the name of Christ. Although this Scripture has already been used in this book it bears repeating:

> For I am jealous for you with godly jealousy. For I have betrothed you to one husband, that I may present you as a chaste virgin to Christ. But I fear, lest somehow, as the serpent

---

361 Grof, 78-79.

deceived Eve by his craftiness, so your minds may be corrupted from the simplicity that is in Christ. For if he who comes preaches another Jesus whom we have not preached, or if you receive a different spirit which you have not received, or a different gospel which you have not accepted; you may well put up with it![362]

Figure 22: Another name for Kundalini is the "serpent power." People overcome by this "serpent power" often shake, twitch and laugh uncontrollably.

[362] 2 Corinthians 11:2-4

16

SPREADING THE FIRE

Catch The Fire.[363] *Share The Fire.*[364] *Into The Fire.*[365] *Spread The Fire.*[366] *Holy Fire.*[367] Check out a cross-section of Christian books and publications. It becomes apparent that a number of people believe a fire has been lit. Not only is this fire burning, proponents of this movement believe the fire is destined to spread around the whole world. This "fire" so many are talking and writing about seems to have a scriptural basis. Advocates of the movement say this fire represents the Holy Spirit. Apparently, you can catch it.[368] You can share it.[369] You can get into it.[370] You can spread it.[371] "It's" supposed to be "holy fire."[372]

---

[363] Guy Chevreau, *Catch The Fire: An Experience of Renewal and Revival,* Harper Perrenial.
[364] Guy Chevreau, *Share The Fire: The Toronto Blessing and Grace-Based Evangelism,* (Revival Press, Shippensbrug, PA, 1997).
[365] Che' Ahn, *Into The Fire: How You Can Enter Renewal and Catch God's Holy Fire,* (Renew Books, Ventura, CA, 1998).
[366] *Spread The Fire*, newsletter from Toronto Airport Christian Fellowship, Issue 1-2000.
[367] Michael L. Brown, *Holy Fire: America on the Edge of Revival,*(Destiny Image, Shippensbrug, PA, 1996).
[368] Chevreau, *Catch The Fire.*
[369] Chevreau, *Share The Fire,* front cover.
[370] Ahn, front cover.
[371] *Spread The Fire.*
[372] Brown.

The Bible does mention a fire that clearly is associated with the Holy Spirit. In the second chapter of Acts, Luke gives an account of some of the events that happened on the day of Pentecost. He wrote:

> And suddenly there came from heaven a noise like a violent, rushing wind, and it filled the whole house where they were sitting. And there appeared to them tongues of fire distributing themselves, and they rested on each one of them. And they were all filled with the Holy Spirit and began to speak with other tongues, as the Spirit was giving them utterance.[373]

So Scripture justifies the use the word *fire* in association with the Holy Spirit. But, it is also reasonable to point out that Scripture warns about a counterfeit unholy spirit that can be identified with the use of the word *fire*. We read about this in the Book of Numbers, where the Bible indicates there are serious consequences when spiritual leaders choose to be disobedient to God:

> Now these are the records of the generations of Aaron and Moses at the time when the Lord spoke with Moses at Mount Sinai. These then are the names of the sons of Aaron: Nadab the first born, and Abihu, Eleazar and Ithamar. These are the names of the sons of Aaron, the anointed priests, whom he ordained to serve as priests. But Nadab and Abihu died before the LORD when they offered strange fire before the LORD in the wilderness of Sinai; and they had no children.[374]

In order to understand why God was so displeased with Nadab and Abihu, we must review the account of this incident as recorded in the Book of Leviticus. The Bible explains that God had consecrated Aaron and his sons as priests, specifically appointed to come before the LORD for the atonement of the sins of the people. God, through Moses, had specified the exact details of how this process was to occur. It is also clear from Scrip-

---

[373] Acts 2:2-4

[374] Numbers 3:1-4

ture that Aaron and his sons knew the importance of being obedient to the LORD.[375]

It is apparent from this account in the Book of Leviticus that Aaron's two sons, Nadab and Abihu were disobedient:

> Now Nadab and Abihu, the sons of Aaron, took their respective fire-pans, and after putting fire in them, placed incense on it, and offered strange fire before the LORD, which he had not commanded them. And fire came out from the presence of the LORD and consumed them, and they died before the LORD. Then Moses said to Aaron. "It is what the LORD spoke saying, 'By those who come near Me I will be treated as holy. And before all the people I will be honored.'" So Aaron, therefore, kept silent.[376]

Although the Bible does not tell us exactly what the term *strange fire* means, it would be safe to say whatever it was, it was displeasing to God. Thus disobedience to God in this instance was related to an unholy fire.

"It's" for Everyone

Signs and wonders! This is a sign Jesus is about to return, many are saying. But is that what the Bible teaches? If you are still unsure, then I would suggest you do your own verse-by-verse search of the Scriptures. When it comes to the last days, there are several warnings.[377] Seeking the miraculous, even in the name of Jesus, could be very misleading. At the very least, Christians should be cautious. But New Wine promoters refuse to accept this line of reasoning. They say they want all God has to offer. Many are so enthusiastic for any experience they will travel from place to place, city to city and even country to country to participate in the latest round of spiritual "blessing."

Even unbelievers are able to participate in these new blessings. According to the concept of power evangelism popularized

---

[375] Leviticus 8:1-36

[376] Leviticus 10:1-3

[377] Matthew 24:22-25; 2 Thessalonians 2:3-12

by the late John Wimber, signs and wonders are essential in order to persuade the lost sheep to become part of the fold.

Che Ahn, the senior pastor of the Harvest Rock Church in Pasadena, California, is convinced that power evangelism is the best way to spread the gospel and reach unbelievers for Jesus Christ. Before his encounter with the Toronto Blessing, he presented the gospel and then allowed the person to either reject or accept Christ. Now he believes that it is much more effective to allow the unbeliever to first encounter the "matchless reality of the Holy Spirit" before trying to "lead the person to the Lord."[378] In his book *Into the Fire,* in a section titled "Changing My Evangelism Philosophy," Che Ahn stated:

> In short, power evangelism takes place when an unbeliever sees and experiences the power of God in a mighty way – such as through miracles or healings, along with a rational presentation of the Gospel. Peter Wagner unapologetically says, "Across the board, the most effective evangelism in today's world is accompanied by manifestations of supernatural power." I personally believe that the primary expansion of Christianity in the Early Church came as a result of power evangelism. It is not new – just far more rare than it needs to be.[379]

While Che Ahn promotes various styles of evangelism in order to bring people to Christ, he believes the "most effective salvation we can demonstrate anywhere on the planet" comes by power evangelism through the manifestation of a supernatural experience he calls a "power encounter." He wrote:

> There is no question in my mind that such demonstrations are the cutting edge of what the Holy Spirit is saying concerning evangelism. It is as old as the Bible. Again and again we observe people believing in the gospel after experiencing signs and wonders. Just look at the Book of Acts![380]

---

[378] Ahn, 89.
[379] Ibid.
[380] Ibid., 89-90.

Pastor Ahn's theory proposes that a power encounter with the Lord pulls down spiritual forces that are hindering people from coming to Christ. He insists: "What better way to experience the kindness of God, than to feel it. Surely it is better felt than taught!"[381]

The Burning in the Bosom

Over the past several years I have had the opportunity to meet with a number of devoted Mormons who have experienced what they believe is a "power encounter" with God. Joseph Smith, the founder of Mormonism promoted the idea of power evangelism enhanced by power encounters, long before John Wimber popularized the idea.

In October of 1999 a friend of mine and I spent several hours interviewing Mormons at the Mormon Tourist Center at the base of Hill Cumorah near Palmyra, New York. Each Mormon we interviewed was convinced they had found the truth because they had experienced what they called a "burning in the bosom." This experience, they said, could also be our experience if we prayed and asked God if Mormonism was the truth.

There are millions of Mormons who believe they are Christians because they have felt this experience called the "burning in the bosom." There is no doubt that these sincere people truly believe as they do because they have had this experience.

I asked a girl who was answering all of my questions if she had ever thought about the possibility that the teachings of their dead leader Joseph Smith could be wrong. To this she responded, "Well, if that were the case, then there would be a lot of Mormons that are knee-deep in doo-doo."

What if this girl's statement is true? According to the Bible, Mormonism is leading people down the road that ends up in hell. Then what about Christians who believe they are Christians because they have had a "power encounter" with Jesus when in reality they have been deceived? We know that Jesus said that

[381] Ibid., 92.

this can happen.[382] Shouldn't we be very cautious about the concept of power evangelism?

Reaching the Masses

According to Che Ahn and others, power evangelism with a power encounter is the best way to reach the masses for Jesus, now and in the future. "Around the world, power evangelism is getting the job done,"[383] Che Ahn stated. In order to demonstrate how effective power evangelism works, Pastor Ahn described an experience that he had with a 15-year-old rebellious Korean-American teenager who attended one of his revival meetings. He wrote:

> I gave the alter call, but Lisa didn't respond. After the altar call, we had a ministry time. I began to pray for people to be filled with the Holy Spirit. People were falling to the ground as the Holy Spirit fell on them. They were "manifesting" or showing the presence on them by shaking or trembling as well. I was wondering what was going through Lisa's mind. I decided to go to her. After introducing myself and chatting for a moment I simply asked Lisa if she would like to give her life to Jesus. She told me she wasn't ready yet.[384]

Ahn described what happened next. Although the girl was indifferent to his suggestion, she indicated he could pray for her if he wanted. Ahn, not wanting to crowd the young girl or add to her discomfort, stood several feet away and prayed. As he recorded in his book:

> "Jesus, please reveal to Lisa how much you love her," I asked quietly. As soon as I said those words, Lisa started to laugh. At first I wondered if she was laughing at me or at what I had prayed. I soon saw that she was trying not to laugh as she made a futile effort to cover her mouth with her hands.

---

[382] Matthew 7:21-23

[383] Ahn, 92.

[384] Ibid., 93-94.

> That is when I knew this laughter was the Holy Spirit flooding her![385]

Now that Lisa was laughing uncontrollably, Pastor Ahn took the next step and approached her. "Don't fight the laughter," he said. "The Holy Spirit is revealing Himself to you!"[386] Then Ahn explained what happened to Lisa along with his interpretation:

> As soon as I lifted my hands, she fell to the floor speaking in tongues. This amazed me. I hadn't led her to the Lord, nor had we prayed the sinner's prayer. In fact she had just told me she wasn't ready to come to Christ. I asked the Lord to give me Scripture concerning what I was witnessing. Immediately Acts 10 came to my mind. As Peter was preaching in the house of Cornelius, the Holy Spirit fell, and the members of the household all began to speak in tongues. Apparently, God who knows the hearts of people must have known that Lisa changed her mind when she experienced that initial touch of the Spirit in laughter. She was then converted and filled with the Holy Spirit all at the same time![387]

So what is the proper biblical analysis of this power encounter? Should we just accept Pastor Che Ahn's interpretation of what happened to Lisa or should we investigate further? Is this the Holy Spirit's new strategy for worldwide evangelism? Can signs and wonders replace the gospel? There are certainly many who are claiming this is so. All around the world this message is being heralded in seminars, conferences and crusades.

Plan Calgary

The strategy is called "Plan Calgary." According to an article by Lorne Gunter that appeared in a Canadian magazine called the *British Columbia Report,* a city in Alberta has been deemed one of four to become a model for the Christian faith. According to this plan, denominationalism will soon be replaced by an in-

---

385 Ibid., 94.
386 Ibid.
387 Ibid., 94-95.

terdenominational unity that will usher in a citywide revival that will see the masses turning to God. Plan Calgary is called a city taking strategy and is just one of the weapons of warfare that is being used by the promoters of the New Apostolic Reformation.[388]

Dr. C. Peter Wagner, internationally known author, speaker and an expert on the subject of church growth, was the inspiration behind Plan Calgary. He believes God has His hand specifically on the city of Calgary and that this location is one of four North American cities that will model spiritual renewal in the next decade. Wagner claimed that Calgary would witness a decrease in crime, poverty, pornography, alcoholism and drug abuse, and an increase in healings, peace and prosperity.[389] In short, the goal is for the devil to be tossed out of Calgary and that the Kingdom of God be established there.

A crusade to retake Calgary for God was presented by Dr. Wagner to 240 evangelical pastors and mainline church leaders in March of 1997. A former professor of church growth at Fuller Theological Seminary in Pasadena, California, Dr. Wagner is known for his innovative ideas. His strategic plan for winning souls apparently was specifically designed for the temperament of western Canadians.[390]

The goal of this plan was to increase Calgary's church attendance rates by one-third. The first phase, centered on a neighborhood-by-neighborhood demographic analysis of the city, required the cooperation of churches of all denominations. The article mentioned that spiritual leaders of nearly 70 of Calgary's 350 churches had already joined in the plan and that organizers expected to add 30 more within a year. Although participants were primarily independent evangelicals, other churches that

---

[388] Lorne Gunter, "The Crusade to Retake Calgary," *British Columbia Report*, April 20, 1998, 28.
[389] Ibid.
[390] Ibid.

were participating included Anglican, Roman Catholic, United Church and Lutheran.[391]

While Plan Calgary may have been new for western Canadians, the idea behind this soul saving strategy has been around for a while. Plan Calgary was based upon Dr. Wagner's "Third Wave" theology. The late John Wimber, was a strong proponent of Third Wave doctrine during his lifetime. His messages and books on the subject of power evangelism added another important dimension to the Kingdom building strategy. According to the idea of power evangelism, the more unity within the body of Christ, the more signs and wonders will appear. These manifestations will be the key to drawing people to Christ, it is believed.

Although this book has already made the point, I want to emphasize it once more. While the Bible teaches that Christian unity is important, Christian unity must be centered on the truth of the cross. However, there are signs that this unity agenda is based on common feelings and experiences. No longer is Scripture sufficient, some of the leaders of the Third Wave claim. Unity is what moves the hand of God – and the more unity, the more signs and wonders. This is what makes power evangelism work, Third-Wavers say.

Plan World

Charisma magazine, January 1997, featured a full two-page advertisement called "Mission to all the World 2000."[392] According to Morris Cerrullo, God spoke to him personally and said: "Son, I am calling you to reach the entire world with the gospel during the next three and one-half years." Then in response to hearing what God had said to him, Cerrullo stated: "I knew right then that this calling was far too big for one man or any one ministry."

---

[391] Ibid.

[392] Morris Cerrullo, "Announcing Mission to All the World 2000," *Charisma*, January 1997, 2-3.

"Mission to all the World 2000" had some very ambitious goals. The advertisement stated:

> STRATEGY: Target ten major world regions and reach the cities and nations of each region through seven-night miracle crusades in ten major stadiums and five-day Schools of Ministry.[393]

The advertisement indicated that Morris Cerrullo had already enlisted the support of several other well-known Christian leaders. For example, C. Peter Wagner, President of Global Harvest Ministries, stated: "Morris has accepted the greatest challenge of any single ministry... and thereby has the greatest potential for evangelistic return of all."[394] Regarding Morris's vision, Dan Cook, Pastor of Westside Pentecostal Church in Abbotsford, British Columbia, Canada said: "This is God! It is doable! There is no doubt this is one of the final drives to bring Christ back."[395] George Otis, President of High Adventure Ministries stated: "This is an answer to prayer. With today's technology we can do it."[396]

A part of the "Mission to all the World 2000" strategy was to raise up 1,000,000 prayer "command centers." As well, six months prior to the miracle crusades, a team of intercessors, called "Prayer Strike Forces," traveled to the crusade sites to saturate the locations with prayer.[397]

A personal letter that also appeared in the advertisement, ended with this passionate plea from Morris Cerrullo:

> Beloved, I believe God has called us to the kingdom for such a time as this. As this millennium draws to a close, we are in a time and place of spiritual destiny, and the anticipation is very high that during the next three and a half years more souls will be saved than during the entire history of the church

---

[393] Ibid., 2.
[394] Ibid., 3.
[395] Ibid.
[396] Ibid., 2.
[397] Ibid., 3.

> put together. It can be done. It ought to be done. It must be done![398]

Yes, anticipation is high. And the fire is spreading in home Bible studies, church meetings, conventions and conferences in thousands of towns and cities in every country of the world. Never before has something like this happened in history. Indeed, this is a "new" thing. According to Bill Hamon:

> Ministers and saints are going to be challenged with the apostolic and prophetic ministries and truths. Old order pastors and denominational leaders always try to protect and warn their people against the new restorational truths, ministries and spiritual experiences that the Holy Spirit is bringing forth in Christ's Church. There are only three options for our response to new truth: We can persecute it, be passive about it or participate and propagate the new restorational truths and ministries.[399]

The New Wine Movement seems to be focused on the goal of establishing a new era of Christianity. Many believe that the New Apostolic Reformation will usher in the greatest revival in the history of the church. The new wave of the Holy Spirit is about to sweep over the entire earth. Signs and wonders will unite unbelievers with believers and the presence of Christ will be manifest and the Kingdom of God will be established here on earth.

Whether or not these predictions are fulfilled, only time will tell. Meanwhile, it is important to always test human predictions and compare them with God's revelation found in His Holy Word.

---

398 Ibid. [emphasis in the original]
399 Hamon, 66.

17

ALPHA

According to the New Wine theology, having a power encounter is the key to power evangelism and power evangelism is the key to global revival. Supporters of this movement see signs and wonders as the equivalent to the voice of God. If you reject God's voice, they say, you are just not spiritual. Knowing and understanding God is directly related to what you feel or experience emotionally.

Until recently it was primarily the Pentecostal Movement that was known for promoting signs and wonders and speaking in tongues as evidence of true spirituality. Other Evangelical Christians were often quite outspoken and critical about their Pentecostal brethren, who they insisted were obsessed with seeking after supernatural experiences.

But a change in this theology has definitely occurred. As one person told me recently, the whole world will soon be Pentecostal. People all over the world from every denomination are "catching the fire."

It is true that the Charismatic Movement is expanding by leaps and bounds. An even more amazing fact is that Catholics are also joining the ranks. Tongues, signs and wonders, healings, casting out demons are available for anyone who professes the name of Christ, even Mormons who are called the Church of Jesus Christ of Latter Day Saints. The only prerequisite many denominations have is that "the moving of the Holy Spirit" never be questioned. When a Christian expresses concern about some of the unusual manifestations that are claimed to be from the Holy Spirit (even though there is no basis in the Scriptures), supporters of the New Wine Movement are often very defensive.

Spreading the Fire through the Alpha Course

The Alpha Program, authored by Nicky Gumbel, an Oxford educated barrister-turned-Anglican priest, has been labeled as the most popular home Bible study course in the history of Christianity. A brochure published for the Alpha Texas Conference in Austin, Texas, held January 8th and 9th, 1998 detailed the goals and objectives of the course. It stated:

> The **Alpha** Course is a ten-week practical introduction to the Christian faith. It is designed primarily for non-church goers and those who have recently become Christians. **Alpha** is a flexible and practical model which can work for a group of any size. Churches and Christian organizations of every background and denomination are discovering it to be a simple and effective way of presenting the gospel of Jesus Christ in a non-threatening manner for people of all walks of life. [400]

The *Charisma* December 1999 issue contained an article that provides additional information about the Alpha program. The article, written by journalist Clive Price, titled "Alpha Course Supporters Urge British To Party With God On New Year's Eve," is introduced the following way:

> Lying on a bed of nails? That does not sound like the most orthodox way of spearheading a $1.6 million evangelistic media campaign for the closing days of the twentieth century. But as British pastor Sandy Miller puts it, the aim of the Alpha Project's millennium initiative is to help people "get the point" of the year 2000. [401]

---

[400] Brochure, The Texas Alpha Conference, January 8-9, 1998, 2.

[401] Clive Price, "Alpha Course Supporters Urge British To Party With God on

Sandy Miller is vicar of Holy Trinity Brompton, an Anglican church located in London, England. Although the Alpha Course was founded in 1991, the effectiveness of the course may not have been realized until later. Originally dedicated to teaching the basics of Christianity, it appears that the Toronto Blessing that was transported to England from Canada in May of 1994 may have impacted the Holy Trinity Brompton leaders. It was then that church leaders of Holy Trinity Brompton received a dose of the "blessing" through Elli Mumford. The following insert taken from my book *New Wine or Old Deception?* provides insight into what happened:

> According to Dave Roberts, editor of the British magazine, *Alpha,* and author of the book *The Toronto Blessing,* published by Kingsway Publications in Great Britain, Elli Mumford's visit to Toronto was transforming: "She had gone there feeling spiritually 'burnt out' and longing for a fresh understanding and vitality in her relationship with Jesus. As she received prayer and encouragement she discovered God anew, much of the time while 'on the carpet' prostrate before God."
>
> On May 24, 1994, Elli Mumford met with several leaders of Holy Trinity Brompton, a charismatic evangelical church in South Kensington. As Mumford prayed at this meeting, "the glory fell." One of the leaders reported back to Sandy Miller, the highly regarded vicar of Holy Trinity Brompton, and it was decided that Elli would preach the following Sunday morning message at Holy Trinity Brompton.
>
> Sunday May 29, 1994, was the day the church caught on fire. After giving her testimony about her "Toronto experience," Elli asked the congregation to stand while she prayed that the Lord would bless and give them all He had. Immediately people began to laugh hysterically, weep, shake, jerk, bark and roar.
>
> "The Holy Spirit Hits South Kensington" was the front-page headline in the London section of *The Independent,* June

New Year's Eve" *Charisma,* December 1999, 38.

21, 1994. Could such strange behavior be from God? People from the "word-of-faith" health and wealth wing of the charismatic movement had been prophesying a great revival for some time. Was this the real thing?

On June 24, 1994, Holy Trinity Brompton staff member Mark Elsdon-Dew reassured the *Church Times* by saying: "Please emphasize that this is not so bizarre or outrageous that sensible people won't want anything to do with it. We try to show common sense and order, but if it is God it would be awful not to have all that He offers."[402]

Alpha Endorsers

Between 1995 and 2000, 750,000 people in Great Britain have attended an Alpha program. There have been a least 7000 different locations where these meetings have occurred.[403] Even North Americans have been impacted. The following *Christianity Today* article titled "A British course for non-Christians aims to transform North American evangelistic outreach," reported on the North American marketing strategy for the Alpha Program:

> Global growth rates for the number of Alpha courses and attendees initially stunned [Alpha Course creator, Nicky] Gumbel. "It was an amazement to us that it would work in any other church but our own," he says. In 1991, four Alpha courses drew 600 people. In 1997, an estimated 500,000 attended courses around the world. Gumbel and Alistair Hanna, a former corporate consultant and now head of Alpha North America, believe that by the year 2001 some 50,000 Alpha courses could be held yearly in the United States and Canada.[404]

---

[402] Roger Oakland, *New Wine or Old Deception?* (The Word For Today, Costa Mesa, CA, 1995), 30-31.

[403] Price, 38.

[404] Doug Leblanc, Debra Fieguth, Mary Cagney, "A British course for non-Christians aims to transform North American evangelistic outreach," *Christianity Today,* February 9, 1998, 37.

Alistair Hanna, the head of Alpha North America has been very active in promoting the program in North America. A brochure called "Alpha: A Model for Dynamic Growth in the Local Church" advertised twenty-two major conferences to be held throughout North America for the year 2000. A number of high profile Christian leaders endorsed Alpha, each one making positive statements.

For example, The Most Reverend and Right Honorable George Carey, Archbishop of Canterbury, England stated: "Alpha is superb and a great blessing to many. I commend it wholeheartedly."[405] Jack Hayford, president of King's Seminary said, "I see Alpha as a strategic tool, sensitively crafted to address today's secularized seekers with satisfying answers to their spiritual hunger."[406] And Cardinal William H. Keeler, Catholic Archbishop of Baltimore stated: "We are hearing wonderful testimony of the good news touching and even transforming the lives of individuals who attended Alpha courses."[407]

While Alpha has been extremely popular in Great Britain, North American interest has increased rapidly. The December 1999 – March 2000 United States edition of *Alpha News* had a major front page headline that proclaimed: "Time Magazine: 'Alpha Miracle.'" The article stated the following:

> The Alpha course is coming to the rescue of the Christian Church in Europe and throughout the world, a recent full-page report in *Time* magazine said.
>
> The magazine is just the latest publication to report on the spread of Alpha. The *New York Times*, the *Los Angeles Times*, the *Boston Herald*, and many other newspapers across the US have carried lengthy articles about the course.

---

[405] "Alpha: A Model for Dynamic Growth in the Local Church," Conferences for 2000, published by Alpha North America, New York, 2000.

[406] Ibid.

[407] Ibid.

Newsweek has also carried a full-page interview with Alpha speaker Nicky Gumbel, describing him as "God's own Adman."

The *Time* magazine article, which appeared in the European edition of the weekly magazine in November, was headlined "Alpha to the Rescue" and reported on the decline of the Christian church in Europe.

The article said, "The miracle formula church leaders are hoping will reverse this religious decline sounds quite old-hat. It's a 10-week introduction to the basics of the Christian faith – what is new or revolutionary in that? Quite a lot, it turns out."

To emphasize the interdenominational aspect of the course, the assistant editor of the Catholic weekly the *Tablet* was quoted. She told *Time*, "This is a significant movement. It's having an amazing success in the Catholic Church." [408]

Alpha Critics

In spite of the overwhelming increase in the number of participants in the program, Alpha has not been free of criticism. Not everyone is quite as enthusiastic as Nicky Gumbel and Alistair Hanna, who have a goal for the Alpha course to be available to North American residents no matter where they live. A *Christianity Today* article stated:

> But not everyone is cheering Alpha forward. Some church leaders have found Alpha teachings too charismatic, too experience-driven, and too negative about traditional churches. Martin Percy, Director of the Lincoln Theological Institute for the Study of Religion and Society of the University of Sheffield, England has commented about Alpha that it is "a package rather than a pilgrimage." In a recent essay he said, "It is a confident but narrow expression of Christianity which expresses

---

[408] *Alpha News*, USA Edition, December 1999-March 2000, 1.

the personal experience of Spirit over the Spirit in the church."[409]

There are others who have expressed their concerns about the Alpha focus on experience. For example, Pastor Darcy Van Horn of the Dunbar Heights Baptist Church of Vancouver, Canada has stated, "There seems to be more of a stress on the gift of tongues, than I think is biblically warranted."[410] Then to qualify this statement he added, "I'm a little leery of people who are not yet saved being pressed to be filled with the Spirit."[411]

However, according to the *Christianity Today* article, Pastor Van Horn has not dismissed the teaching of Alpha altogether. He and other pastors have eliminated certain portions of the Alpha program to remodel the course to their own liking. This has been done despite *"Gumbel's emphasis on the importance of not modifying the curriculum."*[412]

Spiritual Gifts

The Bible teaches that there are spiritual gifts. For the information of those who may be reading this chapter and wondering if I am a cessationsist or "gift basher," it is important that I make the record clear. I believe there are gifts because the Bible teaches there are gifts. I do not believe that gifts have passed away with the New Testament Church. I believe there are legitimate gifts that are in operation today.

But it order to qualify this statement, I must add that there is a very strong trend underway in charismatic circles today to emphasize gifts, to misunderstand what gifts are, or even to add to the list of gifts that are found in the Bible. I have had the privilege of traveling worldwide and making first-hand observations of many different denominations from extremely char-

---

[409] Timothy C. Morgan, "The Alpha-Brits Are Coming," *Christianity Today*, Feb. 9, 1998, 37-38.
[410] Ibid., 39.
[411] Ibid
[412] Ibid. [emphasis mine]

ismatic to extremely conservative. There is a trend to abandon Bible-based Christianity for an experienced-based Christianity.

The apostle Paul addressed the subject of gifts in a very clear message that is outlined in his letter to the church at Corinth as recorded in 1 Corinthians, chapters 13 and 14. While most pastors who teach on the gifts reference these chapters, I have discovered that it is quite rare for these same pastors to teach these two chapters verse by verse. If this were the case, then we would see a much better balance to the gift message. Balanced teaching, of course, is biblical.

Where do pastors and other church leaders get the license to add to or take away from the Scriptures when it comes to the area of the gifts? What man or woman can say with confidence using the Bible as their text, that God is doing a "new thing" even though this "new thing" cannot be identified by any chapter or verse found in the Bible? Of course God cannot be placed in a box, but we must be careful not to embrace something as being of God, just because it appears to be spiritual.

The study guide for the Alpha Program written by Nicky Gumbel is titled *Questions of Life: A Practical Introduction To The Christian Faith.*[413] Most of what Mr. Gumbel teaches about the gifts is biblical, but there are some areas that are not. For example, with regard to "being filled with the Spirit" he writes:

> Physical heat sometimes accompanies the filling of the Spirit and the people experience it in their hands or some other part of their bodies. One person described a feeling of glowing all over. Another said she experienced "liquid heat." Still another described "burning in my arms when I was not hot." Fire perhaps symbolizes the power, passion and purity the Spirit of God brings to our lives.[414]

Then with reference to speaking in tongues, Mr. Gumbel seems to be biblically accurate by stating:

[413] Nicky Gumbel, *Questions of Life: A Practical Introduction To The Christian Faith,* (Cook Ministry Resources, Colorado Springs, 1996).
[414] Ibid., 152.

> Not every Christian speaks in tongues. Yet Paul says, "I would like everyone of you to speak in tongues," suggesting that it is not only for a special class of Christians. It is open to all Christians. There is no reason why anyone who wants this gift should not receive it. Paul is not saying that speaking in tongues is the be-all and the end-all of the Christian life; he is saying that it is a very helpful gift. If you would like to receive it, there is no reason why you should not.[415]

However, later in the same chapter Mr. Gumbel provides a man-made formula for speaking in tongues by stating: "Ask God to fill you with His Spirit and to give you the gift of tongues. Go on seeking Him until you find. Go on knocking until the door opens. Seek God with all your heart. Open your mouth and start to praise God in any language but English or any other language known to you. Believe that what you receive is from God. Don't let anyone tell you that you made it up. Persevere. Languages take time to develop."[416]

Is it our right as believers to receive a gift from God, if God has not given the believer that particular gift? Are all of God's gifts are for all of God's people?

What happens when spiritual gifts, biblical or unbiblical become the focus of our faith? Or what about a gift like speaking in tongues being accepted as the criteria that someone is a true believer? Is it possible that an emphasis on being spiritually enlightened could actually be a tool that may lead to being spiritually deceived? The next chapter will answer this question in detail.

---

[415] Ibid., 159.
[416] Ibid., 162-163.

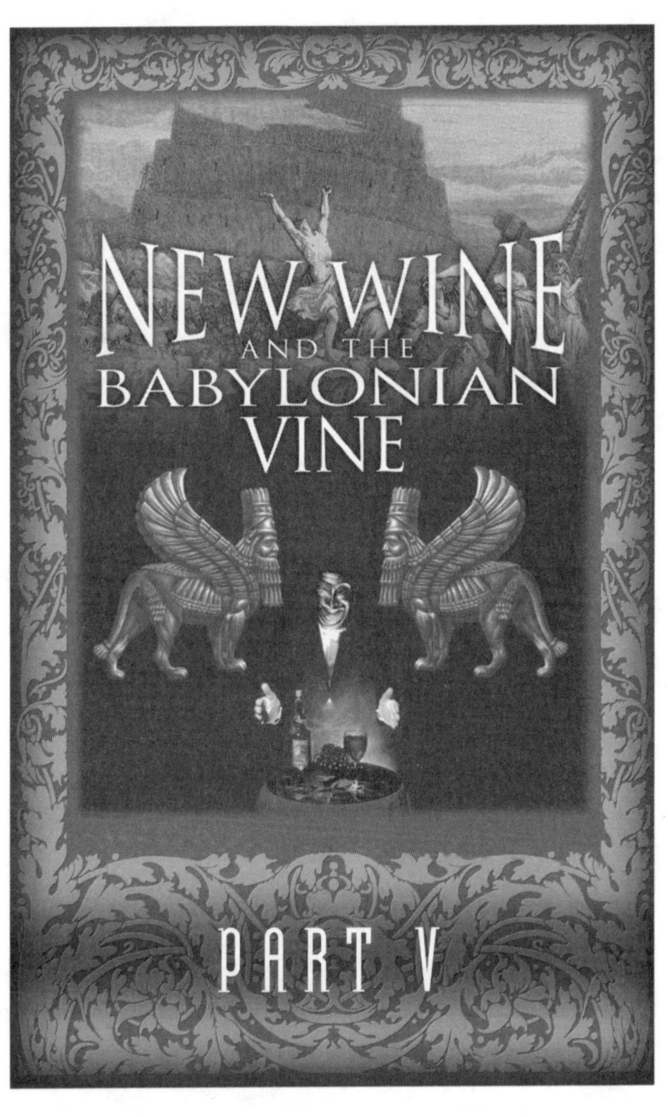

THE BABYLONIAN VINE

18

A SECOND PENTECOST

We know from the words of Jesus Christ that Satan has an agenda to deceive the world in the name of Christ. Throughout history, billions have died and gone to a lost eternity because they have been deceived.[417] The "god of this world"[418] is the master deceiver.[419] We also know as we approach the return of Jesus Christ, Satan's plan intensifies.[420] Billions more will be deceived in the name of Jesus Christ. While the Bible has warned us in advance, the Scriptures indicate deception will be so intense that even God's chosen will not be able to avoid being caught in the trap.[421] Whether or not we accept this warning is our choice.

The previous five chapters of this book have primarily dealt with an experienced-based Christianity that is associated with Protestant denominations. In an earlier part of the book we saw how Catholicism has also been guilty of deviating from the authority of the Bible by embracing teachings, dogmas and experiences that have no biblical basis.

Now as we are in the concluding chapters of this book, it is important to show how both Catholics and Protestants are being

---

417 Matthew 7:21-23
418 2 Corinthians 4:3-4
419 Revelation 12:9
420 1 Timothy 4:1
421 Matthew 24:24

deceived by embracing what is called the "Second Pentecost." While these two groups are convinced that the Holy Spirit is leading and guiding them, there are a number of concerns that need to be addressed. What is this so-called "Second Pentecost" so many Protestants and Catholics are accepting? What about all the ideas and teachings associated with the Charismatic Movement that do not have a biblical basis? Is it possible the New Wine-Charismatic Movement provides a bridge that is preparing Christianity for the reintroduction of the religion of Babylon predicted in the Bible for the end times?

The Latter Rain Returns

Cyclical is biblical. What has happened in the past most surely will happen again. And with reference to the teachings and the practices of the Latter Rain Movement that was born in the late 1940s in Canada, this is exactly what is happening. By June of 1949, the teachings and practices of the Latter Rain Movement that originated in North Battleford, Saskatchewan, divided families, churches and fellowships of believers.

Eventually some pastors and church leaders of various denominations were willing to stand up and express their concerns about the sectarian nature of this movement. One of them was Ernest Williams, General Superintendent of the Assemblies of God in the United States. Dealing with some of the more controversial doctrines of the Latter Rain, he wrote an article that was published in the *Pentecostal Testimony*, an official publication of the Pentecostal Assemblies of Canada. The article stated:

> Does it not look like a bold step to call people out of the congregation that they might, through prophecy and laying on of hands, have gifts and callings imparted to them? Others are named who hope to get to other foreign fields. If they get there they cannot speak the language as they hope to do, raw recruits, what may they suffer? The decay of our bodies and the inroad of disease resulting from the same are not demonism. Think of going to a weakened, afflicted person, charging that the reason the person is sick is because he is possessed of some demon, then trying to name the demon and cast it out. This

> could lead to accusing poor sick people of being possessed with all sorts of demons. Think of the mental reaction on the part of the sufferer.[422]

Williams was not alone in expressing these concerns about Latter Rain doctrine. In the fall of 1949, at the General Council Meeting of the Assemblies of God held in Seattle, Washington, the Council adopted a resolution disapproving the practices of what was termed "The New Order of the Latter Rain." According to the 1949 General Council Minutes, the following statement was read and approved:

> Whereas, we are grateful for the visitation of God in the past and the evidences of His blessings upon us today, and whereas, we recognize a hunger on the part of God's people for a spiritual refreshing and a manifestation of His Holy Spirit, be it therefore resolved, that we disapprove of those extreme teachings and practices, which, being unfounded Scripturally, serve only to break fellowship of like precious faith and tend to confusion and division among the members of the Body of Christ, and it be hereby known that this 23rd General Council disapproves of the so-called "New Order of the Latter Rain": (1) The overemphasis relative to imparting, identifying, bestowing or confirming of gifts by the laying on of hands or of prophecy. (2) The erroneous teaching that the Church is built on the foundation of present-day apostles and prophets. (3) The extreme teaching as advocated by the "New Order" regarding the confession of sin to man and deliverance as practiced, which claims prerogatives to human agency which belong only to Christ.[423]

While the resolution made by the General Council of the Assemblies of God had a major impact on the various Pentecostal denominations throughout North America, there were those who still carried the banner of the "New Order of Latter Rain."

---

422 E.S. Williams, "More About Gifts," *The Pentecostal Testimony,* June 15, 1949, 8.

423 23rd General Council Minutes, Assemblies of God in the USA, Seattle, 1949, 26-27.

These Latter Rain proponents remained active and dedicated to their cause. Many revival churches that had become visible in North America during the Latter Rain remained. Most of these churches were independent and autonomous and became mother churches that spawned other smaller churches that carried on and propagated the Latter Rain teachings.

In addition various beliefs and practices of the Latter Rain Movement found their way into the Charismatic Renewal. It can be documented that the eschatological views of the Latter Rain Movement were adopted by Charismatics throughout the world. One of the promoters of Latter Rain doctrine was J. Preston Eby of El Paso, Texas. Richard Riss, in his book *Latter Rain: The Latter Rain Movement of 1948 and the Mid-Twentieth Century Evangelical Awakening* mentions that men like Eby taught that the Latter Rain Movement would one day be revived. In a Bible study series that was published in 1976, Eby wrote:

> In 1948 – the very year that Israel became a nation – another great deluge fell from heaven, a mighty revival then called the "Latter Rain." In this Restoration Revival God did a work which far transcended the work started in the Pentecostal outpouring of more than 40 years before. All the nine gifts of the Spirit, the five-fold ministries of apostles, prophets, evangelists, pastors and teachers, spiritual praise and worship, and the end-time revelation of God's purpose to manifest His sons, a glorious church, to bring in the kingdom of God, all of this and much more was restored among God's people. And now the great dealings of God; the purgings, the processings, depths of revelation, edification and strengthening, understanding of the ways of the Lord, faith in promise, waiting upon the Lord, development of the nature and character of God – and all of this being laid upon a people who have received the fruit of that second great visitation of God and thus they are being prepared for ***the coming third outpouring*** which shall finally bring the fullness, a company of overcoming Sons of God who have come to the measure of the stature of the fullness of Christ to actually dethrone Satan, casting him out of the heavenlies, and finally binding him in the earthlies, bring-

> ing the hope of deliverance and life to all the families of the earth. This third great work of the Spirit shall usher a people into full redemption – free from the curse, sin, sickness, death and carnality.[424]

Although the above quote is long and difficult to read, it is important to examine it carefully. First, Eby's statement reveals the Latter Rain Movement still had a voice a quarter century after the Latter Rain doctrines were exposed. Second, this statement illustrates that the present New Wine Movement is tied to the Latter Rain teachings that were born fifty years ago. Third, this statement shows that Charismatics today are still promoting the idea that empowered men and women (manifest sons of God) can and will implement a "Church Age." And finally, there is a prediction made of a new outpouring of the Holy Spirit that is extremely interesting in light of current ecumenical alliances between Catholics and Protestants.

Catholic Pentecostals

As I was preparing to write this chapter I was given a book to read with the following title: *As By A New Pentecost: The Dramatic Beginning of the Catholic Charismatic Renewal.*[425] Throughout my life as a researcher, writer, and speaker, I have had many papers, magazines and books placed in my hands that have later turned out to be significant. When I browsed through this book, I could hardly believe what I was reading. The very direction my research was headed was confirmed with each page that I read.

My first response to the book occurred when I read the dedication page. The author, Patti Gallagher Mansfield dedicated her book to "Mary, Spouse of the Holy Spirit, Mother of the Church."[426] The book was written to inform readers about the events surrounding the origin of the Catholic Charismatic Re-

---

[424] J. Preston Eby, "The Battle of Armageddon, Part IV," *Kingdom Bible Studies,* El Paso, TX, September 1976, 10. [emphasis mine]

[425] Patti Gallagher Mansfield, *As By A New Pentecost: The Dramatic Beginning of the Catholic Charismatic Renewal,*(Franciscan University Press, Steubenville, OH, 1992).

[426] Ibid., iii.

newal know as the "Duquesne Weekend." In the introduction, Mansfield stated:

> The retreat of February 17-19, 1967 has become known as the Duquesne Weekend. It is generally accepted as the beginning of the Charismatic Renewal in the Catholic Church. This was the first event at which a group of Catholics experienced the Baptism of the Holy Spirit and the charismatic gifts. While there may be Catholics who were baptized in the Spirit prior to the Duquesne Weekend, this retreat began a widespread movement of Catholic Charismatic Renewal throughout the United States and around the world.[427]

According to Cardinal Suenens who wrote the foreword for the book, the Duquesne Weekend defined and fixed a point in the history of the Catholic Church. He also stated:

> The author links to the Baptism of the Spirit the name of the spiritual maternity of Mary, thereby reminding us that Jesus Christ continues to be born mystically of the Holy Spirit and of Mary and that we should never separate what God has joined together.[428]

This Marian connection with a new outpouring of the Holy Spirit is called "the Second Pentecost." This idea was not entirely new to me. A number of other sources that I had been reading indicated the Marian Movement, the Catholic Charismatic Movement and the Protestant Charismatic Movement all found common ground in the "unity movement." While I will document this further in the next chapter, for now it will be sufficient to state that the information I gleaned from Patti Gallagher Mansfield's book only confirmed these suspicions.

In addition, I wondered if the Latter Rain Movement that predicted the "Third Wave" was what Catholics were now calling the "Second Pentecost." While an ecumenical movement that links Catholics and Protestants has already been well documented, this additional Third-Wave/Second-Pentecost connec-

[427] Ibid., 5.
[428] Ibid., ix.

tion needed to be investigated further. What other ties between the two movements were there? Could it be possible that the Marian apparitions that are so common today could play a further ecumenical role?

The Pope's Prayer

While Cardinal Suenens and Patti Gallagher Mansfield both see the Duquesne Weekend as instrumental in launching the Catholic Charismatic Movement, there seems to be evidence that the groundwork had been laid for this several years before. Even those who consider February 1967 as the beginning of the Catholic Charismatic Renewal at the Duquesne Weekend, will cite the prayer of Pope John XIII at the beginning of the Second Vatican Council as a more significant event. They see the Catholic Charismatic Renewal as a providential answer to the pope's prayer when he called for a new Pentecost in 1961. This prayer stated:

> Renew Your wonders in this our day, as by a new Pentecost. Grant to Your Church that, being of one mind and steadfast in prayer with Mary, the mother of Jesus, and following the lead of the blessed Peter, it may advance the reign of our Divine Savior, the reign of truth and justice, the reign of love and peace. Amen.[429]

Mansfield's book provides interesting insights into the Catholic Charismatic Movement. Apparently Pope John XIII was strongly influenced by charismatic experiences that he had when he visited a small village in Czechoslovakia before he was chosen to be pope. Anna Maria Schmidt, an acquaintance of Mansfield's and a former citizen of this village, told Mansfield about the origins of the Catholic Charismatic Movement that occurred there in the eleventh century. According to Mansfield:

> A beautiful lady, who did not identify herself, appeared on the mountain and taught them to implore the Holy Spirit. As

[429] Prayer of Pope John XIII, *Humanae Salutis,* Second Vatican Council, December 25, 1961. Cf. Walter M. Abbott, S.S., general editor, *The Documents of Vatican II,* (The American Press, New York, 1966), 709 and 793.

> they followed her instructions, they were all filled with the Holy Spirit and received charismatic gifts, such as the discerning of spirits, prophecy, and the gift of tongues.[430]

Mansfield also added further insight from her investigation of Catholic history. She stated that Pope John XIII was influenced to pray for a new Pentecost by Elena Guerra, a woman whom he called "the apostle of the Holy Spirit." Sister Elena Guerra was the foundress of the Oblate Sisters of the Holy Spirit in Lucca, Italy. When she was fifty years old, she was inspired to write to Pope Leo XIII urging him to renew the Church through a return to the Holy Spirit. Sister Elena wrote twelve confidential letters to the Holy Father between 1895 and 1903 calling for renewed preaching on the Holy Spirit. At Sister Elena's suggestion, Pope Leo XIII invoked the Holy Spirit January 1, 1901, the first day of the first year in the twentieth century.[431]

Finally, Mansfield sheds light on an interesting connection between the Catholic Charismatic Movement and the Protestant Charismatic Movement. She stated:

> On the same day (January 1, 1901), an event took place in Topeka, Kansas, that marked the beginning of a great revival in the power and gifts of the Holy Spirit destined to sweep throughout the country and around the world. In Topeka, at 17th and Stone Avenue, (now the site of Most Pure Heart of Mary Catholic Church), stood a huge three-story, thirty room mansion. It was nicknamed "Stone's Folly" after the builder, Erasmus Stone discovered he could not afford to live in it. The mansion then became the home of the Bethel College and Bible School in September 1900. Rev. Charles Fox Parham and his students dedicated themselves to prayer and the study of God's word concerning the Baptism of the Holy Spirit. In fact the highest of the three towers on the mansion was designated as a prayer tower, and a marathon prayer vigil was organized. Twenty-four hours a day, seven days a week, these young people were asking God to baptize one of them or all of them

---

430 Mansfield, 6.
431 Ibid., 7.

> in the Holy Spirit. At about 11:00 on the evening of January 1, 1901 one of the students named Agnes Ozman asked Rev. Parham to lay hands on her head and pray that she would receive the Baptism of the Holy Spirit. That's precisely what happened. Agnes began to speak in tongues and others at the school, including Rev. Parham, had the same experience the following days. This event is generally accepted as the beginning of Pentecostalism. In 1906, a continued outpouring of the Holy Spirit occurred in Los Angeles, and is commonly referred to as the Azusa Street Revival.[432]

An additional explanation of what happened in Topeka, Kansas at the dawn of the twentieth century was written by Robert A. Larden in his book titled *Our Apostolic Heritage.*[433] In this book that documents the official history of the Apostolic Church of Pentecost of Canada, Rev. Larden documented how the Pentecostal doctrine of speaking in tongues as the initial evidence that one had been baptized in the Holy Spirit was established. He wrote:

> One of those who sought God for a more effective witness was Charles Fox Parham. Raised in the Congregational Church, [he] later joined the Methodists. He then associated with the revival movement which eventually separated from the Methodist body called the Holiness Movement. Charles Parham believed that while many obtained real sanctification – there still remained a great outpouring of power for Christians. In the year 1900 Charles Parham opened a Bible School in an abandoned mansion in Topeka, Kansas. Forty students gathered. Twelve ministers were among the men and women that gathered to study God's Word. The prime interest was in the book of Acts. Parham had a speaking engagement in December of that year and instructed the students to search the book of Acts in private study for any distinctive evidence that was consistently associated with the baptism of the Holy Ghost in the

[432] Ibid., 8.

[433] Robert A. Larden, *Our Apostolic Heritage: An Official History of the Apostolic Church of Pentecost of Canada Incorporated,* (Kyle Printing and Stationary, Calgary, 1971).

> early church. On his return the students were unanimous in their conviction that in each case where the baptism of the Holy Ghost was first received the evidence was "speaking in tongues."[434]

It is obvious from this account of the events leading up to the January 1901 occurrences in Topeka, Kansas, that it had already been determined speaking in tongues was not just "a" sign that someone had been filled with the Holy Spirit – it was "the" sign that must be sought. To this day, numerous Pentecostal denominations insist that speaking in tongues is "the" evidence and "the only" evidence for the baptism of the Holy Spirit.

Robert Larden's book also provides an interesting historical account that connects Charles Parham of the Topeka, Kansas group with the Asuza Revival that originated in Los Angeles, California in the early 1900s. Larden wrote:

> Charles Parham never compromised his conviction in regard to revealed truth and the validity of his experience with God… A second Bible School was opened in Houston, Texas in 1905. Among the student body was one called William Seymour.[435]

William Seymour played a significant role in the Asuza Street Revival. Seymour was an ordained minister with the Holiness Movement. He received an invitation to be an associate pastor of a Nazarene church in Los Angeles after the close of the Bible school that was conducted by Parham in Houston, Texas. Larden, writing about Seymour stated:

> It is said by some that he accepted the message of the baptism of the Holy Ghost with the evidence of speaking in other tongues, but had not experienced it personally when he arrived to take up his assignment. Plans were for him to speak nightly in a series of meetings and continue as associate pastor. For his first message at the Nazarene Church he read his text from Acts 2: 4, "And they were filled with the Holy Ghost, and

[434] Ibid., 12.
[435] Ibid., 14.

> began to speak with other tongues as the Spirit gave them utterance." He emphasized the conviction that had come to them at the school in Houston and the confirmation God gave when the greater part of the student body and Brother Parham and received the Holy Ghost baptism with the same evidence as those in the upper room recorded in Acts chapter 2.[436]

Seymour's message was not acceptable to the leaders of the Nazarene church and he was forced to leave. One of the members of the congregation, who was an adherent of Seymour, invited him to hold a service in her home. Larden wrote:

> It was in that home on Bonnie Brae Street on April 9th, 1906 that seven people received the baptism of the Holy Ghost with the evidence of speaking in tongues. The joy of the Lord filled the house. They laughed and shouted, sang and worshipped the Lord all night. The word got around and early the next morning a crowd was gathering, not all could get in. They sought for a larger meeting place and acquired the rent of an old building at 312 Azusa Street. It had one time been a Methodist Church but had been out of use for many years. Old lumber and debris littered the place. They cleaned it out and swept out the accumulated dirt. Planks were acquired and placed on top of empty nail kegs to provide seating for about thirty people. There were about twelve people at that first meeting. With no instruments to lead the singing and no hymn books they worshipped God. Familiar hymns were sung by memory. One of the most common was "The Comforter Has Come." That night two more received the baptism and spoke in tongues. A little flame was lit that was destined to sweep across a nation and envelope the world.[437]

Joined Together

If there are some factors indicating that the Catholic Charismatic Movement and the Protestant Charismatic Movement were joined together at birth January 1, 1901, then what has hap-

---

[436] Ibid., 15.
[437] Ibid., 16.

pened since? Is it possible to examine the two different movements today, compare and contrast them, and see whether or not "what has been joined together" can still be found at least somewhat united?

The answer to these questions can be documented. For example, in the February 1995 edition of *Charisma* we read that a revival that was supposedly happening in Britain was characterized by laughing and spiritual drunkenness. These kinds of experiences united Anglicans, Methodists, Pentecostals, Baptists, and Catholics.[438] Experience-based Christianity has been uniting all Protestants denominations and Catholics worldwide. Although there is no biblical basis for this kind of human behavior, advocates of an experience-based Christianity believe that it is "just people responding to God."[439]

Or consider what took place during the evening sessions at the Orlando 95 Conference, as Catholic and Protestant Charismatics abandoned their differences and worshipped together:

> Haitian Catholics danced conga-style in the aisles singing wildly in Creole. Robed monks and nuns skipped in the aisles along with Pentecostals, Methodists, Mennonites and Episcopalians. Others praised God by dancing around the convention center waving open umbrellas—perhaps to signify that the invisible rain of the Holy Spirit was falling.[440]

The Orlando 95 Conference was addressed by a number of key leaders who all were enthusiastic about this ecumenical gathering. These included Catholic Bishop Sam Jacobs, healing evangelist Benny Hinn, and Pentecostal Bishop Gilbert Patterson. Each speaker urged churches to work together. John Buckley, a Catholic priest from Tampa, Florida, said the conference had broken down walls of prejudice between believers. "This is

---

[438] *Charisma*, November 1995, 54.

[439] *Charisma*, February 1995, 26.

[440]. J. Lee Grady, "Catholics and Protestants Join Forces," *Charisma*, October 1995, 26.

the greatest ecumenical movement in the Christian church," he said.[441]

Charismatic Ecumenism?

The North American Renewal Service Committee (NARSC) is a broad representation of denominations and fellowships committed to sharing the gospel of Jesus Christ in the power of the Holy Spirit and striving for unity in the body of Christ.[442] This ecumenical organization made up of Catholic and Protestant Charismatics was responsible for organizing conferences on the Holy Spirit and World Evangelism in Kansas City in 1977, New Orleans in 1986 and 1987, Indianapolis in 1990 and in Orlando in 1995.[443]

"Celebrate Jesus 2000," held in St. Louis Missouri, June 22-25, 2000 was also sponsored by the North American Renewal Service Committee. This millennial conference was administered by the Franciscan University of Steubenville, Ohio, the Catholic university that had a significant influence in persuading Promise Keepers to reword their statement of faith to be compatible with the Catholic view of the gospel mentioned in chapter seven of this book.

The "Celebrate Jesus 2000" conference was advertised as the "the millennium party you won't want to miss."[444] Among the 47 speakers invited to participate in the conference were John Arnott, Toronto Airport Christian Fellowship; Father Tom Forest, International Director of Evangelization 2000; Father Stan Fortuna, Evangelist, Franciscan Friars of the Renewal; Jack Hayford, The Church on the Way, Van Nuys, California; Steve Hill, Together in Harvest Ministries; Cindy Jacobs, President and Co-founder, Generals of Intercession; Bishop Sam Jacobs, Roman Catholic Diocese of Alexandria, Louisiana; John Kilpatrick, Brownsville, Assemblies of God, Pensacola, Florida; Rick Joyner,

---

441. Ibid., 28.

442 "Celebrate Jesus 2000," brochure, mailed from Christian Conference Office, 1235 University Blvd. Steubenville, OH 43952.

443 Ibid.

444 Ibid.

Morning Star Ministries, Moravian Falls, North Carolina; Sister McKenna, International Healing Ministry; Richard Roberts, President, Oral Roberts University; Father Michael Scanlan, President, Franciscan University of Steubenville, Ohio; and Thomas Trask, General Superintendent of the Assemblies of God.[445]

According to promoters of the conference, "the streams of Christianity are gathering" to become the "River."[446] The brochure stated:

> Join us in St. Louis June 22-25 as thousands of Christians from every stream and tradition honor the 2000th anniversary of the birth of our Savior at the Celebrate Jesus 2000 Congress. This conference promises to be the setting for powerful revival. Gifted speakers and uplifting worship will fill you anew with the living water of the Holy Spirit. International workshops and sessions will give you the tools you need to live out your faith. Fellowship among both Catholic and Protestant will foster mutual respect and remind that Christ died for all. Without a doubt, you'll be prepared to "open wide the doors to Christ" in the third millennium.[447]

While the list of speakers at the "Celebrate Jesus 2000" conference looked like the "who's who" of Charismatic Christianity, there is reason to believe that Steubenville administrators may have stacked the deck with Catholics who have a purely Catholic view of what it means to be a Christian.

One of the "Celebrate Jesus 2000" speakers, Father Tom Forest, the Vatican's representative for "Evangelization 2000," is a staunch promoter of the Catholic agenda to lure the "separated brethren" back to the "Mother of All Churches." At a special session for Catholics held at the Indianapolis conference in 1990, Father Tom Forest went on record by stating:

---

445 Ibid.
446 Ibid.
447 Ibid.

> Our job is to make people as richly and as fully Christian as we can make them by ***bringing them into the Catholic Church.*** So evangelization is never fully successful, its only partial, until the convert is made a member of Christ's body by being led into the [Catholic] church.
>
> No, **you don't just invite someone to become a Christian, you invite them to become Catholics**... Why would this be so important? First of all, there are seven sacraments, and the Catholic Church has all seven. On our altars we have the body of Christ; we drink the blood of Christ. Jesus is alive on our altars... We become one with Christ in the Eucharist...
>
> As Catholics we have Mary, and that Mom of ours, Queen of Paradise, is praying for us till she see us in glory.
>
> As Catholics we have the papacy, a history of popes from Peter to John Paul II... we have the rock upon which Christ did build His Church.
>
> Now as Catholics – now I love this one – we have purgatory. Thank God! I'm one of those people who would never get to the Beatific Vision without it. It's the only way to go....
>
> So as Catholics... ***our job is to use the remaining decade evangelizing everyone we can in the Catholic Church,*** into the body of Christ and into the third millennium of Catholic history.[448]

So will the "streams" of Christianity destined to form the "river" in St Louis in June of 2000, form a river that will eventually flow towards Rome? Has Father Tom Forest changed his views about what is means to be a Christian since his dissertation to Catholics in 1990, or have Protestants been deluded into believing that the Catholic gospel has changed?

---

[448] "Roman Catholic Doubletalk at Indianapolis '90" *Foundation,* July-August 1990, excerpts from talk by Fr. Tom Forest to the Roman Catholic Saturday morning training session.

The Alpha Factor

"Roman Catholic Bishops Applaud Alpha As Course Spreads Through Church."[449] This was the front-page headline of the July-October *Alpha News*. The subheading stated, "Archbishop opens New Zealand Conference." For anyone suspicious that the Alpha program may just be another subtle arm of the ecumenical movement, these headlines are quite significant. The article that follows leaves no doubt.

According to this article, an increasing number of Roman Catholic churches are using the Alpha Course. As well, many Catholic bishops and church leaders are giving the course their blessing, among them Cardinal Thomas Williams, Roman Catholic Archbishop of Wellington. More than 450 people packed London's Westminster Cathedral Hall in May of 1997 for the first Roman Catholic Alpha conference. Sandy Miller and Nicky Gumbel, of Holy Trinity Brompton, led the conference, which had received messages of encouragement from Cardinal Hume, the Archbishop of Westminster.[450]

Bishop Ambrose Griffiths, Roman Catholic bishop of Hexham and Newcastle, introduced the conference. He stated that the Alpha Course is a "powerful evangelistic tool which reaches out precisely to those whom we need." He also said the conference was very important ecumenically. "We should have the humility to learn from other Christians and I am delighted that we are doing this today," he said.[451]

Explaining why Catholics can easily accept the Alpha Course, he further stated: "It is not a complete exposition of Catholic doctrine. No introductory course could possibly do that. But it does not contain anything that is contrary to Catholic doctrine." In addition he said, "What's more, it provides in a wonderful form the basis of Christian belief which many Catholics

[449] *Alpha News,* Holy Trinity Brompton, London, July-October, 1997, 1.
[450] Ibid.
[451] Ibid.

have never cottoned up to. They have been sacramentalised, but never have been evangelized."[452]

After the conference, which included a seminar on how to run an Alpha Course in Catholic context, many delegates expressed excitement and delight at what they had heard. One delegate wrote, "This is an awesome and historic moment in the history of the Church."[453]

Mary and the Holy Spirit

While Protestants and Catholics seem to be finding a unity centered on the gifts of the Holy Spirit, there may be reason to be cautious, especially if you have researched the literature regarding the origins of the Catholic Charismatic Movement. Christian unity must always be centered on the finished work accomplished by Jesus' death on the cross. The gospel is based upon the birth, death and resurrection of Jesus, not on some gift of the Holy Spirit such as speaking in tongues.

According to several statements made by Patti Gallagher Mansfield in her book *As By A New Pentecost,* Mary, the mother of Jesus, is the one who played a key role in the dispensation of the Holy Spirit at the "dramatic beginning of the Catholic Charismatic Renewal" at the Duquesne Weekend in Pittsburgh, February 17-19, 1967. While Jesus is mentioned from time to time in this book, the clear presentation of the gospel is absent. If a nonbeliever were to read the book, they could only assume that a "Pentecostal experience" was the essence of being a Christian. As the book is dedicated to Mary, and as there are many examples of the adoration of Mary in the book, one must wonder if the Catholic Charismatic Movement is more centered on Mary than it is on the gospel of Jesus Christ. For example, with regard to the opening meeting that was held on the Friday night, Patti Gallagher Mansfield stated:

> I believe it was significant to have our attention drawn to Mary at the beginning of our retreat. She was there at the An-

[452] Ibid.
[453] Ibid.

> nunciation when the Word became flesh. She was there at the Nativity to bring forth Jesus into the world. She was there at the Cross when our redemption was won. She was there at Pentecost when the Church was born. In God's plan it was necessary for Mary to be *"with us"* in an explicit way as we experienced a sovereign move of the Holy Spirit that Weekend. The Fathers of the Church call Mary *"the spouse of the Holy Spirit."* How can she fail to be present when the Holy Spirit is at work?[454]

Later that evening, Mansfield went to the chapel where she had what she describes as a supernatural experience. She stated, "I knelt down in the presence of Jesus in the Blessed Sacrament. Then something happened that I was not expecting."[455] She continued:

> I'd always believed by the gift of faith that Jesus is really present in the Blessed Sacrament, but I had never experienced His glory before. As I knelt there that night, my body literally trembled before His majesty and holiness. I was filled with awe in His presence, He was there... the King of Kings, and the Lord of Lords, the Great God of the Universe![456]

Mansfield then began to pray a prayer of unconditional surrender. As she was kneeling before the altar, she found herself prostrate, flat on her face. No one had laid hands on her. She had never had such an experience before.[457]

Later in the evening two girls who were also at the retreat noticed that there was something physically different about her appearance. Taking each of these girls by the hand she led them into the chapel. Writing about this experience, Mansfield stated:

> The three of us knelt before the Lord in the Blessed Sacrament, and I began to pray out loud. I didn't even have the correct terminology; I just prayed from my heart. *"Lord whatever*

---

[454] Mansfield, 35. [emphasis in the original]
[455] Ibid., 39.
[456] Ibid.
[457] Ibid.

> *you just did for me, do it for them!"* I was asking the Lord to baptize them in the Holy Spirit without even realizing it.[458]

These statements certainly sound like the words of a genuinely serious believer who wants to experience a closer walk with her Lord and Savior, Jesus Christ. While Charismatic Protestants use exactly the same terminology when describing their experiences, there is one major difference that needs to be pointed out. Protestants reject the idea that Jesus is present in the Eucharist. The idea that a priest has the power to change a piece of bread or a wafer into the actual body of Christ is called transubstantiation. The faith to believe that this happens is a church dogma that has no biblical basis.

Ms. Gallagher Mansfield has a theory on what she believes is happening which fits well into the context of this book. She states:

> I don't pretend to understand it fully, but I believe the Lord is preparing His people for a new wave of the Holy Spirit. Fr. George Kosicki, C.S.B., and Fr. Gerald Farrell, M.M., have written an insightful book about this new wave of the Spirit entitled *The Spirit and the Bride Say "Come."* In this book they discuss the ***role of Mary*** in the new Pentecost. My own understanding of what God is calling for has been deeply influenced by their reflections.[459]

In the conclusion of her book, Ms. Gallagher Mansfield makes a number of statements that further reveal that her understanding of the new Pentecost is centered on her devotion to Mary. Speaking on behalf of Catholics, she says:

> We Catholics see in this scene a call to entrust ourselves to Mary's motherly care, to welcome her as one of the precious gifts Jesus has given us, and to ask for her powerful intercession. Just as Cana Mary spoke to Jesus on behalf of those in

[458] Ibid. [emphasis in the original]
[459] Ibid., 167. emphasis not in original

> need, we believe that she continues to intercede for the Church today.[460]

Then in this final statement, she clearly explains that to be faithful to the Lord and prepare for the Second Pentecost, we need to look to "Mary" as our spiritual "Mother." She wrote:

> To whatever measure I have been faithful to the Lord, it has been thanks to her example and to her prayer. I believe that an important element in preparing a fresh outpouring of the Holy Spirit is our relationship with Mary as Mother.[461]

The Role of Mary in the Second Pentecost

Catholic Charismatics and Protestant Charismatics focus on the Holy Spirit. We know that the Bible is full of references to the Holy Spirit. The Holy Spirit is a person, not a mystical force that can be invoked. As well, while there was a Day of Pentecost that occurred as recorded in the Book of Acts, what is the biblical basis for proclaiming that there will be a second Pentecost? Jesus said that after He departed the Holy Spirit would come and be with believers as the Comforter. The New Testament teaches that the Holy Spirit is with us and will continue to be with us until Jesus comes for His Church.

The idea that there has to be a special outpouring called a "Second Pentecost" or a "Third Wave" that will draw the masses to Jesus at the end of time is not biblical. If this idea is not biblical, then what is the source? Could this be a major seduction of Christianity? What role does Mary play in the Second Pentecost?

"Mary" and the Second Pentecost

Father Don Stefano Gobbi is the head of the Marian Movement of Priests. He has received hundreds of messages from a supernatural apparition who calls herself "Mary." These messages are recorded and disseminated to 400 plus cardinals and

---

460 Ibid., 171.

461 Ibid.

bishops, more than 100,000 priests, and millions of religious and faithful around the world that constitute "The Marian Movement of Priests." Consider the following Marian messages that are contained in the book *To The Priests, Our Lady's Beloved Sons*:[462]

- Enter all of you into the new and spiritual cenacle of my Immaculate Heart to recollect yourselves in an intense and incessant prayer made with me, your heavenly Mother, in expectation that the great miracle of the Second Pentecost, now close at hand, will be accomplished.[463]

- With an extraordinary cenacle of prayer and fraternity, you celebrate today the solemnity of Pentecost. You recall the prodigious event of the descent of the Holy Spirit, under the form of tongues of fire, upon the Cenacle of Jerusalem, where the Apostles were gathered in prayer, with me, your heavenly Mother. You too, gathered today in prayer in the spiritual cenacle of my Immaculate Heart, prepare yourselves to receive the prodigious gift of the Second Pentecost.[464]

The apparition of Mary not only predicts that she will usher in the Second Pentecost, but she also anticipates that full unity under the Catholic Church will also be achieved during this era:

- The Second Pentecost will come to lead all the Church to the summit of her greatest splendor... Above all, the Holy Spirit will communicate to the Church the precious gift of her full unity and of her greatest holiness. Only then will Jesus bring into her his reign of glory.[465]

- I am for you the way of unity. When I am accepted by the whole Church, then, as Mother, I will be able to reunite

---

[462] Fr. Don Stefano Gobbi, *To The Priests, Our Lady's Beloved Sons,* (The National Headquarters of the Marian Movement of Priests in the United States of America, St. Francis, ME, 1998).

[463] Ibid., 911.

[464] Ibid., 911-912.

[465] Ibid.

my children in the warmth of one single family. For this reason, the reunion of all Christians in the Catholic Church will coincide with the triumph of my Immaculate Heart in the world. This reunited Church, in the splendor of a new Pentecost, will have the power to renew all the people of the earth.[466]

- A true reunification of Christians is not possible unless it be in the perfection of truth. And truth has been kept intact only in the Catholic Church, which must preserve it, defend it and proclaim it to all without fear. It is the light of the truth which will draw many of my children to return to the bosom of the one and only Church founded by Jesus.[467]

Catholic Charismatics and many Protestant Charismatics seem to be embracing a unity that is based upon sharing common supernatural experiences. They believe these supernatural experiences are manifestations of the Spirit of God. But what if Charismatics continue to add extrabiblical experiences to their list of Bible sanctioned "power encounters?"

Among these manifestations is the appearance of a woman Catholics call the Queen of Heaven. This apparitional woman claims that she will usher in a reunification of all Christians with the Roman Catholic Church. Who is this "Queen?" Will this "Queen" effectively convince Protestant Charismatics she is the true mother of Jesus?

---

[466] Ibid., 279.
[467] Ibid., 278.

19

THE RETURN OF THE QUEEN

This book has been written as the result of a personal spiritual journey that has been underway for over two decades. There have been times when I have placed the project on hold realizing that it would be easier and much less of a struggle if I avoided the controversy that connects experienced-based Christianity with Babylonian religious practices that are masquerading in the name of Christ.

Although there have been these times, a motivating factor has always brought me back to the work that was started. To love God with all our hearts and with all our souls means we must abide in His Word. The Bible demands that we love others more than we love ourselves. According to the Bible, people who are embracing another gospel are not only deceived; they are on their way to a lost eternity.

In the Book of Jude we are instructed to stand for the truth. We are to do so with love and concern for others.[468] We should always remember what Paul told the church at Ephesus: our battle is not against flesh and blood, but instead, is against

[468] Jude 17-23

spiritual powers in heavenly places committed to deceiving humans.[469]

God's Word states that deception must not only be identified, it must be exposed. As one reads through the Old Testament it becomes apparent that God has always dealt with deception by speaking to His people through His Word. While there are many examples of this we will look at only one.

God's Warning in the Past

Ezekiel was called as a messenger to warn the children of Israel about their wicked ways and to challenge them to turn away from their sin and return to God. In the third chapter of the Book of Ezekiel we read what God spoke to Ezekiel:

> And He said to me: "Son of man, go to the house of Israel and speak with My words to them. For you are not sent to a people of unfamiliar speech and of hard language, but to the house of Israel, not to many people of unfamiliar speech and of hard language, whose words you cannot understand. Surely, had I sent you to them, they would have listened to you. But the house of Israel will not listen to you, because they will not listen to Me; for all the house of Israel are impudent and hard-hearted. Behold, I have made your face strong against their faces, and your forehead strong against their foreheads. Like adamant stone, harder than flint, I have made your forehead; do not be afraid of them, nor be dismayed at their looks, though they are a rebellious house."[470]

While it is obvious that Ezekiel was called to proclaim a message of warning, it is also apparent that the people of his day were not willing to hear what God was saying to them through the prophet. It is also clear that Ezekiel's call was not an easy one.

Who would want to be unpopular by challenging a majority of the people who believed they were on the road to heaven

---

[469] Ephesians 6:11-14
[470] Ezekiel 3:4-9

when in reality they were headed towards hell? Nevertheless, Ezekiel was commissioned by God to proclaim the warning. If they did not listen then Ezekiel was not to blame. He had done what God had told him to do. Again we read:

> Son of man, I have made you a watchman for the house of Israel; therefore hear a word from My mouth, and give them warning from Me: When I say to the wicked, "You shall surely die," and you give him no warning, nor speak to warn the wicked from his wicked way, to save his life, that same wicked man shall die in his iniquity; but his blood I will require at your hand. Yet, if you warn the wicked, and he does not turn from his wickedness, nor from his wicked way, he shall die in his iniquity; but you have delivered your soul.[471]

While it is true we now live in the age of grace and Ezekiel was a prophet who lived over twenty-five hundred years ago, principles from God's Word are still relevant for us today. When it is possible to identify teachings and practices that are not biblical, the Bible gives us a precedent to address these issues.

Messages from Heaven

She appears as a beautiful translucent woman surrounded by brilliant light. Her countenance is peaceful, her eyes kind and loving. Those who see her relate feeling such joy and pleasure that the term *ecstasy* is often used to describe the experience. She is believed to be the Virgin Mary, the mother of the Lord Jesus and the sightings of her image may be more widespread than most people realize. She has been seen all over the globe - in Medjugorje, Fatima, Lourdes, Guadalupe, Egypt; Russia and all across the U.S.A. Wherever she has appeared millions of faithful followers flock to the shrines that are built in her honor.

Often when the apparition comes, she is accompanied by miraculous signs - healings, bleeding or crying statues, oil extruding from Marian statues and images, rosaries that turn gold, strange lights in the sky, and unusual phenomena in the sun.

[471] Ezekiel 3:17-19

And she has much to say to her followers. Her words are scrupulously written down and distributed among the faithful. She speaks of future events, and most of what she says can be found in the pages of Scripture. However, a critical examination of her messages reveals that she is preaching a false gospel.[472]

While her messages of peace and unity seem harmless, is it possible that she has an agenda that is anticipated in the Bible?[473] What if these apparitions of Mary are not actually Mary? What if the master deceiver is the inspiration behind these extrabiblical messages? There is no doubt people all over the world are experiencing some sort of supernatural phenomenon. The question is however, what are they experiencing? What is the source of these experiences? How can we know?

There are a number of people who have studied the apparitions and have expressed the same concerns that I will be outlining in this chapter. Jim Tetlow, a colleague of mine and a former Catholic, has researched this topic diligently for some time and has written two books and produced a video documentary called *Messages From Heaven: A Biblical Examination of the Apparitions of the Virgin Mary.*[474] While this chapter will touch on the subject of apparitions, Tetlow's books document the Marian apparition phenomenon in depth, comparing "Mary's" messages with the Word of God. The video also examines the possible prophetic significance of various apparitions in light of Bible prophecy. [For more information on the book and the video, see the back of this book.]

The Lady of All Nations

While the "messages from heaven" are somewhat diverse, there are some common factors that can be identified. One of these mentioned earlier in this book is the extrabiblical idea that

---

[472] Jim Tetlow, *Messages From Heaven: A Biblical Exploration of the Apparitions of the Virgin Mary and Other Supernatural Activity in the End Times,* chapters 5-6

[473] Ibid., chapters 1, 4 and 12.

[474] Ibid.

peace in the world can only occur if the pope proclaims a dogma that Mary shares in the act of redemption with her son, Jesus.

Figure 23: Depictions of "Mary" standing upon the serpent are found all over the world. While she often stands on the serpent alone, a few statues show her standing on the serpent with the baby Jesus.

Amsterdam is one of the locations where apparitions of this nature have been received, its messages recorded and exported to the world. Advocates believe that Mary the mother of Jesus appeared to visionary Ida Peerdeman on March 25, 1945. This was the first in a series of about sixty apparitions that supposedly took place from 1945 until 1959 and became known as the "Messages of the Lady of All Nations."[475]

According to a Lady of All Nations Worldwide Action Pamphlet, the reason the messages of Amsterdam are so unique to the history of the Marian Movement is that "Mary is coming in our modern times under a new title THE LADY OF ALL NATIONS and is requesting a final Marian dogma."[476] This dogma, it is stated, will contain a threefold truth: "The Father and the Son wish to send Mary, the Lady of All Nations, in this time as Coredemptrix, Mediatrix, and Advocate. When the

---

[475] *This Time Is Our Time: The Messages of The Lady of All Nations,* (The Lady of All Nations Association, Amsterdam, 1999), 7.

[476] Ibid., 2.

dogma is proclaimed, the LADY OF ALL NATIONS will grant peace, true peace to the world."[477]

The Lady of All Nations doctrines are spreading worldwide. According to a publication entitled *Third International Day of Prayer in Honor of the LADY OF ALL NATIONS,* the Lady of All Nations is not just for one country, she is destined for the people of the world.[478] Six cardinals and forty-seven bishops from thirty-five different countries attended the Third International Day of Prayer held in Amsterdam in 1999 along with over 12,000 other delegates that came from every continent. Even the late Archbishop of New York, His Eminence John Cardinal O'Connor sent his greetings from the United States and expressed his regrets that he was unable to participate in the "celebration to the glory of Our Lady."[479]

The main thrust of the Lady of All Nations Movement is for participants to focus on a prayer. On February 11, 1951, Peerdeman claimed the "Lady" taught her a prayer to the Lord Jesus Christ imploring Him to send the Holy Spirit. In the very next apparition, March 4, 1951, the "Lady" appeared to Peerdeman as "the Lady before the Cross." She was standing upon the globe. Peerdeman claimed that the "Lady" made the following request: "You shall have this image made and spread together with the prayer I recited."[480]

The prayer and the image were to be spread throughout the whole world for the preparation and illustration of a new dogma. According to the "Lady" this new dogma would be the final and greatest dogma: Mary, Coredemptrix, Mediatrix and Advocate. The "Lady" also foretold a great controversy and conflict that would arise over this dogma, which when finally accepted would usher in "a new era for humanity."[481]

---

[477] Ibid.

[478] *Third International Day of Prayer in Honor of the LADY OF ALL NATIONS,* (Family of Mary Coredemptrix, Civitella del Tronto, 1999), (III) – Issue #10.

[479] Ibid., 4.

[480] *This Time Is Our Time,* 8.

[481] Ibid.

This prayer usually is printed along with a painting of the image of the Lady of All Nations. She appears standing on the world. Her arms are extended and three bands of light are projected downward to a large flock of sheep that are being illuminated. A very prominent cross appears behind the "Lady." The prayer states: "Lord Jesus Christ, Son of the Father, send *now* Your Holy Spirit over the earth. Let the Holy Spirit live in the hearts of *all* nations, that they may be preserved from degeneration, disaster and war. May the LADY OF ALL NATIONS, who once was Mary, be our Advocate".[482]

The Worldwide Action Pamphlet distributed by the Lady of All Nations Action Center in St. Louis, Missouri encourages all people to pray this prayer. The pamphlet states: "Let the people pray this short, simple prayer every day. This prayer is short and simple, so that everyone in this quick and modern world can pray it. It is given in order to call down the True Spirit upon the world."[483]

Many of the Peerdeman messages warn the Church of Rome of the seriousness of impending dangers if the new dogma is not adopted and promoted. The "Lady" asks all humanity to take heed of these messages. She calls upon all Christians to unite and to encounter the world with the cross in their hands. Furthermore, the "Lady" commands that the Church be united and become one large community of all peoples.[484]

A Final Marian Dogma

One of the common denominators of the Marian Movement is a very concerted effort to encourage the pope in Rome to proclaim a new Catholic dogma. An excerpt from a feast day homily held in Amsterdam by Bishop Paul Maria Hnilica on Pentecost Sunday, 1999, will confirm this statement. In an article called "The Mother of All Nations Prepares the Hearts for a New Pentecost" we read:

---

[482] Ibid., front cover.
[483] Ibid., 3.
[484] Ibid., 8.

Figure 24: The Lady of All Nations Worldwide Action Pamphlet depicts Mary, as Coredemptrix, Mediatrix, and Advocate.

The Holy Father, the Universal Shepherd of the Church, has felt it his duty to announce to the world the greatness of the mystery of redemption, to which the Mother of Jesus is inseparably united. In his papal emblem one finds a large cross

> inseparably united with a large "M," which represents the presence of the Mother in the entirety of the work of redemption worked by the Son. Many bishops of the world, together with numerous cardinals and millions of faithful venerate Mary under the title: Coredemptrix, Mediatrix, and Advocate. Here in Amsterdam, in the 1940's these three titles were proclaimed by an entire Bishops' Conference. We also want to pray that the light of the Holy Spirit may illumine the entire Church regarding prophecies such as that of Saint Maximilian Kolbe, and regarding the requests placed before the Holy Father – on one part by the People of God, but also by so many shepherds – for the desired dogmatic definition of the coredemption and mediation of Mary. For this dogma would be the coronation of a long theological, mystical, spiritual and pastoral journey, which has illumined the vocation of the Virgin Mary, and which, under his pontificate, seems to have reached a climax.[485]

Initially there was resistance against the "Lady's" apparitions and messages by the majority of the officials of the Catholic Church. In the divided church of the Netherlands they were considered to be inopportune – partially due to ecumenical concerns. However, this has changed significantly. To date, this prayer card has been translated into over seventy languages. Millions of these prayer cards have been distributed all around the world.

On May 31, 1996, official ecclesiastical approval was given for public devotion under the new title "The Lady of All Nations." On this date the bishops of the Haarlem Amsterdam Diocese, Bishop Bomers and Auxillary Bishop Punt, issued a statement declaring that they have no objection to public devotion under the title "The Lady of All Nations."[486]

---

[485] *Third International Day of Prayer in Honor of the LADY OF ALL NATIONS,* 10.

[486] *This Time Is Our Time,* 9.

Figure 25: Cardinals, bishops and priests from around the world stand in front of crowned image of "The Lady of All Nations."

Meanwhile a great international movement has arisen within the Church, and a request has been made for the pope to proclaim a final Marian dogma that would define Mary's role as Coredemptrix, Mediatrix and Advocate. Hundreds of bishops and more than forty cardinals have expressed their support of this new dogma, and more than four million signatures have been collected and presented to the pope to encourage him to proclaim the dogma.[487]

According to the Lady of All Nations Association, a group based in Europe and the United States, this dogma will happen. In their publication called *This Time is Our Time: The Messages of The Lady of All Nations*, the following statement is made:

> To proclaim a dogma means the formulation of a divine truth and thus the providing of a deeper understanding of creation, humanity and salvation. Salvation happens when a human being is touched by God's Love. The dogma of Mary Coredemptrix, Mediatrix, and Advocate explains an essential dimension of salvation: the participation of humanity in the work of redemption – humanity's response to God's redemp-

[487] Ibid.

> tive Love. Mary, realizes this participation in a unique and complete way. She precedes her Son, follows Him and suffers with Him in order to be a light to this world and, as coredeemers, to be builders of the Kingdom of God.[488]

Where would this idea come from that Mary is the "light of the world?" Jesus said that He was the light of the world.[489] It is true that as followers of Jesus, we are to let our "lights shine." But letting our lights shine, means to always let our lives be focused on Jesus, and Jesus alone.

The Bible warns us about the end-times plan of the angel of light.[490] It seems that this unbiblical idea that Mary and humankind share in the redemption process and are co-builders of the Kingdom of God may well be from the Prince of Darkness. Could it be that the apparitions of "The Lady of All Nations" are demonic lies?

Who Is this Queen?

The Book of Revelation warns about a counterfeit religious system. Bible-believing Christians call this global religion the counterfeit bride. John the Apostle labeled this false church the harlot. The Scriptures also indicate the harlot is associated with a "queen." In Revelation chapter eighteen we read:

> For all the nations have drunk of the wine of the wrath of her fornication, the kings of the earth have committed fornication with her, and the merchants of the earth have become rich through the abundance of her luxury. And I heard another voice from heaven saying, "Come out of her, my people, lest you share in her sins, and lest you receive of her plagues. For her sins have reached to heaven, and God has remembered her iniquities. Render to her just as she rendered to you, and repay her double according to her works; in the cup which she has mixed, mix double for her. In the measure that she glorified herself and lived luxuriously, in the same measure give her

488 Ibid.
489 John 8:12
490 2 Corinthians 11:14

> torment and sorrow; for she says in her heart, **'I sit as queen,** and am no widow, and will not see sorrow.' Therefore her plagues will come in one day; death and mourning and famine. And she will be utterly burned with fire, for strong is the Lord God who judges her."[491]

John is not the only prophet who saw there was a queen and that this queen would be judged for the whole world to see at the end of the age. The prophet Isaiah also warned about a deceiving woman called the "virgin daughter of Babylon" who would be judged by God. In the 47th chapter of Isaiah we read:

> Come down and sit in the dust, O virgin daughter of Babylon; Sit on the ground without a throne, O daughter of the Chaldeans! For you shall no more be called Tender and delicate. Take the millstones and grind meal. Remove your veil, take off the skirt, Uncover the thigh, Pass through the rivers. Your nakedness shall be uncovered, yes, your shame will be seen; I will take vengeance, and I will not arbitrate with a man. As for our Redeemer, the LORD of hosts is His name, the Holy One of Israel. Sit in silence, and go into darkness, O daughter of the Chaldeans; for you shall no longer be called **The Lady of Kingdoms**.[492]

Who is this "Lady of Kingdoms" that Isaiah is prophesying about? Apparently she is a female entity that has played a deceptive role and is somehow connected to the pagan religious practices of ancient Babylon. Isaiah's words bring a strong retribution and condemnation upon those who have rejected the true Redeemer, the "Holy One of Israel" - the LORD of hosts is *His* name.

We know from biblical history that a queen, (the Queen of Heaven) has played a significant role in deluding people in the past.[493] Is it possible that this same Queen of Heaven will delude

---

[491] Revelation 18:3-8
[492] Isaiah 47:1-5
[493] Jeremiah 7 and Jeremiah 44

the world once more? Is the apparition of Mary paving the way for the world religion that will worship the Antichrist?

Figure 26: An image of the crowned Queen of Heaven and a baby Jesus is located over the front door of Winchester College in England. The statue was placed there in 1597.

Return of the Goddess

What is Christianity? Is Christianity based upon the Word of God and the teachings of Jesus Christ or is Christianity founded upon messages from heaven attributed to the so-called apparitions of Mary? Or what about other extrabiblical dogmas that have been expounded by church leaders in the past? Who has the authority to add to the canon of Scripture? It is important that we consider the answers to these questions seriously. Humans are designed to be rational thinking beings and to make choices. It is also important that we make correct choices. If we do not, then the Bible teaches there will be serious consequences.

Throughout this book, the premise has been presented that all teachings in the name of Christ should be tested according to the Word of God. As the book is now near completion, I want to make one final plea for all Christians to consider the Word of God as the final authority on all topics relating to Christianity. If we say we are Christians and do not do this, then we willingly open the door for deception.

Regarding the Marian Movement and other experience-based movements that embrace extrabiblical teachings in the name of Christ, the time has come to make a stand. If we do not, then we may well become a part of the counterfeit church. Extrabiblical Christianity can become Babylonian in nature and the harlot that John wrote about in the Book of Revelation can and will materialize.

For those who are still not willing to heed the warnings of the Bible about the reappearance of a Babylonian-like church, consider the following quote taken from the book *Myths of the Female Divine Goddess:*

> But Goddess has never died, and one of the major spiritual and psychological phenomena of our time has been her reemergence as a significant presence in our lives. She has founded a central place in several of the great worlds religions - particularly, Catholicism and Hinduism. Goddess has been revived in modern cults, the spiritual ancestors of which are the earth cults of Demeter, Isis, and Asherah. She has made

herself known in the metaphors, the myths, of modern science – particularly, psychology and climatology. She has expressed herself politically and sociologically in the drive for a new wholeness – a new spiritual, psychological, and physical ecology – that is the power behind what we call the women's movement. Goddess is returning because she is needed.

The return of Goddess in the patriarchal religious context is most clearly illustrated in the progress of the Virgin Mary from her original status in the New Testament as humble birth-giver and grieving mother to that of immaculately conceived Queen of Heaven. The progress was not an easy one. It was consistently resisted by the Church, which in the gospels - the biography of Jesus - finally approved in the fourth century, gave Mary a minor role. But once the divinity of Jesus was established, it was inevitable that Mary, his mother, should be seen as Goddess by a folk mind familiar with the goddesses Asherah, Demeter, and Isis. As Jesus emerged as the New Adam, the new redeeming and edible fruit on the tree – cross that had replaced the forbidden fruit the tree of knowledge in the old Garden of Eden, Mary logically became the sinless New Eve, the balancing feminine principle to the male redeemer. A belief that she had been immaculately conceived, a belief the Roman Catholic Church accepted as dogma only in 1854. Over the centuries, other folk traditions attached themselves to Mary. Special goddess cakes were offered up to her, as they had been earlier to Asherah.[494]

Or finally one more quote from the same book that will further document that Babylonianism is being revived in the name of Christianity:

But as Queen, Mary grew in power. She was the Church itself, in which Christ was contained. She became in a sense the Bride of Christ and was often referred to as such. Once again, Goddess has emerged in union with the sacrificed son-lover. Churches were named for her more often than for other saints

[494] David Leemings and Jake Page, *Myths of the Female Divine Goddess,* (Oxford University Press, New York, 1994), 161-162.

> or for Jesus. Statues and paintings of Mary became and remain objects for both private and public adoration. In these works, Mary is depicted more often as crowned queen than as humble maiden. Sometimes she holds the crowned Christ-king on her lap, much as Isis held the pharaohs of Egypt on hers. Many of the Virgin Mary paintings and statues, especially in France, depict a Black Madonna, linking Mary to other Black Goddesses whose color reflects the dark earth of Goddess's origins. To these objects of devotion, magical powers and sometimes strange rituals and celebrations have been attached.[495]

It is apparent from reading these statements that a revival of Babylonism in the name of Christ is now underway. When we take our eyes off Jesus Christ and His Word, the potential to be deceived in the name of Christ is great.

495 Ibid., 162.

Figure 27: A banner hanging in Winchester Cathedral depicts the crowned Queen of Heaven holding baby Jesus. Notice the moon and the sun.

20

THE EUCHARISTIC JESUS

At this point, the objective for writing this book should be clear. It is infinitely important to pay attention to what God has revealed to us in His Word. If the Bible is really true about statements it makes about the future, it is imperative we pay attention. As the apostle Peter wrote: "And so we have the prophetic word confirmed, which you do well to heed as a light that shines in a dark place, until the day dawns and the morning star rises in your hearts."[496]

The Common Thread

New Wine and the Babylonian Vine: Last Days Delusion in the Name of Christ! When you first glanced at the front cover of this book, you may have been uncertain as to what you would find written on the pages between the front and back cover. Now that you have read through the book to this point, you should have a better idea.

However, for some, there may still be some unanswered questions. The book has examined a number of topics and trends. In the first section, we presented a biblical basis for deception, pointing out that Satan has a master plan to deceive the world - especially in the name of Christ, in the last days before Jesus returns. In the next section, we looked at documentation

---

[496] 2 Peter 1:19

showing that Catholics and Protestants are equally guilty of redefining Christianity by embracing and promoting extrabiblical ideas. We saw how unity is being promoted in the name of Christ, but not always is this unity biblically based. Following this we were able to see how a spirituality based on environmentalism and evolutionism is being promoted in the name of Christ.

The fourth and fifth sections of this book examined the New Wine Movement and the Catholic Charismatic Movement. We saw how both Protestants and Catholics are embracing what they believe is a new wave of the Holy Spirit that is being poured out upon the world.

While the subtitle of this book, *Last Days Delusion in the Name of Christ*, is clearly the theme of *New Wine and the Babylonian Vine*, a number of loose threads still need to be drawn together. Although we have already examined the deception that is currently underway in detail, I felt it was important to add some concluding thoughts for readers to consider. I am convinced the Bible will give us valuable insight about Satan's deceptive plan that will continue to unfold in the future.

The Eucharist and Mary

The apparition of Mary conveys numerous messages given to thousands of visionaries that deal with a variety of topics. One of the main themes consistently reported by those who receive messages from "Mary" is the great importance of the Eucharist. Not only are Catholic apologists like Peter Kreeft stating that experiences centered around the "Host" are important for unity – so are the apparitions of Mary and even manifestations of "Jesus".

The following quote is from an apparition of Mary that occurred in Rome, Italy. Rome, of course is where the "Mother of All Churches" is located. It was here that "Mary" stated that she is the "Mother of the Eucharist":

> Speak about the Mother of the Eucharist, because the Mother of the Eucharist closes history. The Immaculate Con-

> ception opens the History, and the Mother of the Eucharist closes it... All the messages come from God and everywhere that I am appearing, I am speaking about the same things, because through the triumph of the Eucharist the Mother wants all the Churches to be reunited, so that there will be only one Church for all the people.[497]

At this apparition site in Rome, the visionary Marisa Rossi has also received many messages from "Jesus" in the Eucharist. Interestingly, he is also speaking about his great desire for unity, particularly religious unity:

> It is God the Father's wish to reunite all the religions and the races, for them to become only one community and the Eucharist to become the center of all the religions and races...I want all religions to be reunited, the races to be reunited, I want only one religion, only one love, because God is love.[498]

In addition, the apparition of Mary spoke to Father Gobbi, the leader of the Marian Movement of Priests, and stated the importance of the eucharistic reign of Jesus:

> Today I ask all to throw open the doors to Jesus Christ who is coming. I am the Mother of the Second Advent and the door which is being opened on the new era. This new era will coincide with the greatest triumph of the Eucharistic reign of Jesus...The Eucharistic Jesus will release all his power of love, which will transform souls, the Church and all humanity.[499]

From these messages and many others, we can see that "Mary" and the Eucharistic Jesus are preparing the world for a new era of unity under the Roman Catholic Church. They will usher in this new period with mighty signs and wonders. This

---

[497] "Apparitions of Our Lady and Eucharistic Miracles in Rome," Online posting, www.geocities.com/Athens/Forum/6832/msg972.htm, January 23, 2000. Message given on Feb., 16, 1997.

[498] "Our Lady is Appearing in Rome," Online posting, http://www.geocities.com/Athens/Forum/6832/msg976.htm, May 16, 2000. Messages given on June 21, 1997 and June 26, 1997.

[499] Gobbi, pp. 676,640.

fact is well supported, as Marian author and researcher Dr. Thomas Petrisko, made clear in his book *Call of the Ages*:

> While the Blessed Virgin Mary is indeed the great sign spoken of in Chapter 12:1 of the Book of Revelation, the numerous apparitions of Jesus to so many visionaries throughout the world is another phenomenon that deserves close examination. Like Mary's apparitions, these reported visions are not to be taken lightly, for they carry with them incredible miracles and profound messages reportedly from the Lord Himself.[500]

The Eucharistic Jesus: Miracles and Messages

To clarify, it is the "Eucharistic Jesus" and an apparitional "Mary" that have been appearing to many visionaries. This "Jesus" and "Mary" are the ones performing numerous miracles and proclaiming many messages.

John Leary is a visionary, who claims he has heard from "Jesus in the Eucharist" on a number of occasions. John Leary relates one of his experiences:

> At St. Andrew's Church, Edmonton, Alberta, Canada, after Communion, I could see the Host in the monstrance and then it was quickly covered over. Jesus said: "My dear people, today you celebrate My institution of My Blessed Sacrament by My Presence coming into the bread and wine at the Mass. Believe, My faithful, that I am truly present in the consecrated bread and wine. You have witnessed many miracles of My Real Blood coming forth from the Host as evidence to those unbelievers. I tell you, at every Mass you witness My miracle in the Transubstantiation when the bread and wine are made into My Body and Blood. Take advantage of this time to adore Me in exposition of My Host, for a time is coming when this privilege will be taken away. I recommend to all of you to encourage your priests to have Perpetual Adoration of My Host.

[500] Thomas W. Petrisko, *Call of the Ages,* (Queenship Publishing, Santa Barbara, CA, 1995), 17.

I bring many graces to those who can visit Me and give Me praise and adoration."[501]

John Leary receives messages from both the Eucharistic Jesus and the apparition of Mary. He is just one of the increasing number of visionaries who hear from both "Jesus" and "Mary". These phenomena have increased dramatically during our current generation. The Following statement illustrates this point:

> One of the signs of our times is that the announcements of "Marian Apparitions" are multiplying all over the world...Further, there are less frequently occurring but nonetheless awe-inspiring phenomena recorded during the past 1,500 years called Eucharistic Miracles...Both these phenomena have increased dramatically in reported occurrence the last 20 years![502]

It is quite disturbing that these miracles surrounding the Eucharist are providing confirmation to the faithful of the actual physical presence of the body and blood of Jesus Christ under the appearance of the Eucharistic wafer. The Bible commands us to abstain from blood,[503] and that Jesus, who is God, does not dwell in temples made with human hands.[504] These Scriptures and many others reveal that the Catholic doctrine on the Eucharist is unbiblical and even an abomination to God.[505] This doesn't matter though to many, who are sadly more interested in seeking after the miraculous than they are in seeking after the truth.

Eucharistic Experiences

These "Eucharistic Experiences" are extremely interesting in light of another explanation made by Peter Kreeft, author of

---

[501] John Leary, *Prepare for the Great Tribulation and the Era of Peace, Volume VII,* (Queenship Publishing, Santa Barbara, CA, 1997), 57, 58.

[502] "Prologue...a Context for Marian Apparitions and Eucharistic Miracles," Online posting, http://members.aol.com/bjw1106/marian1b.htm, June 6, 2000.

[503] Leviticus 3:17; 7:26,27; Acts 15:20,29; 21:25

[504] I Kings 8:27; Acts 7:48; 17:24

[505] For a thorough comparison of the Catholic Eucharist and the Lord's Supper as described in the Bible, refer to chapter 18 of the book *Messages From Heaven.*

Ecumenical Jihad: Ecumenism and the Culture War. In a chapter titled "The Eucharist and Ecumenism" Kreeft, a former Dutch Reformed Calvanist, now Catholic, makes the following statement in support of the Catholic dogma of the Eucharist. He wrote:

> Once you have swallowed the camel of the Incarnation, why strain at the gnat of the Eucharist? If the eternal Creator-Spirit can become a flesh-and-blood-man, why can't that man's body take on the appearances of bread and wine? The gap between bread and human flesh is only finite; the gap between man and God is infinite. If God can leap the infinite gap, He can certainly leap the finite one.[506]

Of course, its not a matter of whether or not God is able to take on the appearance of bread, the question is: does the Bible teach that Catholic priests have the ability to do this? In Kreeft's pilgrimage from Dutch Reformed Calvanism to Roman Catholicism, it was the dogma of the Eucharist that was the most important for his conversion process. "No Catholic dogma is so distinctive and so apparently anti-ecumenical as the dogma of the Real Presence of Christ in the Eucharist," Kreeft wrote. "Yet this dogma may be the greatest cause of ecumenism and eventual reunion," he continued.[507]

Kreeft also explained in his book how he came to this conclusion. He wrote:

> If I was to become a Catholic, it would be out of love of Christ; and if Christ was really present in the Eucharist, as the Church said He was, then my love for Him would have to draw me there like a magnet, away from a church where Christ was present only subjectively, in the souls of good Protestant Christians, into the Church where He was more fully present, present also objectively, in the Eucharist.[508]

---

[506] Peter Kreeft, *Ecumenical Jihad: Ecumenism and the Culture War,*(Ignatius, San Francisco, 1996), 151.
[507] Ibid., 145.
[508] Ibid., 145-146.

Since his conversion, Peter Kreeft has come to believe that Protestants are missing out on what true Christianity is all about. He stated:

> When I think how much my Protestant brothers and sisters are missing in not having Christ's Real Presence in the Eucharist; when I kneel before the Eucharist and realize I am as truly in Christ's presence as the apostles were but that my Protestant brothers and sisters don't know that, don't believe that – I at first feel a terrible gap between myself and them. What a tremendous thing they are missing! It is as if Christ paid a visit to Capernaum, and a resident of Capernaum didn't bother to come out of his house to see Him. What a point of division the Eucharist is! One of the two sides is very, very wrong. I said before that if Protestants are right, Catholics are making the terrible mistake of idolatrously adoring bread and wine as God. But if Catholics are right, Protestants are making the just-as-terrible mistake of refusing to adore Christ where He is and are missing out on the most ontologically real union with Christ that is possible in this life, in Holy Communion.[509]

Eucharistic Reunion

Now that Peter Kreeft has become an avid supporter of the Catholic Church, he holds out hope that other Protestants will be transformed like himself. He even sees that these separated brethren may one day be drawn back to the Catholic Church by the Eucharistic Jesus along with help from Mary whom he believes may also play a key role. He stated:

> I found that this doctrine, which seemed to repel and divide, at the same time attracted and united. The same with Mary: she – who is a point of division between Catholics and Protestants – she may bring the churches together again and heal the tears in her Son's visible body on earth, she, the very one who seems to divide Catholics from Protestants. The most distinctive Catholic doctrines, especially those concerning the

[509] Ibid., 159-160.

> Eucharist and Mary, may prove to be the most unifying and attracting ones.[510]

There are signs that Kreeft's hopes are being fulfilled. More and more Protestants are testifying that they are being drawn to the Catholic Church, especially through the Eucharist. Some say they have encountered the presence of Christ in a new and exciting way.

One such person is Presbyterian pastor Steven Muse. Muse is one of the contributing authors of *Mary the Mother of All: Protestant Perspectives and Experiences of Medjugore,* published by the Loyola University Press and edited by Sharon E. Cheston.

According to Muse, his visit to Medjugorje was life changing, especially after he encountered the Eucharistic Christ. He wrote:

> The fact remains that never before or since in my life have I had such an encounter with Christ in the Eucharist. I believe this is because I never received the bread and the wine as the Body and the Blood of Christ, so what I loved in my heart and believed in my mind were never experienced as real in the here and now of my bodily presence as I encountered him again and again for the entire week. Sometimes this happened twice a day as I received Communion both in the morning at English Mass, and again in the evening at the Croatian Mass, where I did not even understand what they were saying or singing but only prayed the rosary in my own language with the others as if I had been saying "Hail Marys" all my life. What was true was that the Father, Son and Holy Spirit were real. And *Mary was real.*[511]

---

[510] Ibid., 158.

[511] Sharon E. Cheston, *Mary The Mother of All: Protestant Perspectives and Experiences of Medjugorje,* (Loyola University Press, Chicago, 1992), 57. [emphasis in the original]

Figure 28: A monstrance is a container for the Eucharist. This monstrance is decorated with a sunburst and the moon.

While Muse testified of a real encounter with "Christ" and "Mary" while visiting Medjugorje, other well known Protestants like Benny Hinn have made predictions that "Christ" will be showing up on stage at his crusades. On March 29, 2000 Hinn made the following statement on his television program:

> I'm gonna show you the power of God on young people, I know you may have seen this before, maybe you haven't - if you have, you'll get blessed all over again. I'm in Phoenix Arizona this Thursday and Friday. What you're about to see is gonna happen there, so you in Phoenix make sure you show up for that crusade. Now, what you're gonna see happens usually at the last night at the end of the service for the young people. It's gonna be a powerful crusade, great, great things. Let me tell you something. The Holy Spirit has spoken, He told me He is about to show up. Oh, I gotta tell you this just before we go. I had a word of prophecy from Ruth Heflin, you know who Ruth Heflin is? Ruth prophesied over me back in the seventies. Everything she said has happened. She just sent me a word through my wife and said: The Lord spoke to her audibly and said, that He is going to appear physically in one of our crusades in the next few months. Yeah, She... I'm telling ya she said, the Lord spoke to her audibly and said, tell Benny I'm going to appear physically on the platform in his meetings. Lord, do it in Phoenix, Arizona in the name of Jesus! And in Kenya too, Lord, please, Lord, in fact, do it in every crusade in Jesus' name.[512]

For those who have followed the ministry of Benny Hinn, the previous statement should come as no great surprise. Hinn has previously claimed that "Jesus" materialized to him during a Catholic mass while he was participating in communion at a Catholic church in Amarillo, Texas. Speaking with Paul Crouch on a Trinity Broadcasting Network *Praise the Lord Program* on December 24, 1997 Hinn described this experience:

> The next thing I was feeling was actually the form of a body, the shape of a body. And my body…went totally numb. …And God really gave me a revelation that night, that when we partake communion, it's not just communion, Paul [Crouch]. We are partaking Christ Jesus himself. He did not say, 'Take, eat, this *represents* my body.' He said, 'This *is* my

[512] Benny Hinn with Steve Brock "This is Your Day" Television broadcast, March 29, 2000 from 700 Club Studios, Virginia Beach, VA.

> body, broken for you...' When you partake communion, you're partaking Christ, and that heals your body. When you partake Jesus how can you stay weak? ...sick? ...And so tonight, as we partake communion, we're not partaking bread. We're partaking what *He* said we would be partaking of: 'This is my *body*.'"[513]

Could the entity that appeared to Benny Hinn as Christ in the Eucharist, soon appear to others who seek after signs and wonders more than they seek after the truth? When the apostle Paul prophesied that "lying signs and wonders" and "strong delusion" would usher in the kingdom of the Antichrist,[514] is it possible he was referring to the very thing that Benny Hinn and others are now talking about?

In previous chapters we were able to document the widespread unity developing in the name of Christ. People are so hungry for God that they are willing to forget their doctrinal differences and come together.[515] While Benny Hinn and others may be accurate with their predictions, they are completely off base when it comes to Bible doctrine. However, these manifestations that have been predicted do fulfill Bible prophecy. Jesus said such phenomena would be a sign His return would be soon:

> Then if anyone says to you, 'Look, here is the Christ!' or 'There!' do not believe it. For false christs and false prophets will rise and show great signs and wonders to deceive, if possible, even the elect. See, I have told you beforehand. Therefore if they say to you, 'Look, He is in the desert!' do not go out; or 'Look, He is in the inner rooms!' do not believe it. For as the lightning comes from the east and flashes to the west, so also will the coming of the Son of Man be.[516]

---

[513] *Praise The Lord Show*, Trinity Broadcasting Network, Dec. 27, 1994, emphasis added.

[514] 2 Thessalonians 2: 3-11

[515] Sandra K. Chambers, "Pentecostal Evangelist Calls Christians to Expect the Unusual When Revival Hits," *Charisma,* March 1999, 25.

[516] Matthew 24:24-27

Fire, Evolution and the Eucharist

Some of the ideas of Pierre Teilhard de Chardin were discussed in detail earlier in this book. As I was researching the various claims about the manifestations of the Eucharistic Jesus, I came across another fascinating statement by Teilhard de Chardin. He once wrote:

> As our humanity assimilates the material world, and as the Host assimilates our humanity, the Eucharistic transformation goes beyond and completes the transubstantiation of the bread on the altar. Step by step it irresistibly invades the universe. It is the *fire* that sweeps over the hearth; the stroke that vibrates through the bronze.[517]

There have been a number of occasions in my life when information has come to my attention precisely at a moment in my research helping to fill in an appropriate piece to the puzzle. This was another one of those occasions. While I was aware that Teilhard de Chardin was instrumental in promoting the delusion of evolution, I was somewhat surprised to see that his views were also connected with the manifestation of a Eucharistic Jesus. Second, Chardin's view that a spiritual "fire" was associated with the manifestation of the Eucharistic Christ was also interesting.

The following day I decided to do more research on some of Teilhard de Chardin's teachings. I discovered a book called *Christ in All Things: Exploring Spirituality With Teilhard de Chardin.*[518] As I glanced through the book I was reminded about Teilhard de Chardin's vision for a global spirituality, a global religion based on evolution in the name of Christ. In a chapter called "Spirituality And Evolution," author Ursula King stated: "Teilhard envisaged a closer coming together of different religions and their collaboration in working toward common aims beneficial for the whole human community." Then a few pages later King outlined another of Teilhard de Chardin's major goals. She

---

[517] Pierre Teilhard de Chardin, *The Divine Milieu*, (Harper and Rowe, New York, 1965), 125-26. [emphasis mine]

[518] Ursula King, *Christ In All Things: Exploring Spirituality with Teilhard de Chardin*, (Orbis Books, New York, 1997).

wrote: "To make people *'see and make them feel'*[519] the presence of God everywhere was Teilhard's primary aim."

I found these two statements by Teilhard de Chardin very significant in light of the documentation that I had already assembled for *New Wine and the Babylonian Vine.* First, Teilhard's idea that a transformative force called "a fire" would sweep over the world, to me, was more than coincidental. I wondered: *could the "fire" that de Chardin was calling for be the same "fire" that is presently being promoted by Charismatic Christians?* Second, a eucharistic experience that could help people "see" and "feel" the "presence of the Divine" was also fascinating. According to Jesus, there would be many counterfeits masquerading in His name. And third, Teilhard emphasized the formation of a new religion that would be based upon a unity of religions and associated with the dogma of evolution in the name of Christ.

Although I had already come to the conclusion that evolution played a significant role in the preparation of the counterfeit bride, the statements made by Teilhard de Chardin from Ursula King's book made it clearer to me than ever before. For example, in a chapter titled "Christ in All Things," King wrote:

> Teilhard was looking for a God of evolution, a God whose image is truly commensurate with the complex dimensions of our universe; a God who is not an outsider, a prime mover, but is deeply involved in the entire cosmic process of which we form an integral part; a truly living God, with us here and now, fully incarnate in matter and all-becoming. For him, the essence of Christianity is a belief in the unification of the world in God through incarnation. It is because of these central beliefs that Teilhard saw Christianity – not western Christianity as we know it, but a much more inclusive and all-embracing Christianity – as a "religion of action," a religion of evolution, and a religion of the future.[520]

---

519 Ibid., 59 [emphasis mine]

520 Ibid., 63.

This "religion for the future," a "religion of action," based upon a "religion of evolution," was described by Pierre Teilhard de Chardin in an essay he wrote in 1916. He stated:

> Since Jesus was born, and grew to his full stature, and died, everything has continued forward because Christ is not yet fully formed: he has not yet gathered about him the last folds of his robe of flesh and of love which is made up of his faithful followers. The mystical Christ has not yet attained to his full growth; and therefore the same is true of the cosmic Christ. Both of these are in the state of being and becoming; and it is from the prolongation of this process of becoming that all created activity ultimately springs. Christ is the end-point of evolution, even the natural evolution, of all beings and therefore evolution is holy.[521]

Teilhard de Chardin's vision of a religion based on evolution that would eventually unite all religions and beliefs to embrace a cosmic mystical christ is happening. The counterfeit bride that John called the harlot[522] is being prepared for the counterfeit christ and the indoctrination of evolution that has happened throughout the world continues to play a major role.

The Scriptures Say

There will be doctrines of demons![523] There will be many that are deceived by many, in the name of Christ![524] There will be a great apostasy![525] There will be false prophets![526] There will be a strong delusion![527] There will be lying signs and wonders![528] Evil men and impostors will grow worse and worse, deceiving

---

[521] Ibid., 72.
[522] Revelation 17:1
[523] 1 Timothy 4:1
[524] Matthew 24:5
[525] 2 Thessalonians 2:3
[526] Matthew 24:24
[527] 2 Thessalonians 2:11
[528] Matthew 24:24

and being deceived.[529] There will be false appearances of false christs.[530]

So what about these so-called manifestations or appearances of a Eucharistic Christ? Will these continue to become even more popular and acceptable? Is it possible that Muslims, Hindus, and other religions will also embrace the Eucharistic Jesus as a basis for a global spiritual unity?

Based upon insight from the Scriptures, Bible-believing Christians should be able to analyze the Eucharistic Jesus and Marian messages and make predictions for the future. According to Scripture, more and more people will be deceived into believing that "Christ" is appearing here, there or everywhere.[531] Some will believe that Christ can be found in the "inner rooms."[532]

The Pope and the Eucharist

According to Catholic doctrine, when a confirmed Catholic partakes of the "Blessed Sacrament," Christ's physical body actually nourishes the body of the person who has eaten the Host. In other words Christ is in them, because they have eaten His body. Also when they drink the wine, they have swallowed His blood.

In order to understand the significance of this belief called transubstantiation, it is important to review a message made by Pope John Paul II during the General Audience held in the middle of the 47th International Eucharistic Congress, June 21, 2000. In his homily, the pope spoke of the Eucharist as the source and focus of the Catholic Church's missionary task. In his own words:

> The Congress puts the Eucharist at the center of the Great Jubilee of the Incarnation and expresses all its spiritual, ecclesial and missionary depth. It is from the Eucharist, in fact, that

[529] 2 Timothy 3:13
[530] Matthew 24:24
[531] Matthew 24:23
[532] Matthew 24:26

> the Church and every believer draw the indispensable strength to proclaim and bear witness before all to the Gospel of salvation. The celebration of the Eucharist, the sacrament of the Lord's Passover, *is in itself a missionary event*, which plants the fertile seed of new life in the world. This *missionary* aspect of the Eucharist is explicitly recalled by St Paul in the Letter to the Corinthians: "As often as you eat this bread and drink this cup, you proclaim the Lord's death until he comes" (1 Cor. 11:26). [533]

Further elaborating on what the pope called the "missionary aspect of the Eucharist," he continued his message:

> The Eucharist is a "missionary" sacrament not only because the grace of mission flows from it, but also because it contains in itself the principle and eternal source of salvation for all. The celebration of the Eucharistic sacrifice is therefore the most effective missionary act that the Ecclesial Community can perform in the history of the world. [534]

While Pope John Paul's message used terms like "missionary" and "salvation" in association with "the celebration of the Eucharistic sacrifice," it is important to point out that many Catholics have been confused by actually believing that it is the Catholic Church and the sacraments that provide salvation, rather than faith in Jesus Christ alone. And with regard to "the missionary" focus that accompanies the "Eucharistic experience," there is reason to be concerned about this as well. According to Pope John Paul's message given at the General Audience in Rome June 21, 2000:

> this reflection on the meaning and missionary content of the Eucharist cannot fail to mention those outstanding *"missionaries"* and witnesses to the faith and love of Christ who are *the martyrs.* The relics of the martyrs, preserved since antiquity beneath the altars where the memorial of the "Victim whose

[533] "Holy Father's Homily for Corpus Christi: The Living Father Comes Down from Heaven – Eucharist Spurs Christians to mission," L'Osservatore Romano, Online posting, www.vatican.va/news_services/or/or_eng/text.html #4, July 3, 2000. Message given June 28, 2000. [Emphasis mine]

[534] Ibid

> death has reconciled us" is celebrated, are a clear sign of the power flowing from Christ's sacrifice. This spiritual energy spurs all who are nourished by the Body of the Lord to offer their lives for him and for their brothers and sisters by giving themselves without reserve and, if necessary, even by shedding their blood.[535]

This "missionary" motivation that is derived from the "spiritual energy" that comes from the "relics" associated with the "missionary martyrs" is troubling to me. Again note what the pope said: **"this spiritual energy spurs all who are nourished by the Body of the Lord to offer their lives for their brothers and sisters by giving themselves without reserve and, if necessary, even by shedding their blood."** Further to this the pope added:

> May the International Eucharistic Congress, through the intercession of Mary, Mother of the Christ offered in sacrifice for us, help to make believers more conscious of the missionary responsibility that stems from their participation in the Eucharist. The "Body given" and the "Blood poured out" (cf. Lk 22: 19-20) are the highest criterion they must always use in giving themselves for the world's salvation.[536]

All serious Bible believing Christians should be alarmed by the pope's statement. Consider the ramifications! First, by making this statement, the pope further substantiated the link between "Mary" and the Eucharist. Second, with this announce ment the pope has once again sanctioned the adoration of the Eucharist as the focal point for evangelizing of the world. Third, his plea is a call to the faithful for "missionary" action – even to the point of "shedding of blood."

With regard to the shedding of blood, perhaps it would be appropriate to be reminded of the blood that was shed during the Counter-Reformation centuries ago. We know that Bible-believing Christians were martyred and their blood shed because

[535] Ibid

[536] Ibid

they refused to accept the Catholic dogma that the presence of Christ's body was in the Eucharist. Is it possible that history will repeat itself again?

Could it be possible that the world is being set up for the greatest delusion in the history of mankind? Is it reasonable to suggest that these appearances of "Mary" and the Eucharistic Jesus are a major part of Satan's last days plan to deceive the world in the name of Christ?

Besides coming up with biblical answers to these questions, there are still other pieces of the puzzle that need to be discovered. How could genuine sincere Bible-believing Christians fall for such a seductive plan? How could those who once professed "the faith" fall away from "the faith" because "they did not receive the love of the truth, that they might be saved."[537]

Or what about Muslims who believe Islam is the only true religion? What about New Agers who believe that anything and everything is God? How about Hindus and Buddhists? How could all of these groups ever join together in the name of Christ? The next chapter will provide some insights.

---

[537] 2 Thessalonians 2:10

21

QUEEN OF ALL

The Bible! What an incredible God-given message that helps us understand what is going on in the world today! If you have read through this book, you will know that one of my major goals has been to point people to the Word of God. If you want to have insight and understanding about the past, the present, and the future, you must study the Bible.

Paul, writing to Timothy stated: "All Scripture is given by inspiration of God, and is profitable for doctrine, for reproof, for correction, for instruction in righteousness, that the man of God may be complete, thoroughly equipped for every good work."[538] In his letter to the Thessalonians, Paul warned the body of Christ about events that would precede the Second Coming of Jesus Christ:

> But concerning the times and the seasons, brethren, you have no need that I should write to you. For you yourselves know perfectly that the day of the Lord so comes as a thief in the night. For when they say, "Peace and safety!" then sudden destruction comes upon them, as labor pains upon a pregnant woman. And they shall not escape. But you, brethren, are not in darkness, so that this Day should overtake you as a thief. You are all sons of light and sons of the day. We are not of the night nor of darkness. Therefore let us not sleep, as others do,

[538] 2 Timothy 3:16

> but let us watch and be sober. For those who sleep, sleep at night, and those who get drunk are drunk at night. But let us who are of the day be sober, putting on the breastplate of faith and love, and as a helmet the hope of salvation. For God did not appoint us to wrath, but to obtain salvation through our Lord Jesus Christ, who died for us, that whether we wake or sleep, we should live together with Him.[539]

The Bible proclaims there is a time coming when the world will embrace a counterfeit peace. Also, the Bible warns us that there is no reason for anyone who reads the Bible to be duped by this end-times delusion. We have been told certain things in advance. We are to be vigilant and awake, ready to respond with a zeal for the truth, always with love.

Global Control

Previous chapters have already established that a counterfeit church will play a major role in preparing for the counterfeit peace. This counterfeit church which the Bible calls the harlot, will be established in the name of Christ. We also know that deceptive signs and wonders will play a major role. But there is still one more piece to the prophetic jigsaw puzzle. How can the acceptance of a global religion that identifies itself with Christ trick the world into believing that peace has been established? Could it be possible that someone or something has a spiritual solution to the global problems we face?

The Bible indicates that this harlot's false religion will encompass the globe.[540] Her counterfeit church will consist of people from all nations, multitudes, and tongues. How will she convince "Christians," and people of other religions to join with her? How will she sit on many waters and reign over the entire earth?[541]

A Christmas Day 1998 issue of the *Los Angeles Times* may provide a possible answer to this hypothetical question. In an

---

[539] 1 Thessalonians 5:1-10
[540] Isaiah 47:5; Revelation 17:15
[541] Revelation 17:1, 18

article entitled "Mary's Rising Popularity Goes Beyond Faith" we read:

> A growing number of Americans from all Christian denominations are reaching out to the Virgin Mary as a comforting conduit of spirituality and a symbol of peace in troubled times...Reported sightings of Mary have steadily increased across the globe in recent years...Her maternal gaze seems to have an ecumenical appeal...It's not just Catholics who are interested in Mary and following the apparitions...Each day, thousands of people bring their troubles to the sites where the Virgin is claimed to have appeared.[542]

The idea that messages from heaven could possibly be the key to world peace may seem absurd to some. However, the faithful who are making pilgrimages to visit the numerous locations where Marian apparitions are happening are convinced. They and many others believe the only answer for world peace is for global religious and political leaders to pay heed to what some have called the "final warning." Messages that are coming from the "Queen of Heaven" have one common theme. "Mary" is demanding she be given her "rightful place" as a heavenly conduit in order for world peace to be achieved. As an example, from Medjugorje, the "Queen of Peace" stated:

> Dear children, today I invite you to peace. I have come here as the Queen of Peace and I desire to enrich you with my Motherly Peace. I invite you to become carriers and witnesses of my peace to this unpeaceful world. Let peace rule in the whole world."[543]

This Queen of Peace seems to be gathering a lot of support. Leaders from a number of religious viewpoints are embracing the idea that the peace process can only be accomplished when the world's religions come together. Even Protestant pastors are in support of the "peace plan," citing the Marian Movement as

---

[542] Elaine Gale, "Mary's Rising Popularity Goes Beyond Faith," *Los Angeles Times*, Dec. 25, 1998, A41.

[543] "Message given July 25, 1990," Online posting, http://www.medjugorje.org/msg90.htm, Sept. 28, 1998.

key to the successful future of mankind. Consider the following statement by Charles Dickson, author of *A Protestant Pastor Looks at Mary*:

> A Muslim student visiting Rome wants especially to see the Church of Santa Maria Maggiore. Surprised? The poetry of a Syrian mystic is replete with Marian devotion. Surprised? Martin Luther recommended prayer to Mary. Surprised? An American Pentecostal minister begins to visit shrines of Marian apparitions. Surprised? Muslims refer to Mary as Il-Sittneh, or Our Lady. Surprised? A chapter in the Koran is named after her. Surprised? Mary's deep kindness as a mother is portrayed in Chinese art. Surprised? And now a Presbyterian minister has written a book recommending praying the rosary. Still surprised?...a closer investigation of both past history and current events points out that Mary has a universal appeal that transcends our cultural, geographical, and even religious boundaries."[544]

Muslims and Mary?

Think of the regions of our world today that are potential time bombs - powder kegs waiting to be ignited by some religious dispute. Can anyone imagine how religious differences could be resolved in these areas? Who alive on planet earth today could act as a mediator or diplomat that has the ability to bring about a peaceful resolution? Certainly for such an historic event to occur, a supernatural miracle would be required. There are some who are saying that Marian apparitions and the messages that "Mary" gives from heaven provide such a possibility.

While the title of this section may seem strange to the reader, it is appropriate, as we will see. How could the Mary of the Bible have any influence on the millions of Muslims who follow Allah?

Those who have studied the Muslim's holy book, known as the Koran, may be aware of the answer. First, the Koran portrays

[544] Charles Dickson. *A Protestant Pastor Looks at Mary*, (Our Sunday Visitor Publishing, Huntington, IN, 1996), 60.

Jesus Christ as a prophet, unique in His preincarnate nature, miraculous birth, miracles and moral stature. Muslims revere Jesus Christ. As the Koran states:

> The angels said to Mary: "God [Allah] bids you rejoice in a Word from Him. His name is the Messiah, Jesus son of Mary. He shall be noble in this world and in the world to come, and shall be one of those who are favored. He shall preach to men in his cradle and in the prime of manhood, and shall lead a righteous life."[545]

It is interesting to note that in the Koran, Jesus is almost exclusively referred to as "Jesus son of Mary," rather than "Son of God." The Koran vehemently denies that Jesus is the Son of God, yet it holds both Jesus and Mary in high esteem. More important to our context, is the fact that Mary is arguably more highly honored than Jesus in the Koran and in the Muslim world. The Muslims, like the Catholics, refer to her as "Our Lady." She is also venerated as a pure and holy saint in the Islamic world.

Furthermore, Mary is mentioned no less than 34 times in the Koran. In addition, the 19th surah (chapter) of the Koran is named after Mary. Based on these facts alone, it is apparent that "Our Lady" is surely seen as blessed above all women by orthodox Muslims. In addition, consider the following three quotes taken directly from the Koran:

> And remember the angels' words to Mary. They said: "God has chosen you. *He has made you pure and exalted you above womankind.*"[546]

> *The Messiah, the son of Mary, was no more than an apostle*: other apostles passed away before him. *His mother was a saintly woman.*[547]

---

[545] N. J. Dawood, translator, *The Koran,* (Penguin Putnam, Inc., New York, 1997), 46,47, surah 3:40 - 3:46.
[546] Ibid., 46, surah 3:40. [emphasis not in original]
[547] Ibid., 88, surah 5:75. [emphasis not in original]

> Whereupon he [Jesus] spoke and said: "I am the servant of God. He has given me the Book and ordained me a prophet. His blessing is upon me wherever I go, and He has exhorted me to be steadfast in prayer and to give alms as long as I shall live. *He has exhorted me to honor my mother and has purged me of vanity and wickedness"*[548]

Muslims and Apparitions of Mary

While it is apparent that Mary is considered by adherents of the Islamic faith to be the most blessed woman ever, does this necessarily imply that Muslims would respond to Marian apparitions or signs and wonders as many Catholics, Protestants, and Orthodox Christians have done? Would Muslims listen to these apparitions and heed the messages? In order to answer this question, we can consider an apparition of Mary that appeared to millions of Muslims in the 20th century.

At a Coptic Orthodox church in Zeitoun, Egypt, a suburb of Cairo, a remarkable series of events occurred. A woman that onlookers believed was Mary, appeared in the form of an apparition, performing signs, wonders, and healings. This same woman appeared several nights each week for years. The vast majority of spectators were Muslim. Here is a description of the events surrounding the Zeitoun apparitions:

> The Zeitoun apparitions...were seen by everyone present ... the persons present at apparitional events there varied from several thousand to over two hundred thousand per night. Total witnesses perhaps numbered into the millions..
>
> Several nights each week, thousands of Muslims (who constituted most of the crowds) fell to their knees on prayer rugs spread wherever space permitted, and wept before the magnificent, wondrous, glorious form of Our Lady from Heaven. All witnesses agree that the Lady seemed to be composed of light that usually was intense, yet lessened occasionally. At times, the light of the apparition dimmed enough for the slight

[548] Ibid., 216, surah 19:29. [emphasis not in original]

bluish coloration of her mantle to be seen, also revealing radiant flesh tones that could be perceived in her face.

The apparitions of "Mary, the Mother of Jesus" were serenely animate, moving from one side of the church roof to another, as if to provide a direct view to all the surrounding throng, from which many called to her to come their way. She often responded to the singing or chanting of the crowd, appearing to bow in acknowledgment, greeting and blessing. Sometimes she made gestures of prayer, or held out and waved what appeared to be an olive branch. At other times, thousands watched her radiant form, which was often aglow with bluish white light, as she held in her left arm what certainly appeared to be the baby Jesus.

The Zeitoun apparitions seemed to affect all witnesses, including hundreds who were spontaneously healed. Many such cases have been documented by Dr. Shafik Abd El Malik, M.B., B.Ch., M.D., Faculty of Medicine, Ain Shams University, who headed a commission of seven doctors to study the miraculous cures. Cancer of various types, severe thyroid diseases, rheumatoid arthritis, blindness, chronic inability to speak, severe hypertension and hemiplegia, paralysis of the hand, severe hernia, complete evulsion of both biceps brachialis, acute subconjunctival hemorrhage of the left eye, chronic nephritis, severe chronic asthma, a severe finger infection, for which amputation was planned, and other conditions, too numerous to recount here, apparently were instantly cured, as verified by extensive medical evidence.[549]

Think about the implications - millions of Muslims responding to an apparition of Mary, falling to their knees and quoting from the Koran. Why did these followers of Allah respond to these signs and wonders? Why were they so sure that this apparitional woman was Mary? If events like these repeat in the 21st century for the entire world to behold, will the Islamic

[549] Ray Stanford, *Fatima Prophecy,* (Ballantine Books, New York 1988), 44-49.

community follow "Mary"? While we can't state with certainty what will happen, the following quotes taken directly from the Koran may lend some insight:

> *We [Allah] made the son of Mary and his mother a sign to mankind,* and gave them shelter on a peaceful hillside watered by a fresh spring. Apostles! Eat of that which is wholesome, and do good works: I have knowledge of all your actions. Your community is but one community, and I am your only Lord: therefore fear me. Yet men have divided themselves into factions, each rejoicing in his own doctrines. Leave them in their error till a time appointed.[550]

> And to the woman [Mary] who kept her chastity, We [Allah] breathed into her of Our spirit, *and made her and her son a sign to all mankind.* Your community is but one community, and I am Your only Lord. Therefore serve Me. *Men have divided themselves into factions, but to Us shall they all return."*[551]

In addition, the Koran appears to lay a heavy emphasis on past and future signs as evidence that the Day of Judgment is at hand. The Koran states:

> The Day of Reckoning for mankind is drawing near, yet they blithely persist in unbelief. They listen with ridicule to each fresh warning that their Lord gives them: their hearts are set on pleasure… Yet though We showed them signs, the communities whom We destroyed before them did not believe either. Will they believe?[552]

Concerning this "Hour of Doom," which appears to be the Day of Judgment, Allah states: "We will show them Our signs in all the regions of the earth and in their own souls, until they clearly see that this [The Koran] is the truth."[553]

---

[550] *Koran*, 243, surah 23:49. [emphasis not in the original]
[551] Ibid., 233, surah 21:87. [emphasis not in the original]
[552] Ibid., 227, surah 21:1.
[553] Ibid., 338, surah 41:50.

Is it possible that signs from "Mary" will persuade Muslims that she is a sign from Allah? Could this be one of the "lying signs and wonders" that Jesus warned about in Matthew chapter twenty-four?[554] Is it reasonable to speculate that "Mary," through signs and wonders could convince many Muslims to become part of a world religion that contains the name of Christ? Might these same false signs and wonders deceive the world?

Muslims and Catholics

The Koran infers that Allah inspired the Bible, though Jews and Christians have corrupted the text.[555] Also, it is interesting to note that both Muslims and the Roman Catholic Church believe that Allah and the God of the Bible are the same. Quoting from the Catholic Catechism we read:

> The plan of salvation also includes those who acknowledge the Creator, in the first place amongst whom are the Muslims; these profess to hold the faith of Abraham, and together with us they adore the one, merciful God, mankind's judge on the last day.[556]

How will the Muslims be included in this plan of salvation? Could the apparitions that perform numerous signs and wonders, impact "Christians" and Muslims who worship the same God? Could they possibly unite on this basis? Insight from the late Catholic priest Father Malachi Martin, in his popular book, *The Keys of this Blood*, may help answer these questions:

> In reckoning the future of Islam, Pope Paul takes into account that as a genuinely religious faith, it preserves certain fundamental truths that the Holy Spirit reveals to all people of good will; and that, in God's providence, Islam can be a threshold from which its adherents can be prepared to accept

---

[554] Matthew 24:24

[555] Abdiyah Akbar Abdul-Haqq, *Sharing Your Faith with a Muslim*, Minneapolis, Minnesota, (Bethany House Publishers, Minneapolis, MN, 1980), chapters 3 and 4 p. 242-243

[556] *Catechism of the Catholic Church,* (An Image Book, published by Doubleday, New York, 1994), paragraph 841.

the only historical revelation made by God in this world. There will come a day, John Paul believes, when the heart of Islam - already attuned to the figures of Christ and of Christ's Mother, Mary - will receive the illumination it needs. In the meantime, the Pontiff knows that Islam will stand against him and his church and his geopolitical vision.[557]

An Old Mother for a New Age

It is one thing to see how Muslims and Catholics could find common ecumenical ground based on signs, wonders, and miracles associated with Marian apparitions. No doubt this would be one of the greatest religious miracles in history, encompassing over one-third of the world's population. But there is another large group that would need to be tied into the one world religion.

There are hundreds of millions of people in the world today who believe in the gods of Eastern religion. These would include the millions who have converted to eastern religion through what is commonly called the New Age Movement. It is interesting that Hindus, Buddhists, Native American Indian religions, New Agers and other similar groups already emphasize goddess worship and the earth as our living, breathing "Mother." These groups teach that all religions are similar and that we must unite to solve the myriad of problems facing mankind.

The book entitled *Mary's Message to the World* contains hundreds of revelations from "Mary," which fall in line with both New Age thinking and eastern religious beliefs. Though many Catholics would deny that this is the same Mary that appears at Catholic apparition sites, the major Catholic Marian apparitions have never discredited a single apparition around the world. On the contrary, all apparitions emphasize that she is appearing everywhere with the same message. *Mary's Message to the World* can be found at almost any New Age bookstore and may represent one of the bridges between the Catholic Mary and the

---

[557] Malachi Martin, *The Keys of this Blood*, (Simon & Schuster, New York, 1990), 285.

"Mary" who espouses New Age thinking. Here are a few of "Mary's" messages to the world:

> Each religion is worshiping, underneath the outer trappings, its Creator. It is the same Creator! Whether you pray facing the east or facing an altar, or on Saturday or Sunday, it is all worship…Allow us to view the world as a whole and each nation, each religion, as part of this Great Whole. Be tolerant, one of the other. All religions are man-made, inspired by the Creator. All words which have been written in the Holy Books have been written by men in unity with the Creator.[558]

> I would like for all men to return to their original selves and to comprehend their own natures, which are Divine. Tell the people of this world that unless they repent in their hearts and souls of their selfish ways, they will lose lifetimes of spiritual growth.[559]

> I have purposely not addressed the elements of the Catholic Church because this message is not for one religion, but for all religions and for all people. I love the people of this world no matter what culture they live in or religion they believe in…I have learned to love as God loves us, ignoring cultural and religious differences. One religion or one culture is not better than another. Each has its uniqueness and its beauty of faith and of creed.[560]

It is interesting that the Most Rev. Frank R. Bugge, Australian Archdiocese, Catholic Church of Antioch, has endorsed the book from which these quotes were taken. He writes: "I have read and shared this book widely. All are impressed with the accuracy of the messages. It is indeed a book of the greatest importance for humanity in this age."[561]

---

[558] Annie Kirkwood, *Mary's Message to the World*, (A Perigee Book, New York, 1991), 145.
[559] Ibid., 154.
[560] Ibid., xvi.
[561] Ibid., inside front cover.

It is not surprising that these revelations from "Mary" emphasize the need for all to come together. Another central point of "Mary's" messages is that we are living at a period of history known as the end of time. She pleads with people of all religious persuasions to lay down their differences and unite around her Queenship. An additional example will illustrate this theme:

> I will be appearing in many places in these next few years. If my apparitions increase, perhaps the general population will take notice and question. I come to give you the same message I have given at Fatima, Lourdes, Mexico, and in many other places…I am concerned with all who are now living on Earth, for this is the 'end time.' This is the time which John foresaw in his writings of Revelation… My presence will not be denied because there will be much evidence of the supernatural. There will be miracles…I wish to warn the Muslim nations and to allow them to consider that Allah and God are the same Spirit…I will continue to appear to men until the last day. I will be making more and more appearances.[562]

"Mary" goes on to state that she is appearing throughout Russia, Yugoslavia, Canada, South America, Korea, Europe, the Middle East -- all over the world: "Have I not told you I would be appearing all over the world and I will be manifesting myself in many different areas and ways?"[563]

Once more, not surprisingly, "Mary's" message is to unite: "It is imperative that the world join together at this time to pray to God. Pray for peace on Earth and among men. I seek to embrace all people with my love. I wish to encircle all people on Earth in a safety net which will save your souls."[564] And finally this proclamation: "It is only as a whole unit that mankind can advance. Soon a giant leap forward will occur."[565]

This giant leap forward that "Mary" suggests will happen is typical New Age doctrine. But as we have seen, the Scriptures

---

[562] Ibid., 40-44.
[563] Ibid., 42,43.
[564] Ibid., 168,169.
[565] Ibid., 155.

reveal that the idea is not new - it is just the same old lie that Satan has used to deceive the world over and over again.

Reemergence of the Goddess

Within New Age and eastern religious circles, many acknowledge the great importance and reemergence of the goddess. She has always played a major part in their beliefs and worship. And accordingly, books like *The Goddess Re-Awakening* are predicting her triumphant come-back:

> But the presence of the Goddess herself has never departed from her holy place in our consciousness, and now, as we enter what many feel to be a "new age," we sense that the Goddess is somehow making her way back to us. But in just what guise is so far unclear."[566]

Furthermore, those who hold Eastern and New Age beliefs are open to whatever form this returning goddess might assume. According to Caitlin Matthews, author of *Sophia Goddess of Wisdom*, this goddess has appeared in many varying forms in the past, and is sure to return soon. Matthews writes:

> I have accordingly looked for the Goddess of Wisdom under many names and titles, including Nature, the World-Soul, the Blessed Virgin and the Shekinah, as well as her more usual designations. Each of them has retained some part of the Goddess's image which, like a shattered mirror, waits to be reassembled…Nothing is going to delay the Goddess's second coming, whether in the guise of Sophia or under any other form.[567]

> The re-emergence of the Divine Feminine - the Goddess - in the twentieth century has begun to break down the conceptual barriers erected by orthodox religion and social conservatism.

---

[566] Beatrice Bruteau, compiled by Shirley Nicholson, *The Goddess Re-Awakening*, (The Theophical Publishing House, Wheaton, Il, 1994), 68.
[567] Caitlin Matthews, *Sophia Goddess of Wisdom*, Hammersmith, London, (Thorsons - An Imprint of Harper Collins Publishers, London, 1992), 11,332.

> For the first time in two millennia, the idea of a Goddess as a central pivot of creation is finding a welcome response.[568]

Author Carol Christ explains more about this enthusiastic response for the re-emergence of the Divine Feminine in her book *Rebirth of the Goddess*:

> One of the most unexpected developments of the late twentieth century is the rebirth of the religion of the Goddess in western cultures...In America, Europe, Australia and New Zealand, hundreds of thousands of women and increasing numbers of men brought up in biblical religions are rediscovering the language, symbols, and rituals of the Goddess.[569]

Buddhist and Hindu Goddesses

An entire book could easily be written describing the rebirth of the goddess currently taking place in cultures and religions around the world. However, for the purposes of this book, a few more examples of the widespread worship and significance of this female deity will be sufficient. For example, Buddhists have a profound and intimate adoration for their female Savioress who is called, Goddess Tara:

> Perhaps because such a concept was too abstract for many people, there gradually grew up within Mahayanna Buddhism a need for a female figure...This figure came to be Tara, the Savioress, whose name means star. Veneration of Tara seems to have begun around the seventh or eight century in India...The worship of the Goddess Tara is now one of the most widespread of Tibetan cults ... from highest to lowest, the Tibetans realize with Tara a personal and enduring relationship, unmatched by any other single deity... Tara, in other words, is the Divine Mother of Tibetan Buddhism, a tender, beautiful,

---

[568] Ibid., 8.

[569] Carol P. Christ, *Rebirth of the Goddess*, (Addison-Wesley Publishing Co., Reading, MA., 1997), preface.

> intimately and personally concerned deity who protects all who turn to her...[570]

This description of the Goddess Tara is remarkably similar to the descriptions given by visionaries who see the "Blessed Virgin Mary." And Buddhism is not unique when it comes to their worship and affection given to their beloved goddess - all of the Eastern Religions worship female deities. For example, the Hindu religions are unmatched in their veneration of goddesses, as author David R. Kinsley describes:

> One of the most striking characteristics of the ancient and multifaceted Hindu religious traditions is the importance of goddess worship. A considerable number of goddesses are known in the earliest Hindu scriptures, the Vedic hymns. In contemporary Hinduism the number and popularity of goddesses are remarkable. No other living religious tradition displays such an ancient, continuous, and diverse history of goddess worship.[571]

There is no end of documentation with regard to the importance of the female deities to the religions and cultures of the world. Whether we refer to the holy woman of Native American Indians, known as the "White Buffalo Calf Pipe Woman," or we refer to the "Shing Moo" or "Holy Mother" of the Chinese, one thing is consistent, all are worshipping a powerful, yet loving goddess.

Christian Paganism

It is apparent that the worship of a female deity is common to pagan religion. In addition, the worship of this female deity is global, it is a major theme throughout history, and it is still popular throughout the world today.

---

[570] Andrew Harvey and Anne Baring, *The Divine Feminine: Exploring the Feminine Face of God Around the World*, (Conari Press, Berkeley, CA, 1996), 140.

[571] David R. Kinsley, *Hindu Goddesses: Visions of the Divine Feminine in the Hindu Religious Tradition*, (University of California Press, Los Angeles, 1989), 1.

While the Bible teaches there is one God and that it is an abomination to worship other gods, the Catholic Church seems to be silent regarding the worship of pagan goddesses. As an example, an article taken from the *Los Angeles Times* called "Parallel Faiths of Jesus and African Deities Meld in Cuba," will demonstrate this point:

> Santiago, Cuba - Pope John Paul II gently placed a tiny, jewel-encrusted crown on the 18-inch-high figure before him, then lovingly draped a golden rosary on her hand. And with that simple act in a public square at noon Saturday, tens of thousands of Cubans erupted in unison: "Long live our Virgin of Charity! Long live our patron saint! Long live the queen of Cuba!"[572]

According to the article, this event electrified Cuba's Roman Catholics "bringing tears of joy to a multitude of believers." But at the same moment that Pope John Paul II crowned the beloved saint of Cuba's Catholic believers, his blessing also "swept through the souls of millions of Cubans who never prayed to Jesus Christ."[573]

In order to clarify what was happening a further statement from the Los Angles Times article would be appropriate:

> For them, (non-Christians who do not pray to Jesus) the small wooden figure in Santiago's Antonio Maceo Plaza was not the Virgin Mary – who legend has it, miraculously appeared to three fishermen just above the waves of the Cuban coast 400 years ago, becoming the singular symbol of faith for Cuba's devout Catholics. For them - the followers of the Afro-Cuban religion of Santeria - the statue is Ochun, the flirtatious deity who was sent by Orofi across the oceans from Central Africa to protect the slaves in the copper mines and cane fields of the New World. And for them, the pope had crowned Santeria's goddess of beauty, sexuality, promiscuity and the river,

---

[572] Mark Fineman, "Parallel Faiths of Jesus and African Deities Meld in Cuba," *Los Angles Times*, January 25, 1998, p A8

[573] Ibid

> one of the main Orisha deities presiding over a religion that guides millions of lives here (Cuba)[574]

So what was the significance of this event? Did the pope crown a pagan goddess unaware that he had endorsed Ochun, the female goddess of Santeria, actually believing that it was a statue of the Virgin Mary? If this was the case, plenty of time has passed for him so that he could have made a public announcement explaining that he had made a terrible mistake.

Miracles from "Mary" and the Eucharistic Jesus

Apparently the Queen of Heaven, who appears under many names and titles, is capable of masquerading as a goddess that is compatible with the faith of numerous pagan religions. While the devoted truly believe that their Queen of Heaven is Mary, the mother of Jesus, it appears this female deity may very well be the same Queen of Heaven that Jeremiah warned the Children of Israel about as recorded in the Book of Jeremiah, chapters seven and forty-four.

She is the one who is credited with many miraculous manifestations. And she proclaims that she will usher in the reign of the Eucharistic Jesus. Those who have studied these manifestations are expecting even greater signs and wonders centered around the Queen and the Eucharist, in the near future. For example, world-renowned Marian researcher Dr. Thomas Petrisko states in his book *Call of the Ages,* that since 1917, many revelations of future miracles have been given to Marian visionaries. He concludes, from studying hundreds of visionaries' messages, that there will be a worldwide "warning" followed by great miracles that will confirm the Virgin Mary's apparitions:

> After the warnings will come the great miracles. Some of these miracles are to be wondrous signs to the world that God

---

574 Ibid

exists and that Jesus Christ is Lord. Others will confirm the Virgin Mary's apparitions throughout the world.[575]

Marian researchers Ted and Maureen Flynn agree that the great miracle will be Marian. In addition, they state, the miracle will be Eucharistic:

> The miracle will be Eucharistic...We must be ready to receive an unmistakable proof from God, through the miracle, that the Holy Eucharist is the center of our life in the Church and that Jesus is truly present to us in the Eucharist.[576]

New Wine and the Babylonian Vine

This chapter has laid out a possible scenario regarding an end–times delusion in the name of Christ. Based upon current events that are taking place along with an understanding that can only come from the Bible, this scenario is not only reasonable, it is possible.

But can we make predictions based upon the Bible, about what lies ahead? If the apparitions of Mary and the Eucharistic Jesus are to continue, would it be possible that even more powerful supernatural signs and wonders will occur and attract more and more people. Is it also logical to predict that the Roman Catholic Mary and the Eucharist Jesus will become the center of world attention? Will the Roman Catholic Church eventually becoming the most influential and powerful spiritual organization on planet earth?

Throughout this chapter we have been discussing current trends associated with the Marian Movement. Several possible scenarios have been presented that could provide insight into how this movement could draw the world into the final spiritual delusion that Satan has planned to deceive the world in the name of Christ.

---

[575] Thomas W. Petrisko, *Call of the Ages*, (Queenship Publishing, Santa Barbara, CA, 1995), 197,198.

[576] Ted and Maureen Flynn, *The Thunder of Justice*, (MaxKol Communications, Sterling, VA, 1993), 324,325.

However, there is one additional key factor that is important for us to consider. What about sincere Bible-believing, Bible-loving, God-fearing Christians? How could a large group of people who sincerely love Jesus and His Word be duped into falling for lying signs and wonders that would lead them astray?

Throughout the latter section of this book we have carefully examined current trends. We were able to present documented evidence to show how many Christians are more willing to base their faith on experience than on the Word of God. We also know that the Bible teaches there will be a great departure from the faith in the last days. Apostasy plays a significant role in setting up the counterfeit bride as "Christians" stray further and further away from the truth. It would follow then, that Satan's plan to deceive Christians into embracing another gospel can and will materialize. It is also reasonable then, to consider another possible scenario – God-fearing, God-loving, Bible-believing Christians falling for the messages from the Queen of Heaven!

Since the mid 1990s when I started researching the New Wine Movement, I have noticed a number of signs that Protestant Charismatic Christians are being persuaded towards the Catholic view of Mary. For example, consider some of the ideas being promoted by Rev. Mark Pearson, president of the Institute for Christian Renewal and rector of Trinity Church Plaistow, New Hampshire and a theologian associated with the Charismatic Episcopal Church. In an article that he wrote called "Who is the Virgin Mary?" for *Charisma*, December 1996, he stated the following:

> Though Roman Catholics often place too much importance on Mary, it's too bad that Protestants tend to ignore her. We have much to learn from the mother of the Christ child.[577]

Rev. Pearson further clarified his view on unbiblical Catholic dogmas. He stated: "Some doctrines about Mary held by the Roman Catholic Church may not necessarily be wrong. In many

---

[577] Mark Pearson, "Who is the Virgin Mary?" *Charisma*, December 1996, 63.

cases the biblical witness is not that clear or it is silent."[578] Then justifying the Catholic position on Mary by adding to what the Bible teaches, the Protestant theologian stated:

> First, the assumption of Mary could have happened. It happened to Enoch and Elijah for sure and possibly to Moses. Second, Mary could have been a virgin perpetually. Reformers thought so. Biblical scholars are divided on whether the Greek word for Jesus' "brothers" means biological brothers or could mean close relatives.[579]

Pearson's views are not atypical. What Pearson wrote in *Charisma,* could have been written by a number of other Protestant Christians whose forefathers may well have died for their stand for biblical Christianity during the Counter Reformation. Pearson made another statement that further attempts to nullify what the Reformers gave their lives to defend. He wrote:

> There are signs that the Protestant-Roman Catholic divide are starting to listen to each other and jointly go back to the Scriptures. Who would have believed years ago that there ever would have been a Roman Catholic charismatic, much less millions of them? Who would have thought that in the "convergence movement" Pentecostal pastors would embrace liturgical worship and higher view of the sacraments? Who would have imagined that David du Plessis not only would visit the Marian shrine in Medjugorie but also proclaim how much he liked it.[580]

Although Rev. Pearson says this ecumenical unity is happening because Catholics and Protestants are jointly going back to the Scriptures, I am certain that this is a distortion of the truth. Although Mary does deserve special recognition because she is the mother of Jesus, when the Bible is silent on an issue, no person has the right to establish a doctrine based on what the Bible does not proclaim.

---

578 Ibid., 66.

579 Ibid.

580 Ibid.

I am convinced that Pearson's comments about Mary are just a glimpse of the apostasy that is to come. Discernment, in many Protestant Charismatic circles has become a thing of the past. In February of 2000, while touring the Trinity Broadcasting Network studio located on Bear Street in the city of Costa Mesa, California, I made another observation that confirmed this point.

On the second floor of a building owned by the world's largest Christian television network, was a statue of "The Queen of Heaven." She is wearing her crown. Baby Jesus is cradled in her left arm.

One final example will conclude this chapter and the documentation that supports the connection between the New Wine Movement and the Babylonian vine. On the front cover of the January 1999 issue of *Charisma,* graphic artist Attila Hejja illustrated his conception of a model church for the third millennium. This illustration was obviously chosen by the editor of *Charisma* to represent the magazine's feature article. The subtitle next to the illustration stated: "FASTEN YOUR SEATBELT. A CHRISTIAN REVIVAL COULD SWEEP THE WORLD IN THE NEXT 25 YEARS."[581]

I was amazed when I saw this *Charisma* magazine for the first time. The similarity between Attila Hejja's front cover illustration and the layout and design of St. Peter's Basilica and St. Peter's Square in Rome, is apparent. The obelisk is central to both structures. As previously documented, obelisks are phallic symbols associated with the worship of the Queen of Heaven. Could this Queen of Heaven someday become the Queen of All?

581 *Charisma*, December 1999, front cover.

Figure 29: A statue of a crowned "Queen of Heaven" is located on the second floor of Trinity Broadcasting Network's Costa Mesa studio. Photo taken February 1, 2000.

Figure 30: Front cover of *Charisma,* December, 1999

Figure 31: St. Peter's Church and Square: "The Mother of All Churches"

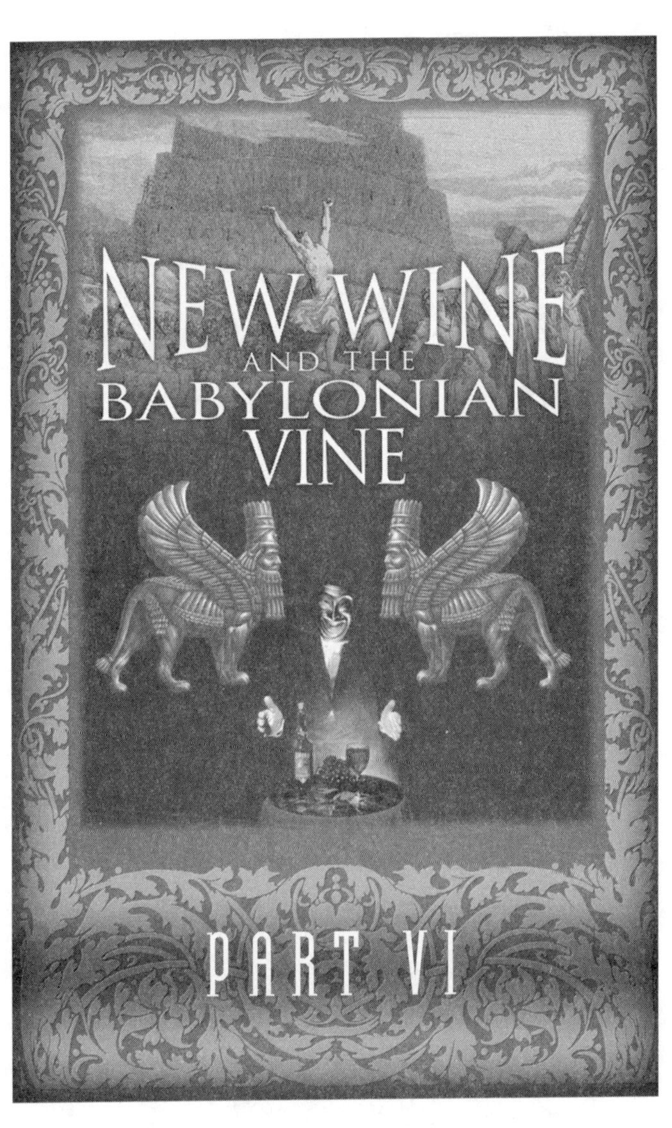

THE CHALLENGE

22

REFORMATION BEFORE REVIVAL

Since becoming a Christian, God has given me a desire to witness for Jesus Christ and tell the lost about God's saving grace. My whole life is now dedicated to being a vehicle that God can use through which the gospel message can be shared wherever God leads.

My primary objective for writing this book has been to point people to the true gospel while reminding Christians that God has an adversary who has a plan to delude people in the name of the Savior. Now, with this final chapter I want to challenge you, the reader to respond accordingly.

Christian books are written and published primarily for two reasons. The first reason is for popularity. Authors write books and publishers publish them because they are attempting to meet a need they believe exists in the Christian marketplace. In some cases Christian books fulfill a biblical mandate. In other cases, they do not.

The second reason for writing a book is to make a statement or proclaim a message that the author feels compelled to communicate. *New Wine and the Babylonian Vine,* was not written for the sake of popularity. The reason this book was written was because I wanted to communicate a message that burned in my heart – a message that I believe needs to be shared.

There are so many who are making predictions about a great revival that lies ahead. Of course, a revival is what every Christian prays for.

More than a generation ago, A.W. Tozer surveyed the spiritual landscape of his day. He wrote:

> When Christians meet these days one word is sure to be heard constantly repeated: that word is revival. In sermon, song, and prayer we are forever reminding the Lord and each other that what we must have to solve all our spiritual problems is a "mighty, old-time revival." The religious press, too, has largely gone over to the proposition that that revival is the one great need for the hour, and anyone who is capable of preparing a brief for revival is sure to find many editors who will publish it.
>
> So strongly is the breeze blowing for revival that scarcely anyone appears to have the discernment or the courage to turn around and lean into the wind, even though the truth may easily lie in that direction....
>
> It is my considered opinion that under the present circumstances we do not want revival at all. A widespread revival of the kind of Christianity we know in America might prove to be a moral tragedy from which we would not recover in a hundred years.[582]

A Biblical Exhortation

Why would anyone want to write a book that goes against the flow? Who would dare turn their back to the wind and make a stand against the great end-times Christian revival that so many insist is happening in the name of Christ? The answer is

---

[582] A.W. Tozer, *Keys to the Deeper Life*, Clarion Classics, Zondervan Publishing House, 1984, pp. 17-18

quite simple. In order to please God, we must trust and believe in His Word.

When the discussion arises about whether or not we are experiencing a global revival in the name of Jesus, it is important to ask two questions. Is the revival in accordance with God's divine will? Is the revival based upon sound biblical principles that are found in His Word? If we are in violation of God's will, we will not please Him at all, no matter how sincere and well intentioned our objectives may be.

In order to illustrate what I am saying it is important to present a biblical example. In the First Book of Chronicles we read about David's attempt to please the Lord by bringing the ark of God to Jerusalem. The Bible states:

> And David said unto all the congregation of Israel, if it seem good unto you, and that it be of the LORD our God, let us send abroad unto our brethren every where, that are left in all the land of Israel, and with them also to the priests and Levites which are in their cities and suburbs, that they may gather themselves unto us. And let us bring again the ark of our God to us: for we inquired not at it in the days of Saul. And all the congregation said that they would do so: for the thing was right in the eyes of all the people.[583]

In this situation we see that a decision was made to bring the ark to Jerusalem based on what seemed to be "the right thing in the eyes of the people." The people David consulted with were the leaders of the Jewish nation. These chosen vessels of God believed they were making the right decision. There is no doubt they were attempting to perform a service to their God to bring glory and honor to Him. It would appear then, from man's perspective, "the thing" that "was right in the eyes of the people," was the right thing to do.

But as we consider the full council of God we see what was right in man's eyes, was totally wrong from God's perspective. God, in His Word, had given specific instructions regarding how

[583] 1 Chronicles 13:2-4

the ark was to be transported and who was allowed to touch the ark.[584] God's divine and sovereign will had been written down in advance. The decision that seemed right to the leaders of Israel was the wrong decision according to God. As a result of man's disobedience, we read:

> And they carried the ark of God in a new cart out of the house of Abinadab: and Uzza and Ahio drove the cart. And David and all Israel played before God with all their might, and with singing, and with harps, and with psalteries, and with timbrels, and with cymbals, and with trumpets. And when they came unto the threshing floor of Chidon, Uzza put forth his hand to hold the ark; for the oxen stumbled. And the anger of the LORD was kindled against Uzza, and he smote him, because he put his hand to the ark: and there he died before God. And David was displeased, because the LORD had made a breach upon Uzza: wherefore that place is called Perezuzza to this day. And David was afraid of God that day, saying, How shall I bring the ark of God home to me?[585]

The consequences of being genuinely sincere, but sincerely deceived, were catastrophic for Uzza and the children of Israel. From this Old Testament example we have a written record in the Word of God that should be helpful for us today. It is always important to consider what God has revealed in His Word. If we do not, there is a very strong possibility we will be led astray.

The Final Word

We have come to the final section of this book. While a number of concluding thoughts have come to my mind regarding a few final challenging statements, I have come to the conclusion that it would be more important to let the Word of God to be the final word. Please read the following Scriptures and pray that God will reveal to you His will for your life according to His Word. My prayer is that you will respond accordingly.

---

[584] Numbers 1:50 and Numbers 7:9

[585] 1 Chronicles 13:7-12

That which has been is what will be, that which is done is what will be done, and there is nothing new under the sun. Is there anything of which it may be said, "See, this is new"? It has already been in ancient times before us. There is no remembrance of former things, nor will there be any remembrance of things that are to come by those who will come after.[586]

Will you steal, murder, commit adultery, swear falsely, burn incense to Baal, and walk after other gods whom you do not know, and then come and stand before Me in this house which is called by My name, and say, 'We are delivered to do all these abominations'?[587]

The children gather wood, the fathers kindle the fire, and the women knead dough, to make cakes for the queen of heaven; and they pour out drink offerings to other gods, that they may provoke Me to anger. "Do they provoke Me to anger?" says the LORD. "Do they not provoke themselves, to the shame of their own faces?" Therefore thus says the Lord GOD: "Behold, My anger and My fury will be poured out on this place; on man and on beast, on the trees of the field and on the fruit of the ground. And it will burn and not be quenched."[588]

Assemble yourselves and come; Draw near together, you who have escaped from the nations. They have no knowledge, who carry the wood of their carved image, and pray to a god that cannot save. Tell and bring forth your case; Yes, let them take counsel together. Who has declared this from ancient time? Who has told it from that time? Have not I, the LORD? And there is no other God besides Me, a just God and a Savior; there is none besides Me. Look to Me, and be saved, all you ends of the earth! For I am God, and there is no other.[589]

---

[586] Ecclesiastes 1: 9-11
[587] Jeremiah 7: 9-10
[588] Jeremiah 7: 18-20
[589] Isaiah 45: 20-22

The earth mourns and fades away, the world languishes and fades away; the haughty people of the earth languish. The earth is also defiled under its inhabitants, because they have transgressed the laws, changed the ordinance, broken the everlasting covenant. Therefore the curse has devoured the earth, and those who dwell in it are desolate. Therefore the inhabitants of the earth are burned, and few men are left. The new wine fails, the vine languishes, all the merry-hearted sigh.[590]

Then one of the seven angels who had the seven bowls came and talked with me, saying to me, Come, I will show you the judgment of the great harlot who sits on many waters, with whom the kings of the earth committed fornication, and the inhabitants of the earth were made drunk with the wine of her fornication. So he carried me away in the Spirit into the wilderness. And I saw a woman sitting on a scarlet beast which was full of names of blasphemy, having seven heads and ten horns. The woman was arrayed in purple and scarlet, and adorned with gold and precious stones and pearls, having in her hand a golden cup full of abominations and the filthiness of her fornication. And on her forehead a name was written: MYSTERY, BABYLON THE GREAT, THE MOTHER OF HARLOTS AND OF THE ABOMINATIONS OF THE EARTH.[591]

Beloved, while I was very diligent to write to you concerning our common salvation, I found it necessary to write to you exhorting you to contend earnestly for the faith which was once for all delivered to the saints.[592]

For certain men have crept in unnoticed, who long ago were marked out for this condemnation, ungodly men, who turn the grace of our God into lewdness and deny the only Lord God and our Lord Jesus Christ.[593]

---

590 Isaiah 24:3-7
591 Revelation 17:1-5
592 Jude 3
593 Jude 4

But I fear, lest somehow, as the serpent deceived Eve by his craftiness, so your minds may be corrupted from the simplicity that is in Christ. For if he who comes preaches another Jesus whom we have not preached, or if you receive a different spirit which you have not received, or a different gospel which you have not accepted; you may well put up with it! [594]

Many will say to Me in that day, "Lord, Lord, have we not prophesied in Your name, cast out demons in Your name, and done many wonders in Your name?" And then I will declare to them, "I never knew you; depart from Me, you who practice lawlessness!" Therefore whoever hears these sayings of Mine, and does them, I will liken him to a wise man who built his house on the rock: and the rain descended, the floods came, and the winds blew and beat on that house; and it did not fall, for it was founded on the rock. But everyone who hears these sayings of Mine, and does not do them, will be like a foolish man who built his house on the sand: and the rain descended, the floods came, and the winds blew and beat on that house; and it fell. And great was its fall. [595]

But take heed to yourselves, lest your hearts be weighed down with carousing, drunkenness, and cares of this life, and that Day come on you unexpectedly. For it will come as a snare on all those who dwell on the face of the whole earth. Watch therefore, and pray always that you may be counted worthy to escape all these things that will come to pass, and to stand before the Son of Man. [596]

Therefore take heed to yourselves and to all the flock, among which the Holy Spirit has made you overseers, to shepherd the church of God which He purchased with His own blood. For I know this, that after my departure savage wolves will come in among you, not sparing the flock. Also from among yourselves men will rise up, speaking perverse things, to draw away the disciples after themselves. Therefore watch,

[594] 2 Corinthians 11:3-4

[595] Matthew 7:22-27

[596] Luke 21:34-36

and remember that for three years I did not cease to warn everyone night and day with tears. So now, brethren, I commend you to God and to the word of His grace, which is able to build you up and give you an inheritance among all those who are sanctified.[597]

But you, beloved, remember the words which were spoken before by the apostles of our Lord Jesus Christ: how they told you that there would be mockers in the last time who would walk according to their own ungodly lusts. These are sensual persons, who cause divisions, not having the Spirit. But you, beloved, building yourselves up on your most holy faith, praying in the Holy Spirit, keep yourselves in the love of God, looking for the mercy of our Lord Jesus Christ unto eternal life. And on some have compassion, making a distinction; but others save with fear, pulling them out of the fire, hating even the garment defiled by the flesh. Now to Him who is able to keep you from stumbling, And to present you faultless before the presence of His glory with exceeding joy, to God our Savior, who alone is wise, be glory and majesty, dominion and power, both now and forever. Amen.[598]

I charge thee therefore before God, and the Lord Jesus Christ, who shall judge the quick and the dead at his appearing and his kingdom; Preach the word; be instant in season, out of season; reprove, rebuke, exhort with all longsuffering and doctrine. For the time will come when they will not endure sound doctrine; but after their own lusts shall they heap to themselves teachers, having itching ears; and they shall turn away their ears from the truth, and shall be turned unto fables. But watch thou in all things, endure afflictions, do the work of an evangelist, make full proof of thy ministry.[599]

---

[597] Acts 20:28-32

[598] Jude 17-25

[599] 2 Timothy 4:1-5

For God so loved the world that He gave His only begotten Son, that whoever believes in Him should not perish but have everlasting life.[600]

[600] John 3: 16

In Memory

Of our son

Bryce Dean Oakland

June 23, 1974

August 5, 2001

Through his death,
there has been new life.
May God, by His grace,
use this book
and our lives,
to reach the lost
with the gospel
of
Jesus Christ.

Additional Resources

For a catalogue of additional resources
that will include an audio pack and video for

New Wine and the Babylonian Vine

Contact Understand The Times

PO Box 27239
Santa Ana, CA
U.S.A.
92799

or

PO Box 1160
Eston, Sask.
Canada
SOL 1AO

or call

1.800.689.18888

or

www.undertandthetimes.org